本书由陕西省"一带一路"知识产权语言服务人才培养中心资助出版

英美最高法院版权裁判文书选译

(2010—2020)

YINGMEI ZUIGAO FAYUAN BANQUAN
CAIPAN WENSHU XUANYI

汤 玲 张小号／译

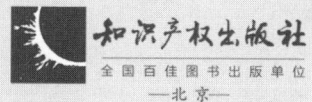

知识产权出版社
全国百佳图书出版单位
—北京—

图书在版编目（CIP）数据

英美最高法院版权裁判文书选译 . 2010—2020/汤玲，张小号译 .—北京：知识产权出版社，2021.10
ISBN 978-7-5130-7791-0

Ⅰ. ①英… Ⅱ. ①汤… ②张… Ⅲ. ①版权-法律文书-汇编-英国-2010—2020②版权-法律文书-汇编-美国-2010—2020 Ⅳ. ①D971.234②D956.134

中国版本图书馆 CIP 数据核字（2021）第 210055 号

内容简介

本书选取了英美两国最高法院2010—2020年的七个有代表性的版权判例，较为全面地展现了版权领域司法保护的最新发展动态，并在翻译过程中加上必要的注释，便于读者理解。

本书适合知识产权律师、法官等专业人士参考阅读。

责任编辑：龚卫　　　　　　　　　执行编辑：李叶
责任印制：刘译文　　　　　　　　封面设计：段维东

英美最高法院版权裁判文书选译（2010—2020）

汤玲　张小号　译

出版发行	知识产权出版社有限责任公司	网　址	http://www.ipph.cn
电　话	010-82004826		http://www.laichushu.com
社　址	北京市海淀区气象路50号院	邮　编	100081
责编电话	010-82000860 转 8745	责编邮箱	laichushu@cnipr.com
发行电话	010-82000860 转 8101	发行传真	010-82000893
印　刷	天津嘉恒印务有限公司	经　销	各大网上书店、新华书店及相关专业书店
开　本	720mm×1000mm　1/16	印　张	18.25
版　次	2021年10月第1版	印　次	2021年10月第1次印刷
字　数	280千字	定　价	88.00元

ISBN 978-7-5130-7791-0

出版权专有　侵权必究
如有印装质量问题，本社负责调换。

前 言
Preface

中共中央办公厅、国务院办公厅 2019 年 11 月印发的《关于强化知识产权保护的意见》提出，要进一步发挥知识产权制度激励创新的基本保障作用，并要求"建立国外知识产权法律修改变化动态跟踪机制"。英国和美国是典型的判例法传统国家，关注英美国家最高法院版权判例，对于掌握版权制度的最新发展动态、准确预测和积极应对版权司法保护领域出现的新问题，具有重要的理论和实践意义。

本书选取了英美两国最高法院 2010—2020 年所作的七个代表性版权裁判文书作为翻译素材。其中，美国联邦最高法院的裁判文书共五个，英国最高法院的裁判文书共两个，分别是：

（1）里德爱思唯尔公司等（上诉人）诉欧文·穆奇尼克等案（*REED ELSEVIER, INC., et al., Petitioners, v. Irvin MUCHNICK et al.*），认为登记作品是提出版权侵权主张的先决条件，但版权人未遵从该要求的不影响联邦法院对针对侵犯未登记作品版权的行为所提出权利主张的对物管辖权。

（2）劳伦斯·戈兰等（上诉人）诉小埃里克·H. 霍尔德总检察长等案（*Lawrence GOLAN, et al., Petitioners v. Eric H. HOLDER, Jr., Attorney eneral, et al.*），认为国会制定颁布的《乌拉圭回合协定法案》第 514 条，并未逾越国会依据《宪法》版权条款所享有的立法权限。

（3）葆拉·佩特拉（上诉人）诉米高梅电影公司等案（*Paula PETRELLA, Petitioner v. METRO-GOLDWYN-MAYER, INC., et al.*），认为《版权法案》第 507 条（b）款规定的诉讼时效限制仅允许版权人在胜诉后获得起诉之日起倒推三年内的追溯性赔偿，这一限制已经考虑到了迟误问题，法院不应

再以权利人怠于起诉为由，阻止其主张三年内的损害赔偿。

（4）新闻界公益公司（上诉人）诉华尔街在线有限责任公司等（被上诉人）案（*FOURTH ESTATE PUBLIC BENEFIT CORPORATION*，*Petitioner v. WALL – STREET. COM*，*LLC*，*et al.*），认为只有当版权行政部门准予登记作品，登记手续才算完成，版权人才能提起版权侵权之诉，但版权人可以就登记前和登记后所发生的侵权行为主张损害赔偿。

（5）里米尼街公司等（上诉人）诉甲骨文美国公司等案（*RIMINI STREET*，*INC.*，*et al.*，*Petitioners v. ORACLE USA*，*INC.*，*et al.*），认为《版权法案》第505条所称之"全部费用"应限于规范费用的一般性条款（即《美国法典》第28卷第1821条和第1920条）所规定的六项费用，不应作扩大解释。

（6）卢卡斯影业有限公司等（上诉人）诉安斯沃斯及另一人（被上诉人）案［*Lucasfilm Limited and others*（*Appellants*）*v. Ainsworth and another*（*Respondents*）］，认为电影中所用的道具头盔因具有实用性而不构成雕塑作品。

（7）公共关系顾问协会（上诉人）诉报纸许可协会等（被上诉人）案［*Public Relations Consultants Association Limited*（*Appellant*）*v. The Newspaper Licensing Agency Limited and others*（*Respondents*）］，认为在互联网上浏览受版权保护资料所涉技术过程并不构成版权侵权。

本书提供了"案例摘要与裁判要旨"及裁判文书译文和原文。案例摘要与裁判要旨为译者添加，目的是降低读者阅读理解裁判文书的难度；随附在译文之后的裁判文书原文来自英美最高法院的官方网站。此外，书中原文及译文中的"＊＊880（数字）"或"＊880（数字）"是指判例收录在相关判例汇编中的页码，方便读者查找。

同已有此类图书相比，本书集中关注版权主题并同时提供了裁判文书译文及原文，以全面展现英美裁判文书的语言风格、框架结构和文本内容。

本书提供了了解版权领域最新发展动态的第一手资料，对于知识产权专业语言学习者和服务提供者而言，通过提供尽可能准确的版权裁判文书译文并附上原文供对比，有助于提升专业语言服务能力。

本书受陕西省"一带一路"知识产权语言服务人才培养中心资助。两位译者分工如下：汤玲负责第一到第六个判例的翻译；张小号负责第七个判例的翻译，并负责全书统稿校对。感谢王亚楠、武静雯、姚欢、陈琛、刘静、吴智敏、李欣欣和刘天华等同学前期投入大量的时间和精力。

一直以来，裁判文书翻译是个复杂课题。因时间和译者能力所限，不足之处敬请读者谅解。

目 录
Contents

美国联邦最高法院篇

里德爱思唯尔公司等(上诉人)诉欧文·穆奇尼克等 ………… 3
REED ELSEVIER, INC., et al., Petitioners, v. Irvin MUCHNICK et al. ………… 24

劳伦斯·戈兰等(上诉人)诉小埃里克·H. 霍尔德总检察长等 ………… 41
Lawrence GOLAN, et al., Petitioners v. Eric H. HOLDER, Jr., Attorney General, et al. ………… 63

葆拉·佩特拉(上诉人)诉米高梅电影公司等 ………… 83
Paula PETRELLA, Petitioner v. METRO-GOLDWYN-MAYER, INC., et al. ………… 117

新闻界公益公司(上诉人)诉华尔街在线有限责任公司等(被上诉人) …… 147
FOURTH ESTATE PUBLIC BENEFIT CORPORATION, Petitioner v. WALL-STREET.COM, LLC, et al. ………… 158

里米尼街公司等(上诉人)诉甲骨文美国公司等 ………… 169
RIMINI STREET, INC., et al., Petitioners v. ORACLE USA, INC., et al. ………… 181

英国最高法院篇

卢卡斯影业有限公司等(上诉人)诉安斯沃斯及另一人(被上诉人) …… 193

Lucasfilm Limited and others(Appellants) v. Ainsworth and another(Respondents) ……………………………………………… 213

公共关系顾问协会(上诉人)诉报纸许可协会等(被上诉人) ………… 235
Public Relations Consultants Association Limited (Appellant) v. The Newspaper Licensing Agency Limited and others (Respondents) …………………………………………………………… 256

美国联邦最高法院篇

里德爱思唯尔公司等（上诉人）

欧文·穆奇尼克等

第 08-103 号
开庭日期：2009 年 10 月 7 日
裁决日期：2010 年 3 月 2 日

案情摘要与裁判要旨

《美国法典》第17卷第411条（a）款要求版权人在提起版权侵权主张前先办理作品登记手续。在一合并审理的版权侵权集体诉讼中，原告称各自拥有至少一项一般为报纸或杂志自由撰稿作品的版权，他们已根据第411条（a）款登记了作品。但该集体诉讼的原告既包括已登记作品的作者，也包括尚未登记作品的作者。双方请求联邦地区法院确认集体诉讼和解集体并批准和解协议。

联邦地区法院确认了集体诉讼和解集体并批准了和解协议，但遭到了部分自由撰稿人的反对。在上诉环节，联邦第二巡回上诉法院主动提出了一个问题，即第411条（a）款是否剥夺了联邦法院对涉及未登记版权侵权主张的对物管辖权，并裁决认为，联邦地区法院无权确认集体诉讼和解集体或批准和解协议。

联邦最高法院认为，第411条（a）款之登记要求是提出版权侵权主张的先决条件，版权人未遵从该要求的，不影响联邦法院对涉及未登记作品侵权主张的对物管辖权。联邦最高法院遂撤销联邦第二巡回上诉法院裁决，将案件发回重审。

托马斯大法官发表了判决意见，罗伯茨首席大法官、斯卡利亚大法官和肯尼迪大法官以及艾略特大法官持赞同意见；金斯伯格大法官部分赞同判决意见，赞同判决结果；斯蒂文斯大法官和布雷耶法官对金斯伯格大法官的意见表示赞同；索托马约尔法官未参与本案讨论或判决。

除某些例外情形,《版权法案》要求版权人在提起版权侵权主张之前对其作品进行登记[《美国法典》第17卷第411条(a)款(2006年版,增补卷2)]。本案中,联邦第二巡回上诉法院认为,版权人未遵从第411条(a)款的登记要求,剥夺了联邦法院对其版权侵权主张进行裁决的权力。我们对此不予认同。第411条(a)款的登记要求是提起版权侵权主张的前提条件,与联邦法院的对物管辖权无关。

A

《宪法》授予国会:"为促进科学进步……授予作者有限时间内……利用其作品的垄断权"(《宪法》第1条第8款第8项)。国会行使这项权力,制定了一套全面的立法方案,以规范"固定在任何有形介质上独创作品"的"版权保护"的存在和范围[《美国法典》第17卷第102条(a)款(2006年版)]。该方案赋予版权人分发、复制或公开表演作品的"垄断性权利"(法定例外情形除外)(第106条)。"任何侵犯法案赋予版权人专有权利者","都是版权侵权人"[第501条(a)款]。侵权发生时,版权人"**有权遵从第411条之要求,提起诉讼**"[第501条(b)款(黑体字为本法院特作强调)]。

本案涉及第501条(b)款所指的"第411条之要求"。第411条(a)款规定,除某些例外情况,"在版权按照本卷要求进行预登记或登记前,不得对侵犯任何美国作品版权的行为提起民事诉讼"[1]。这项规定是**1242法案救济方案的一部分。它设定了原告在提起侵权主张和援引法案救济条款之前通常必须要满足的要求——版权登记。我们要回应第411条(a)款是否也剥夺了联邦法院裁决涉及未登记作品侵权主张案件的对物管辖权。

B

本案的相关诉讼程序始于我们对 New York Times Co. v. Tasini 案[《美国判例汇编》第533卷,起始页483;《最高法院判例汇编》第121卷,起始

页2381；《美国判例汇编律师版·第二辑》第150卷，起始页500（2001年裁决）]发表判决意见之后。在 Tasini 案中，本法院维持了联邦第二巡回上诉法院的裁决，认为几个在线数据库所有者和印刷出版商未事先征得六名自由撰稿人同意便以电子方式复制了他们的作品，侵犯了版权（同上，引证页493；《最高法院判例汇编》第121卷，起始页2381）。基于这一裁决，继联邦巡回上诉法院在 Tasini 案发表判决意见后，我们申明了适用于其他自由撰稿人所提起版权侵权主张的主要责任理论。在我们作出裁决之后，一些因 Tasini 案而中止审理的其他诉讼继续进行，并由多区诉讼司法小组协调在纽约南区联邦地区法院合并审理。

合并审理案件的起诉状称，具名的原告各自至少拥有一项版权，通常基于为报纸或杂志撰写文章的自由撰稿人，他们已根据第411条（a）款为这些文章办理了登记手续。然而，此次集体诉讼的原告，既包括已经登记作品的作者，也包括尚未登记作品的作者（调卷令申请附录94）。

由于诉讼规模越来越大，越来越复杂，联邦地区法院建议当事人考虑调解。三年多来，自由撰稿人、出版商（及其保险人）和电子数据库（及其保险人）进行了磋商。最后，在2005年3月，以上当事人达成和解协议，准备"在出版业实现全球和平"["关于电子数据库中的文学作品版权诉讼"，《联邦上诉法院判例汇编·第三辑》第509卷，起始页116，引证页119（联邦第二巡回上诉法院2007年裁决）]。

以上当事人向联邦地区法院提出了申请确认集体诉讼和解集体并批准和解协议的动议，但遭到了包括欧文·穆奇尼克在内的10名自由撰稿人（以下简称"穆奇尼克等被上诉人"）的反对。联邦地区法院驳回了反对意见，依据《联邦民事诉讼规则》第23条（a）款和（b）款3项确认了自由撰稿人集体诉讼和解集体，根据第23条（e）款确认该和解协议公平、合理和恰当，并作出了最终判决。穆奇尼克等被上诉人以缺乏对物管辖权为由，敦促联邦地区法院驳回案件，不得确认集体诉讼和解集体并批准和解协议。

穆奇尼克等被上诉人遂提出上诉，再次以程序性和实体性理由反对和解。在口头辩论前不久，联邦上诉法院主动要求各方就第411条（a）款是否剥夺联邦法院对涉及未登记作品版权侵权主张的对物管辖权问题出具意见。即使和解协议涉及未登记作品，所有各方都提交了意见，认为联邦地区法院拥有批准和解协议的对物管辖权。

**1243 联邦巡回上诉法院援引了两个联邦巡回上诉法院的判例，认为第 411 条（a）款的登记要求涉及管辖权［见《联邦上诉法院判例汇编·第三辑》第 509 卷，引证页 121（引述 *Well-Made Toy Mfg. Corp. v. Goffa Int'l Corp.* 案，《联邦上诉法院判例汇编·第三辑》第 354 卷，起始页 112，引证页 114-115，联邦第二巡回上诉法院，2003 年裁决；以及 *Morris v. Business Concepts, Inc.* 案，《联邦上诉法院判例汇编·第三辑》第 259 卷，起始页 65，引证页 72-73，联邦第二巡回上诉法院，2001 年裁决）］，并判决指出，由于集体诉讼涉及未登记作品的版权侵权主张，联邦地区法院无权确认集体诉讼和解集体，也无权批准和解协议［《联邦上诉法院判例汇编·第三辑》第 509 卷，引证页 121（引述"巡回上诉法院普遍认为第 411 条（a）款是管辖权上的要求"）］[2]。

沃克法官为少数意见法官。他认为，"第 411 条（a）款更像 *Arbaugh v. Y & H Corp.* 案［《美国判例汇编》第 546 卷，起始页 500；《最高法院判例汇编》第 126 卷，起始页 1235；《美国判例汇编律师版·第二辑》第 163 卷，起始页 1097（2006 年裁决）］"中非管辖权上的雇员数量要求限制，而不是 *Bowles v. Russell* 案［《美国判例汇编》第 551 卷，起始页 205；《最高法院判例汇编》第 127 卷，起始页 2360；《美国判例汇编律师版·第二辑》第 168 卷，起始页 96（2007 年裁决）］中管辖权上的法定时效限制（《联邦上诉法院判例汇编·第三辑》第 509 卷，引证页 129）。因此，他认为，第 411 条（a）款的登记要求并不影响联邦法院对涉及未登记作品侵权主张的对物管辖权（同上）。

我们批准了版权人和出版商的调卷令状申请，并将他们提出的问题提炼为第 411 条（a）款是否限制了联邦法院对版权侵权行为的对物管辖权［《美国判例汇编》第 555 卷，起始页 1211；《最高法院判例汇编》第 129 卷，起始页 1523；《美国判例汇编律师版·第二辑》第 173 卷，起始页 655（2009 年裁决）］。由于无人支持联邦巡回上诉法院关于版权登记为管辖权上要求的主张，我们指派了法庭之友来捍卫联邦巡回上诉法院的裁决[3]［《美国判例汇编》第 556 卷，起始页 1161；《最高法院判例汇编》第 129

卷，起始页 1693；《美国判例汇编律师版·第二辑》第 173 卷，起始页 1053（2009 年裁决）］。现推翻原判决。

A

"管辖权"是指"法院的审判权"［*Kontrick v. Ryan* 案，《美国判例汇编》第 540 卷，起始页 443，引证页 455；《最高法院判例汇编》第 124 卷，起始页 906；《美国判例汇编律师版·第二辑》第 157 卷，起始页 867（2004 年裁决）］。因此，"管辖权上的"一词仅适用于涉及"界定案件类别（对物管辖权）和人员（对人管辖权）"权限的规定［同上，参见 *Steel Co. v. Citizens for Better Environment* 案，《美国判例汇编》第 523 卷，起始页 83，引证页第 89；《最高法院判例汇编》第 118 卷，起始页 1003；《美国判例汇编律师版·第二辑》第 140 卷，起始页 210（1998 年裁决）："对物管辖权"指的是"法院裁决案件的法定或宪法**权力**"（黑体字为强调）。又见 *Landgraf v. USI Film Products* 案，《美国判例汇编》第 511 卷，起始页 244，引证页 274；《最高法院判例汇编》第 114 卷，起始页 1483；《美国判例汇编律师版·第二辑》第 128 卷，起始页 229（1994 年裁决）："管辖权立法说的是'法院的权力，而不是当事人的权利或义务'"（引用 *Republic Nat. Bank of Miami v. United States* 案，《美国判例汇编》第 506 卷，起始页 80，引证页 100；《最高法院判例汇编》第 113 卷，起始页 554；《美国判例汇编律师版·第二辑》第 121 卷，起始页 474，1992 年裁决）（托马斯法官对此表示赞同）］。

虽然管辖权的定义可能在理论上表达得很清楚，但在实践中，管辖条件和索赔处理规则之间的区别可能会让人产生困惑。法院，包括本法院在内，有时错误地将索赔处理规则或 **1244 起诉理由的要素视为管辖权上的限制，特别是当这一定性并非案件核心时，因此并未去仔细分析。参见 *Arbaugh v. Y & H Corp.* 案，《美国判例汇编》第 546 卷，起始页 500，引证页 511-512；《最高法院判例汇编》第 126 卷，起始页 1235（2006 年裁决）（引述了具体案例）；*Steel Co.* 案，《美国判例汇编》第 523 卷，引证页 91；

《最高法院判例汇编》第 118 卷，起始页 1003（同样引述了具体案例）。我们最近的案例表明，人们明显希望减少这种"捎带式的管辖权裁决"（同上），因为这类裁决很容易忽略真正的管辖权条件和起诉理由限制这一非管辖权要素之间的"关键区别"（Kontrick 案，见前，引证页 456；《最高法院判例汇编》第 124 卷，起始页 906。另见 Arbaugh 案，《美国判例汇编》第 546 卷，引证页 511；《最高法院判例汇编》第 126 卷，起始页 1235）。

鉴于管辖权上的规定和索赔处理规则之间存在重要区别。参见 Arbaugh v. Y & H Corp. 案，《美国判例汇编》第 546 卷，引证页 514；《最高法院判例汇编》第 126 卷，起始页 1235，我们奉劝联邦法院和诉讼当事人谨慎使用"管辖权上的"一词，以"提高"准确性（Kontrick 案，见前，引证页 455；《最高法院判例汇编》第 124 卷，起始页 906）。在 Arbaugh 案中，我们描述了区分"管辖权上的"条件与索赔处理要求或索赔要素的一般方法：

"如果立法机关明确规定，将制定法的适用门槛限制视为管辖权上的要求，那么法院和诉讼当事人将得到明确指导，不会再就这一焦点问题进行争论。但是，当国会没有将制定法的适用限制与管辖权相关联时，法院应视该制定法与管辖权无关。"参见《美国判例汇编》第 546 卷，引证页 515-516；《最高法院判例汇编》第 126 卷，起始页 1235（省略引用和脚注）。

Arbaugh 案的原告根据 1964 年《民权法案》第七节提起诉讼，该法案规定，"对雇主来说……歧视"是非法的，尤其是基于性别的歧视 [《美国法典》第 42 卷，第 2000e-2 条（a）款（1）项]。但是，雇员只能向拥有"15 名或以上雇员"的雇主提起第七节中的诉讼 [第 2000e 条（b）款]。Arbaugh 案谈到了雇员数量要求究竟是"影响联邦法院的对物管辖权，或者与之相反，是对 1964 年《民权法案》第七节关于救济索赔实质性条件的描述"（《美国判例汇编》第 546 卷，引证页 503；《最高法院判例汇编》第 126 卷，起始页 1235）。我们认为属于后者。

我们的判决主要是基于对第 2000e 条（b）款文本的考查，1964 年《民权法案》第七节的雇员数量要求就出现在这一条文中。第 2000e 条（b）款没有"明确说明"第七节的雇员数量门槛"应视为管辖权上的要求"（同上，引证页 515-516，以及脚注 11；《最高法院判例汇编》第 126 卷，起始页 1235）。在本法院之前的与第七节相关的判例中，并不能得出这样的结论：尽管雇员数量要求缺乏明确的管辖权标签，但它仍然施加了管辖权上的限制（同上，引证页 511-513；《最高法院判例汇编》第 126 卷，起始页 1235）。同样，第 2000e 条（b）款的文字表述和结构也没有表明国会将该要求"列为"管辖权上的要求（同上，引证页 513-516；《最高法院判例汇编》第 126 卷，起始页 1235）。正如我们所述的那样，雇员数量要求在不同于 1964 年《民权法案》第七节 2000 条 e 款至 5（f）（3）款（授予管辖权）的条款中，与《美国法典》第 28 卷规定多样性管辖权的第 1332 条将"争议金额作为对物管辖权的门槛要素区分开来……"（Arbaugh 案，《美国判例汇编》第 546 卷，引证页 514-515；《最高法院判例汇编》第 126 卷，起始页 1235）。因此，雇员数量要求不能被合理地解读为"用管辖权用语或以任何方式指向联邦地区法院的管辖权"［同上，引证页 515；《最高法院判例汇编》第 126 卷，起始页 1235（引述 Zipes v. Trans World Airlines, Inc. 案，《美国判例汇编》第 455 卷，起始页 385，引证页 394；《最高法院判例汇编》第 102 卷，起始页 1127；《美国判例汇编律师版·第二辑》第 71 卷，起始页 234，1982 年裁决）］。因此，我们"避免"将雇员数量要求解释为"挤占了第 1331 条或第七节的管辖权条款"［Arbaugh 案，见前，引证页 515；《最高法院判例汇编》第 126 卷，起始页 1235（省略内部引号）］。

＊＊1245 针对第 411 条（a）款，我们现采用同样的处理方法。

B

第 411 条（a）款规定：

"除根据第 106A 条（a）款对侵犯作者权利的行为提起诉讼外，并遵从（b）款之规定，在根据本卷对版权主张进行预登记或登记之前，不得对侵犯任何美国作品版权的行为提起民事诉讼。然而，在任何情况下，如果符合版权登记规定所需的样本、申请表和费用提交给版权局后，登记申请遭到拒绝的，只要将起诉的通知连同起诉状副本送达版权登记官，则登记申请人有权针对侵权行为提起民事诉讼。版权登记官可自行决定在通知送达后 60 天内出庭，就版权主张应否予以登记的问题，作为诉讼一方当事人发表意见，但如果版权登记部门未参与诉讼，法院对该问题的管辖权也不能被剥夺（省略脚注）。"

我们必须要考虑第411条（a）款是否"明确规定"其登记要求是"管辖权上的要求"（Arbaugh案，见前，引证页515；《最高法院判例汇编》第126卷，起始页1235）。第411条（a）款并未对此进行明确规定，但法庭之友对此不予认同，认为第411条（a）款最后一句中包含了"管辖权"一词，并争辩说，在那里使用该词表明第411条（a）款第一句也属于管辖权要求［下级法院指定法庭之友陈述意见（以下简称"法庭之友意见"）第18页］。但这里提及的"管辖权"显然不具有法庭之友所赋予它的分量。法庭之友所依据的判决指出：

"版权登记官可自行决定在通知送达后60天内出庭，就**版权主张应否予以登记的问题**，作为诉讼一方当事人发表意见，但如果版权登记部门未参与诉讼，法院对该问题的管辖权也不能被剥夺。"参见第411条（a）款（黑体字为本法院特作强调）。

国会在1976年《版权法案》（《美国制定法大全》第90卷，第2583页）中增加了这句话，以阐明即使版权登记官出席侵权诉讼程序，联邦法院依然可以确定"版权主张应否予以登记的问题"。这一阐明是必要的，因为法院解释了第411条（a）款的先导条款[4]，该先导条款禁止被版权登记官**拒绝**作品登记的版权人起诉侵权行为，直至**首先**提起针对登记官的职责履行诉讼。参见 Vacheron & Constantin-Le Coultre Watches, Inc. v. Benrus Watch Co. 案，《联邦上诉法院判例汇编·第二辑》第260卷，起始页637，引证页640-641（联邦第二巡回上诉法院，1958年裁决）：诠释了第411条（a）款的前导条款。1976年《版权法案》修正案明确规定，联邦法院显然拥有裁定"**该问题**"的裁判权［第411条（a）款（黑体字为本法院特作强调）］——**应否予以登记**的问题——无论版权登记官是否成为**侵权诉讼**的一方当事人。因此，这里使用"管辖权"一词，并没有说明联邦法院是否拥有对物管辖权，以对侵犯未登记作品版权的行为进行裁决。

此外，与第七节规定的雇员数量要求一样，第411条（a）款的登记要求并不在授予联邦法院对相应版权主张的对物管辖权的条款中＊＊1246（见Arbaugh案，见前，引证页514-515；《最高法院判例汇编》126卷，起始页1235）。根据《美国法典》第28卷第1331条和第1338条，联邦地区法院拥有对版权侵权行为的对物管辖权。但无论是第1331条（赋予联邦法上问题的对物管辖权），还是第1338条（a）款（具体到版权侵权主张），都没有要求版权人在起诉侵权之前对作品进行登记，以作为管辖的前提条件（Arbaugh案，《美国判例汇编》第546卷，引证页515；《最高法院判例汇编》第126卷，起始页1235："1964年《民权法案》第七节的管辖权规定"没有"设定任何类似于《美国法典》第28卷第1332条的最低索赔金额要求"）。

也没有任何其他因素表明可以将《美国法典》第17卷第411条（a）款的登记要求解读为"使用管辖权相关术语或以任何方式提及地区法院的管辖权"[Arbaugh案，见前，引证页515；《最高法院判例汇编》第126卷，起始页1235（引用Zipes案，《美国判例汇编》第455卷，引证页394；《最高法院判例汇编》第102卷，起始页1127）]。首先，同时也是最重要的，第411条（a）款**明确允许**法院在以下三种情况下裁决涉及未登记作品的侵权主张：作品并非美国作品，侵权索赔涉及第106A条下的署名权和保护作品完整权，或者版权人申请登记作品但遭到拒绝。另外，如果作者"宣告获得作品版权的意愿"，并"按照（a）款要求，在作品首次传播后三个月内进行作品登记"，则第411条（c）款允许法院对某些未登记作品的侵权行为进行裁决[第411条（c）款1至2项]。将以上三种例外情形视为具有管辖权意义，至少会显得有些不同寻常。[5]

正如我们在Zipes案判决所表明的那样，将Arbaugh案中的雇员数量要求视为根据1964年《民权法案》第七节提出索赔的一个要素，而非提起诉讼的先决条件，并不能改变这一结论。Zipes案（Arbaugh案的判决依据）认为，1964年《民权法案》第七节关于遭受性别歧视索赔人在向联邦法院提起民事诉讼之前应及时向平等就业机会委员会❶提出歧视指控的要求，并非管辖权上的要求。参见《美国判例汇编》第455卷，引证页393；《最高法院判例汇编》102卷，起始页1127；见《美国法典》第42卷第2000e-5条（f）款（1）项，规定了遭受性别歧视的索赔人在向平等就业机会委员会提出指控后必须提起诉讼的具体期限。制定法中要求当事人在提起诉讼

---

❶ EEOC，Equal Employment Opportunity Commission的缩写，即平等就业机会委员会。——译者注

前应采取行动的这一法定条件，并不能自动成为"诉讼**管辖权**的先决条件"[Zipes 案，《美国判例汇编》第 455 卷，引证页 393；《最高法院判例汇编》第 102 卷，起始页 1127（黑体字为本法院特作强调）]。相反，在分析是否为管辖权要求时，必须集中关注该要求的"法律特征"（同上，引证页 395；《最高法院判例汇编》第 102 卷，起始页 1127），这是我们通过查看这一法定条件的文本、上下文和相关历史适用得出的（同上，引证页 393-395；《最高法院判例汇编》102 卷，起始页 1127）。另见 National Railroad Passenger Corporation v. Morgan 案，《美国判例汇编》第 536 卷，起始页 101，引证页 119-121；《最高法院判例汇编》第 122 卷，起始页 2061；《美国判例汇编律师版·第二辑》第 153 卷，起始页 106（2002 年裁决）。同理，我们将索赔人**1247 在提起诉讼前必须完成或满足的其他类型的门槛要求视为非管辖权上的要求。[6]

《美国法典》第 17 卷第 411 条（a）款中的登记要求就属于这一类。第 411 条（a）款规定了提出索赔主张的先决条件，既未被明确标记为管辖权上的要求，也没有出现在授予联邦法院管辖权的条款中，并且还允许出现国会立法规定的例外。参见第 411 条（a）款至（c）款，因此，第 411 条（a）款规定了一种提起诉讼的先决条件，符合我们处理非管辖权上要求的判例。

C

法庭之友坚持认为，本法院 Bowles 案的判决（《美国判例汇编》第 551 卷，起始页 205；《最高法院判例汇编》第 127 卷，起始页 2360；《美国判例汇编律师版·第二辑》第 168 卷，起始页 96）将迫使我们得出与今天结论相反的结论。法庭之友援引 Bowles 案的判决意见认为，即使国会没有明确将法定条件标记为管辖权上的要求，如果对该条件一贯解释为管辖权上的要求并且国会没有反对这种解释，那么法院就应将其视为管辖权上的要求（法庭之友意见第 26 页）。具体来说，法庭之友依据 Bowles 案的一个脚注提出，与 Bowles 案一样，这里将法定条件定性为非管辖权上的要求并不恰当，因为这样做会推翻"一个世纪的先例"，该先例将第 411 条（a）款的登记要求定义为管辖权上的要求（法庭之友意见第 26 页，引用 Bowles

案,见前,引证页209,以及脚注2;《最高法院判例汇编》第127卷,起始页2360)。该论点着眼于Bowles案的结果,而非我们的分析。

任何制定法中未明确标记为管辖权性质的法定条件,只要长期被法院当作管辖权要求,就应视为管辖权上的要求,这并非Bowles案的主张。该案也不认为应将所有制定法中的时效限制视为管辖权上的限制。[7] 相反,**1248 Bowles案的主张是,应结合语境,包括本法院过去很多年对类似条款的解释,来判断制定法是否将特定要求与管辖权相关联。

在Bowles案中,我们讨论了《美国法典》第28卷第2107条(该条要求民事诉讼当事人必须在收到判决书之日起30日内提交上诉状),以及《联邦上诉程序规则》第4条(该条"将第2107条付诸实践")(《美国判例汇编》第551卷,引证页208;《最高法院判例汇编》第127卷,起始页2360)。在分析了第2107条的特定语言以及本法院对第2107条所施加限制类型的过往处理(即上诉的法定期限)之后,我们得出结论——国会已将这一法定条件列为管辖权要求。因此,我们在Bowles案里关注提起上诉法定条件的过往处理,与Arbaugh案的框架一致。实际上,Bowles案强调指出,本法院一直将第2107条及其他制定法(尤其是联邦巡回上诉法院设立前出台的制定法)中设定的条件视为管辖权上的要求。参见《美国判例汇编》第551卷,引证页209-210,以及脚注2;《最高法院判例汇编》第127卷,起始页2360。

因此,Bowles案表明,这里的相关问题不在于第411条(a)款本身是否长期被标记为管辖权上的要求(如法庭之友所言),而是在于第411条(a)款设定的限制类型,在没有制定法明确规定的情况下,是否属于应被视为管辖权上要求的类型。Bowles案中的法定时效属于我们长期主张的"用管辖权术语组织言语"的类型,即使没有"管辖权"标签,第2107条的文本或上下文语境,或者本法院对这种限制的过往处理,都没有理由背离这一观点。然而,Zipes案和Arbaugh案的情况并非如此。

在本案,经过同样的分析,我们得出以下结论:第411条(a)款并不涉及联邦法院的对物管辖权。虽然在过往判例中,第411条(a)款曾被当作"管辖权上的"要求来处理,但这只是分析中的一个因素,且不是决定性因素。以上讨论的其他因素表明,第411条(a)款的登记要求更类似于

我们在 *Zipes* 和 *Arbaugh* 两起案件中所考虑的非管辖权上的要求，而不像是 *Bowles* 案中所争论的法定时效限制。[8] 因此，我们的结论是，第 411 条（a）款的登记要求并非管辖权上的要求，尽管以前曾将其作为管辖权上的要求对待过。[9]

III

法庭之友辩称，即使第 411 条（a）款并非管辖权上的要求，本法院仍应基于禁止反言规则，维持上诉法院撤销**1249 联邦地区法院批准和解协议并驳回案件的裁定。据法庭之友所说，上诉人先前在诉讼中曾称版权登记是管辖权上的要求，这一说法应阻止他们反击的权利，来对抗主张作者未成功登记作品的反对声音。法庭之友敦促我们通过杜绝当事人"根据当时的紧急情况故意改变立场"，来防止出现当事人"在法庭上反复无常"的状况。参见法庭之友意见第 58 页（引用 *New Hampshire v. Maine* 案，《美国判例汇编》第 532 卷，起始页 742，引证页 750；《最高法院判例汇编》第 121 卷，起始页 1808；《美国判例汇编律师版·第二辑》第 149 卷，起始页 968，2001 年裁决）。

我们也认为，当事人在向地区法院和上诉法院所提交材料中的一些陈述与他们在庭上的论点相矛盾，但我们拒绝适用禁止反言规则。正如我们在 *New Hampshire* 案中所解释的那样，这一原则通常适用于"一方当事人成功地说服法院接受了该方当事人先前的立场，而在接下来的诉讼程序中，如果法院接受与之前不一致的立场，会产生第一或第二法院被误导的印象"[出处同上（省略内部引号）]。

本案不存在这一情形，原因有二。其一，当事人在协商或捍卫和解协议时，就已经发表声明。当事人律师在谈判中援引有利于其客户立场的具有约束力的联邦巡回上诉法院先例，对于这一行为，我们并不做任何指责。或许更重要的是，在批准和解协议时，联邦地区法院没有采纳上诉人关于第 411 条（a）款属于管辖权要求的解读。其二，当上诉法院要求上诉人就第 411 条（a）款是否限制了联邦地区法院的对物管辖权陈述意见时，他们

辩称没有，上诉法院驳回了他们的论点（上诉人反答辩状第 3a-5a，以及脚注 2）。因此，本案中接受上诉人的论点不会产生对他们有利的"不一致的法院裁决"。参见 New Hampshire 案，见前，引证页 751；《最高法院判例汇编》第 121 卷，起始页 1808（省略内部引号）。故而，我们认为，联邦地区法院有权裁决当事人批准和解协议的请求。

IV

我们关于第 411 条（a）款并未限制联邦法院对物管辖权的主张，意味着即使上诉法院错误地解读了第 411 条，我们也无需再回应当事人诸如地区法院是否有权批准和解协议等争辩。本法院得出了联邦地区法院有批准和解的管辖权的裁判结论，但我们对和解协议本身并不发表意见。

我们也不愿回应以下问题：鉴于第 411 条（a）款的登记要求是提起诉讼的强制性先决条件——就如同以下三案的门槛条件：*Arizona v. California* 案［《美国判例汇编》第 530 卷，起始页 392，引证页 412-413；《最高法院判例汇编》第 120 卷，起始页 2304；《美国判例汇编律师版·第二辑》第 147 卷，起始页 374（2000 年裁决）：已决案件辩护］，*Day v. McDonough* 案［《美国判例汇编》第 547 卷，起始页 198，引证页 205-206；《最高法院判例汇编》第 126 卷，起始页 1675；《美国判例汇编律师版·第二辑》第 164 卷，起始页 376（2006 年裁决）：人身保护诉讼时效］，以及 *Hallstrom v. Tillamook County* 案［《美国判例汇编》第 493 卷，起始页 20，引证页 26、31；《最高法院判例汇编》第 110 卷，起始页 304；《美国判例汇编律师版·第二辑》第 107 卷，起始页 237（1989 年裁决）：《1976 年资源保护和恢复法案》通知条款］——联邦地区法院是否可以或应当顺理成章地驳回涉及未登记作品的版权侵权主张。

……

本法院推翻联邦第二巡回上诉法院的裁决，并将此案发回，要求上诉法院按照本法院意见重新审理此案。

此令。

索托马约尔大法官未参与本案的讨论或裁决。

**1250 金斯伯格大法官部分赞同判决意见,并赞同判决结果;史蒂文斯大法官和布雷耶大法官认同金斯伯格大法官的下述观点。

我同意本法院对《美国法典》第 17 卷第 411 条（a）款的定性［《美国法典》第 17 卷第 411 条（a）款，2006 年版，增补卷 2］。该条款指示作者在提起侵权诉讼前办理版权登记，这是"提起版权侵权主张的前提条件，与联邦法院的对物管辖权无关"（见上，第 1241 页）。我也认为 Arbaugh v. Y & H Corp. 案 ［《美国判例汇编》546 卷，起始页 500;《最高法院判例汇编》第 126 卷，起始页 1235;《美国判例汇编律师版·第二辑》第 163 卷，起始页 1097 （2006 年裁决）］ 是一个决定性先例（见上，引证页 1244），并且认为 Bowles v. Russell 案 ［《美国判例汇编》第 551 卷，起始页 205;《最高法院判例汇编》第 127 卷，起始页 2360;《美国判例汇编律师版·第二辑》第 168 卷，起始页 96 （2007 年裁决）］ 并未提出有用的建议。然而，这两例判决意见之间存在着不可否认的冲突。为了避免继续争论"管辖权上的"要求具体是指什么，我将阐述一下我对法院在 Arbaugh 和 Bowles 这两起案件判决意见的理解，以及我调和这些裁决的理由。

在 Arbaugh 案中，我们认为，将 1964 年《民权法案》第七节覆盖的范围限制为至少雇佣 15 名雇员的雇主［《美国法典》第 42 卷，第 2000e-2 条（a）款（1）项］，这并非管辖权上的要求。在论及"15 名雇员人数限制……'没有用管辖权术语组织语言，也没有以任何方式提及联邦地区法院的管辖权'"。参见《美国判例汇编》第 546 卷，引证页 515;《最高法院判例汇编》第 126 卷，起始页 1235（引用 Zipes v. Trans World Airlines, Inc. 案，《美国判例汇编》第 455 卷，起始页 385，引证页 394;《最高法院判例汇编》第 102 卷，起始页 1127;《美国判例汇编律师版·第二辑》第 71 卷，起始页 234 页，1982 年裁决）。之后，Arbaugh 案的判决意见宣布并应用了一条"易于管理的明确标准"：

"如果立法机关明确规定，将制定法的适用门槛限制视为管辖权上的要求，那么法院和诉讼当事人将得到明确指导，不会再就这一焦点问题进行争论。但是，当国会没有将制定法的适用范围限制与管辖权相关联时，法院应视该制定法与管辖权无关。将这一条'易于管理的明确标准'应用于本案，我们认为，适用第七节的雇员人数门槛是原告提出救济主张的要素之一，而非管辖权要求。"参见《美国判例汇编》第 546 卷，引证页 515-516；《最高法院判例汇编》第 126 卷，起始页 1235（省略引用和脚注）。

正如上面引用的段落所指出的那样，与 Arbaugh 案法院预计一致，所有联邦法院此后都坚持适用 Arbaugh 案主张的"明确标准"。

然而，Bowles 案则与之不同。本案中，法院内部分歧很大，多数意见法官认为，提起上诉的时效限制是"强制性的且是管辖权上的"要求。参见《美国法典》第 28 卷第 2107 条（a）（c）款；《美国判例汇编》第 551 卷，引证页 209；《最高法院判例汇编》第 127 卷，起始页 2360（省略内部引号）。Bowles 案提到 Arbaugh 案的目的只是说明 Arbaugh 案涉及一项制定法，该制定法规定了"雇员数量要求，而非时效限制"（《美国判例汇编》第 551 卷，引证页 211；《最高法院判例汇编》第 127 卷，起始页 2360）。Bowles 案解释道，第 2107 条的时效限制之所以是"管辖权上的"要求，一方面是因为时效限制包含在制定法中，而非仅仅包含在联邦诉讼规则中（同上，引证页 210-213；《最高法院判例汇编》第 127 卷，起始页 2360）；另一方面"本法院一直认为在规定的时间内上诉是'强制性的且是管辖权上的'要求"（同上，引证页 209；《最高法院判例汇编》第 127 卷，起始页 2360）。只要忠实于 Arbaugh 案和类似推理的决定，那么 Bowles 案的少数意见法官就会得出以下结论：法定时效限制"只有在国会明确同意的情况下才具有管辖权意义"。参见《美国判例汇编》第 551 卷，引证页 217；《最高法院判例汇编》第 127 卷，起始页 2360（苏特大法官的意见）。

**1251 Bowles 案和 Arbaugh 案的裁决可以相互调和，不会扭曲任一裁决结果：Bowles 案"依赖于本法院长期以来的裁决，裁决内容不涉及国会制定法干涉的领域"[Union Pacific R. Co. v. Locomotive Engineers 案，《美国判例汇编》第 558 卷，起始页 67 页，引证页 82；《最高法院判例汇编》第 130 卷，起始页 584，引证页 597；《美国判例汇编律师版·第二辑》第 175 卷，起始页 428（2009 年裁决）（引述 Bowles 案，《美国判例汇编》第 551 卷，引证页 209-211；《最高法院判例汇编》第 127 卷，起始页 2360）]。在 Bowles 案之后，我们在 John R. Sand & Gravel Co. v. United States 案［《美国判例汇编》第 552 卷，起始页 130；《最高法院判例汇编》第 128 卷，起始页

750;《美国判例汇编律师版·第二辑》第169卷,起始页591（2008年裁决）]中也是如此处理。在那一案件中,本法院判决描述道,主要基于遵循先例的立场,联邦索赔法院的诉讼时效要求自然而然考虑诉讼的及时性（同上,引证页136；《最高法院判例汇编》第128卷,起始页750；"上诉人只有说服本法院,让本法院认识到已经推翻或现在应推翻本法院的先例,才能辩护成功"）。

简而言之,*Arbaugh*案和*Bowles*案都得出了第411条（a）款并非管辖权上要求的结论。第411条（a）款"没有用管辖权术语组织语言,也没有以任何方式提及联邦地区法院的管辖权"（*Zipes*案,《美国判例汇编》第455卷,引证页394；《最高法院判例汇编》102卷,起始页1127）。因此,*Arbaugh*案提出的"易于管理的明确标准"发挥了控制作用。参见《美国判例汇编》第546卷,引证页516；《最高法院判例汇编》第126卷,起始页1235。

*Bowles*案也没有偏离这一判断。和我一样,法庭之友阅读了*Bowles*案的判决意见,敦促本法院将第411条（a）款视为管辖权上的要求,以免我们背离"一个世纪以来的先例"。参见下级法院指定法庭之友陈述意见,第26页（引用*Bowles*案,《美国判例汇编》第551卷,引证页209,以及脚注2；《最高法院判例汇编》第127卷,起始页2360）；同上,引证页1247。但在*Bowles*案和*John R. Sand & Co.*案中,如前所述,我们基于本法院由来已久的判决意见,将相关规定视为"管辖权上的"要求,包括*Bowles*案[《美国判例汇编》第551卷,引证页209-210；《最高法院判例汇编》第127卷,起始页2360（引述*Scarborough v. Pargoud*等案,《美国判例汇编》第108卷,起始页567；《最高法院判例汇编》第2卷,起始页877；《美国判例汇编律师版》第27卷,起始页824,1883年裁决）],*United States v. Curry*案[霍华德《美国判例汇编》第6卷,起始页106；《美国判例汇编律师版》第12卷,起始页363（1848年裁决）]和*John R. Sand & Gravel Co.*案（《美国判例汇编》第552卷,引证页136；《最高法院判例汇编》第128卷,起始页750）。法庭之友引用了200多条将第411条（a）款定性为管辖权要求的判决意见,但没有一条判决意见来自本法院,而且大多数意见是"捎带式的管辖权裁决",并"无先例的效力"。参见*Arbaugh*案,《美国判例汇

编》第546卷，引证页511；《最高法院判例汇编》第126卷，起始页1235（引用 Steel Co. v. Citizens for Better Environment 案，《美国判例汇编》第523卷，起始页83，引证页91；《最高法院判例汇编》第118卷，起始页1003；《美国判例汇编律师版·第二辑》第140卷，起始页210，1998年裁决）。见 Arbaugh 案，第546卷，引证页514-515；《最高法院判例汇编》第126卷，起始页1235；同上，引证页1243-1244）。

……

基于上述原因，我赞同判决结果，并部分赞同判决意见。

注释

[1] 该法案的其他条款，主要是第408条至第410条，详细说明了登记程序，并为了鼓励版权人登记作品，确立了救济动因。参见如第410条（c）款和第412条（《美国法典》第17卷第412条，2006年版，增补卷2）。

[2] 见 La Resolana Architects, PA v. Clay Realtors Angel Fire 案［《联邦上诉法院判例汇编·第三辑》第416卷，起始页1195，引证页1200-1201（联邦第十巡回上诉法院，2005年裁决）］；Positive Black Talk Inc. v. Cash Money Records Inc. 案［《联邦上诉法院判例汇编·第三辑》第394卷，起始页357，引证页365（第五巡回上诉法院，2004年裁决）］；Xoom, Inc. v. Imageline, Inc. 案［《联邦上诉法院判例汇编·第三辑》第323卷，起始页279，引证页283（联邦第四巡回上诉法院，2003年裁决）］；Murray Hill Publications, Inc. v. ABC Communications, Inc. 案［《联邦上诉法院判例汇编·第三辑》第264卷，起始页622，引证页630，以及脚注1（联邦第六巡回上诉法院，2001年裁决）］；Brewer-Giorgio v. Producers Video, Inc. 案［《联邦上诉法院判例汇编·第三辑》第216卷，起始页1281，引证页1285（联邦第十一巡回上诉法院，2000年裁决）］；Data Gen. Corp. v. Grumman Systems Support Corp. 案［《联邦上诉法院判例汇编·第三辑》第36卷，起始页1147，引证页1163（联邦第一巡回上诉法院，1994年裁决）］。

[3] 我们任命黛博拉·琼斯·梅里特作为法庭之友，就案件进行陈述和辩护，以支持上诉法院的判决。梅里特女士圆满地履行了职责。

[4] 见1909年3月4日法案第12条（《联邦立法大全》第35卷，第1078页）。

[5] 对比 Zipes 案（《美国判例汇编》第455卷，引证页393-394、397；《最高法院判例汇编》102卷，起始页1127：依据以下事实，即国会至少在某些情况下已经"批准了"不符合制定法申请要求的向 EEOC 索赔者授予第七节救济的案例，认为申请要求并非管辖权上的要求）；United States v. Cotton 案（《美国判例汇编》第535卷，起始页625，引证页630；《最高法院判例汇编》第122卷，起始页1781；《美国判例汇编律师版·第二辑》第152卷，起始页860，2002年裁决："管辖权"应指法院审理案件的权力，这一权力"永远不能被剥夺或放弃"）。

[6] 见 Jones v. Bock 案，参见《美国判例汇编》第549卷，起始页199，引证页211；《最高法院判例汇编》第127卷，起始页910；《美国判例汇编律师版·第二辑》第166卷，起始页798（2007年裁决）[1995年《监狱诉讼改革法案》（PLRA）的穷尽行政救济规则要求，"在用尽现有的行政救济措施前……犯人不得根据本法第1983条或任何其他联邦法律就监狱条件提起诉讼"，《美国法典》第42卷第1997条 e（a）款]，该案将此视为一种肯定性辩护，即使"毫无疑问，根据1995年《监狱诉讼改革法案》，穷尽行政救济是强制性的，在穷尽行政救济之前，不能向法庭提起诉讼"]；Woodford v. Ngo 案，见《美国判例汇编》第548卷，起始页81，引证页93；《最高法院判例汇编》第126卷，起始页2378；《美国判例汇编律师版·第二辑》第165卷，起始页368（2006年裁决）（同上）。

[7] 例如，Bowles 案区分了 Scarborough v. Principi 案 [《美国判例汇编》第541卷，起始页401；《最高法院判例汇编》第124卷，起始页1856；《美国判例汇编律师版·第二辑》第158卷，起始页674（2004年裁决）：将根据《平等诉诸司法法案》提起诉讼后律师费用主张的明确法定时效限制定性为非管辖权上的要求。见《美国判例汇编》第551卷，引证页211；《最高法院判例汇编》第127卷，起始页2360页]。正如本法院所解释的那样，Scarborough 案的时效限制"涉及**一种救济方式**……该救济附属于已经拥有完全管辖权的法院的判决"。参见《美国判例汇编》第551卷，引证页211；《最高法院判例汇编》第127卷，起始页2360（引用 Scarborough 案，见前，

引证页 413;《最高法院判例汇编》第 124 卷,起始页 1856;黑体字为本法院特作强调)。Bowles 案还区分对待 Kontrick v. Ryan 案[《美国判例汇编》第 540 卷,起始页 443;《最高法院判例汇编》第 124 卷,起始页 906;《美国判例汇编律师版·第二辑》第 157 卷,起始页 867(2004 年裁决)]和 Eberhart v. United States 案[《美国判例汇编》第 546 卷,起始页 12;《最高法院判例汇编》第 126 卷,起始页 403;《美国判例汇编律师版·第二辑》第 163 卷,起始页 14(2005 年裁决):全体参审法官共同议决]。在这些案件中,由于一些时效限制是由联邦程序规则施加的,不具有管辖权意义,因此算不上管辖权上的要求(见《美国判例汇编》第 551 卷,引证页 210-211;《最高法院判例汇编》第 127 卷,起始页 2360)。Kontrick 案涉及在破产程序中"适用于反对债务清偿的时效限制"(《美国判例汇编》第 540 卷,引证页 453;《最高法院判例汇编》第 124 卷,起始页 906)。在该案中,我们首先分析了《美国法典》第 28 卷第 157 条(b)(2)(J)款,该条款"赋予了对债务清偿异议案件的管辖权",并指出该条不包含及时性要求(Kontrick 案,《美国判例汇编》第 540 卷,引证页 453;《最高法院判例汇编》第 124 卷,起始页 906)。相反,"适用于反对债务清偿的时效限制"规定在《破产规则》中,该规则明确规定,"不得被解释为扩大或限制法院的管辖权")(同上,引用《联邦破产程序规则公告》第 9030 条)。紧接着,在 Eberhart 案中,"与 Kontrick 案非常相似"的某些规则也被视为非管辖权上的要求(《美国判例汇编》第 546 卷,引证页 15;《最高法院判例汇编》第 126 卷,起始页 403)。

[8] 这一判决反映了我们在 Zipes 案中的观点,即 1964 年《民权法案》第七节的 EEOC 申请要求并非管辖权上的要求,尽管本法院自己所作的一些判决已经将其定性为管辖权上的要求。参见《美国判例汇编》第 455 卷,引证页 393;《最高法院判例汇编》102 卷,起始页 1127(注意到"在早期案件中,该要求的法律性质不存在争议")。另见 National Railroad Passenger Corporation v. Morgan 案,见《美国判例汇编》第 536 卷,起始页 101,引证页 109、121;《最高法院判例汇编》第 122 卷,起始页 2061;《美国判例汇编律师版·第二辑》第 153 卷,起始页 106(2002 年裁决)(依据 Zipes 案的分析)。

［9］法庭之友支持登记为管辖权上要求的其余论点——版权登记的政策目标支持将第411条（a）款的登记条款解释为管辖权上的要求（法庭之友意见，第45页），同样站不住脚。仅仅因为一个条件促进了国会重要目标的达成，就将其列为管辖权上的要求，这一点我们不予认可。参见 *Arbaugh v. Y & H Corp.* 案，《美国判例汇编》第546卷，起始页500，引证页504、515-516；《最高法院判例汇编》第126卷，起始页1235；《美国判例汇编律师版·第二辑》第163卷，起始页1097（2006年裁决）（主张1964年《民权法案》第七节的雇员数量要求是非管辖权上的要求，尽管它服务于重要的政策目标，即"鼓励小型企业免除1964年《民权法案》第七节的责任"）。

例如，*Eberhart v. United States* 案，见《美国判例汇编》第546卷，起始页12；《最高法院判例汇编》第126卷，起始页403；《美国判例汇编律师版·第二辑》第163卷，起始页14（2005年裁决）（全体参审法官共同议决）。*Scarborough v. Principi* 案，见《美国判例汇编》第541卷，起始页401；《最高法院判例汇编》第124卷，起始页1856；《美国判例汇编律师版·第二辑》第158卷，起始页674（2004年裁决）。*Kontrick v. Ryan* 案，见《美国判例汇编》第540卷，起始页443；《最高法院判例汇编》第124卷，起始页906；《美国判例汇编律师版·第二辑》第157卷，起始页867（2004年裁决）。

REED ELSEVIER, INC., et al., Petitioners, v.

Irvin MUCHNICK et al.

No. 08–103.

Argued Oct. 7, 2009.

Decided March 2, 2010.

https://www.supremecourt.gov/opinions/09pdf/08–103.pdf

Subject to certain exceptions, the Copyright Act (Act) requires copyright holders to register their works before suing for copyright infringement. 17 U. S. C. § 411(a) (2006 ed., Supp. II). In this case, the Court of Appeals for the Second Circuit held that a copyright holder's failure to comply with § 411(a)'s registration requirement deprives a federal court of jurisdiction to adjudicate his copyright infringement claim. We disagree. Section 411(a)'s registration requirement is a precondition to filing a claim that does not restrict a federal court's subject-matter jurisdiction.

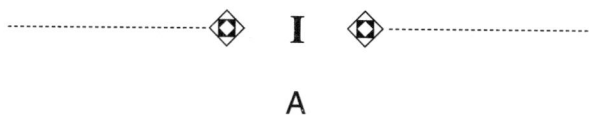

I

A

The Constitution grants Congress the power "[t]o promote the Progress of Science and useful Arts, by securing for limited Times to Authors...the exclusive Right to...their...Writings." Art. I, § 8, cl. 8. Exercising this power, Congress has crafted a comprehensive statutory scheme governing the existence and scope of "[c]opyright protection" for "original works of authorship fixed in any tangible medium of expression." 17 U. S. C. § 102(a) (2006 ed.). This scheme gives copyright owners "the exclusive rights" (with specified statutory exceptions) to distribute, reproduce, or publicly perform their works. § 106. "Anyone who violates any of the exclusive rights of the copyright owner as provided" in the Act "is an infringer of the copyright." § 501(a). When such infringement occurs, a copyright owner "is entitled, *subject to the requirements of section* 411, to institute an action" for copyright infringement. § 501(b) (emphasis added).

This case concerns "the requirements of section 411" to which § 501(b) refers. Section 411(a) provides, *inter alia* and with certain exceptions, that "no civil action for infringement of the copyright in any United States work shall be instituted until preregistration or registration of the copyright claim has been made in accordance with this title."[1] This provision is * * 1242 part of the Act's remedial scheme. It establishes a condition—copyright registration—that plaintiffs ordinarily must satisfy before filing an infringement claim and invoking the Act's remedial provisions. We address whether § 411(a) also deprives federal courts of subject-matter jurisdiction to adjudicate infringement claims involving unregistered works.

B

The relevant proceedings in this case began after we issued our opinion in *New York Times Co. v. Tasini*, 533 U. S. 483, 121 S. Ct. 2381, 150 L. Ed. 2d 500 (2001). In *Tasini*, we agreed with the Court of Appeals for the Second Circuit that several owners of online databases and print publishers had infringed the copyrights of six freelance authors by reproducing the authors' works electronically without first securing their permission. See *id*., at 493, 121 S. Ct. 2381. In so holding, we affirmed the principal theory of liability underlying copyright infringement suits that other freelance authors had filed after the Court of Appeals had issued its opinion in *Tasini*. These other suits, which were stayed pending our decision in *Tasini*, resumed after we issued our opinion and were consolidated in the United States District Court for the Southern District of New York by the Judicial Panel on Multidistrict Litigation.

The consolidated complaint alleged that the named plaintiffs each own at least one copyright, typically in a freelance article written for a newspaper or a magazine, that they had registered in accordance with § 411(a). The class, however, included both authors who had registered their copyrighted works and authors who had not. See App. 94.

Because of the growing size and complexity of the lawsuit, the District Court referred the parties to mediation. For more than three years, the freelance authors, the publishers (and their insurers), and the electronic databases (and their insurers) negotiated. Finally, in March 2005, they reached a settlement agreement that the parties intended "to achieve a global peace in the publishing industry." *In re Literary Works in Electronic Databases Copyright Litigation*, 509 F. 3d 116, 119 (C. A. 2 2007).

The parties moved the District Court to certify a class for settlement and to approve the settlement agreement. Ten freelance authors, including Irvin Muchnick (hereinafter Muchnick respondents), objected. The District Court overruled the objections; certified a settlement class of freelance authors under Federal Rules of Civil Procedure 23(a) and (b)(3); approved the settlement as fair, reasonable, and adequate under Rule 23(e); and entered final judgment. At no time did the Muchnick respondents or any other party urge the District Court to dismiss the case, or to refuse to certify the class or approve the settlement, for lack of subject-matter jurisdiction.

The Muchnick respondents appealed, renewing their objections to the settlement on procedural and substantive grounds. Shortly before oral argument, the Court of Appeals *sua sponte* ordered briefing on the question whether § 411(a) deprives federal courts of subject-matter jurisdiction over infringement claims involving unregistered copyrights. All parties filed briefs asserting that the District Court had subject-matter jurisdiction to approve the settlement agreement even though it included unregistered works.

**1243 Relying on two Circuit precedents holding that § 411(a)'s registration requirement was jurisdictional, see 509 F. 3d, at 121(citing *Well-Made Toy Mfg. Corp. v. Goffa Int'l Corp.*, 354 F. 3d 112, 114 – 115 (C. A. 2 2003); *Morris v. Business Concepts, Inc.*, 259 F. 3d 65, 72 – 73 (C. A. 2 2001)), the Court of Appeals concluded that the District Court lacked jurisdiction to certify a class of claims arising from the infringement of unregistered works, and also lacked jurisdiction to approve a settlement with respect to those claims, 509 F. 3d, at 121 (citing "widespread agreement among the circuits that section 411(a) is jurisdictional"). [2]

Judge Walker dissented. He concluded "that § 411(a) is more like the [nonjurisdictional] employee-numerosity requirement in *Arbaugh* [v. Y & H Corp., 546 U. S. 500, 126 S. Ct. 1235, 163 L. Ed. 2d 1097(2006),]" than the jurisdictional statutory time limit in *Bowles v. Russell*, 551 U. S. 205, 127 S. Ct. 2360, 168 L. Ed. 2d 96(2007). 509 F. 3d, at 129. Accordingly, he reasoned that § 411(a)'s registration requirement does not limit federal subject-matter jurisdiction over infringement suits involving unregistered works. *Ibid.* We granted the owners' and publishers' petition for a writ of certiorari, and formulated the question presented to ask whether § 411(a) restricts the subject-matter jurisdiction of the federal courts over copyright infringement actions. 555 U. S. 1211, 129 S. Ct. 1523, 173 L. Ed. 2d 655(2009). Because no party supports the Court of Appeals' jurisdictional holding, we appointed an *amicus curiae* to defend the Court of Appeals' judgment. [3] 556 U.

S. 1161, 129 S. Ct. 1693, 173 L. Ed. 2d 1053 (2009). We now reverse.

II

A

"Jurisdiction" refers to "a court's adjudicatory authority." *Kontrick v. Ryan*, 540 U. S. 443, 455, 124 S. Ct. 906, 157 L. Ed. 2d 867 (2004). Accordingly, the term "jurisdictional" properly applies only to "prescriptions delineating the classes of cases (subject-matter jurisdiction) and the persons (personal jurisdiction)" implicating that authority. *Ibid.*; see also *Steel Co. v. Citizens for Better Environment*, 523 U. S. 83, 89, 118 S. Ct. 1003, 140 L. Ed. 2d 210 (1998) ("'subject-matter jurisdiction' refers to 'the courts' statutory or constitutional *power* to adjudicate the case" (emphasis in original)); *Landgraf v. USI Film Products*, 511 U. S. 244, 274, 114 S. Ct. 1483, 128 L. Ed. 2d 229 (1994) ("[J]urisdictional statutes 'speak to the power of the court rather than to the rights or obligations of the parties'" (quoting *Republic Nat. Bank of Miami v. United States*, 506 U. S. 80, 100, 113 S. Ct. 554, 121 L. Ed. 2d 474 (1992) (THOMAS, J., concurring))).

While perhaps clear in theory, the distinction between jurisdictional conditions and claim-processing rules can be confusing in practice. Courts—including this Court—have sometimes mischaracterized claim-processing rules or elements of a **1244 cause of action as jurisdictional limitations, particularly when that characterization was not central to the case, and thus did not require close analysis. See *Arbaugh v. Y & H Corp.*, 546 U. S. 500, 511–512, 126 S. Ct. 1235 (2006) (citing examples); *Steel Co.*, 523 U. S., at 91, 118 S. Ct. 1003 (same). Our recent cases evince a marked desire to curtail such "drive-by jurisdictional rulings," *ibid.*, which too easily can miss the "critical difference[s]" between true jurisdictional conditions and nonjurisdictional limitations on causes of action, *Kontrick, supra*, at 456, 124 S. Ct. 906; see also *Arbaugh*, 546 U. S., at 511, 126 S. Ct. 1235.

In light of the important distinctions between jurisdictional prescriptions and claim-processing rules, see, e. g., *id.*, at 514, 126 S. Ct. 1235, we have encouraged federal courts and litigants to "facilitat[e]" clarity by using the term "jurisdictional" only when it is apposite, *Kontrick, supra*, at 455, 124 S. Ct. 906. In *Arbaugh*, we described the general approach to distinguish "jurisdictional" conditions from claim-processing requirements or elements of a claim:

"If the Legislature clearly states that a threshold limitation on a statute's scope shall count as jurisdictional, then courts and litigants will be duly instructed and will not be left to wrestle with the issue. But when Congress does not rank a statutory limitation on coverage as jurisdictional, courts should treat the restriction as nonjurisdictional in character." 546 U. S., at 515–516, 126 S. Ct. 1235 (citation and footnote omitted).

The plaintiff in *Arbaugh* brought a claim under Title VII of the Civil Rights Act of 1964, which makes it unlawful "for an employer...to discriminate," *inter alia*, on the basis of sex. 42 U. S. C. § 2000e–2(a)(1). But employees can bring Title VII claims only against employers that have "fifteen or more employees." § 2000e(b). *Arbaugh* addressed whether that employee numerosity requirement "affects federal-court subject-matter jurisdiction or, instead, delineates a substantive ingredient of a Title VII claim for relief." 546 U. S., at 503, 126 S. Ct. 1235. We held that it does the latter.

Our holding turned principally on our examination of the text of § 2000e(b), the section in which Title VII's numerosity requirement appears. Section 2000e(b) does not "clearly stat[e]" that the employee numerosity threshold on Title VII's scope "count[s] as jurisdictional." *Id.*, at 515–516, and n. 11, 126 S. Ct. 1235. And nothing in our prior Title VII cases compelled the conclusion that even though the numerosity requirement lacks a clear jurisdictional label, it nonetheless imposed a jurisdictional limit. See *id.*, at 511–513, 126 S. Ct. 1235. Similarly, § 2000e(b)'s text and structure did not demonstrate that Congress "rank[ed]" that requirement as jurisdictional. See *id.*, at 513–516, 126 S. Ct. 1235. As we observed, the employee numerosity requirement is located in a provision "separate" from § 2000e–5(f)(3), Title VII's jurisdiction-granting section, distinguishing it from the "amount-in-controversy threshold ingredient of subject-matter jurisdiction in ...diversity-of-jurisdiction under 28 U. S. C. § 1332." *Arbaugh*, 546 U. S., at 514–515, 126 S. Ct. 1235. Accordingly, the numerosity requirement could not fairly be read to " 'speak in jurisdictional terms or in any way refer to the jurisdiction of the district courts.' " *Id.*, at 515, 126 S. Ct. 1235 (quoting *Zipes v. Trans World Air-*

lines, Inc., 455 U. S. 385, 394, 102 S. Ct. 1127, 71 L. Ed. 2d 234 (1982)). We thus "refrain[ed] from" construing the numerosity requirement to "constric[t] § 1331 or Title VII's jurisdictional provision." *Arbaugh*, *supra*, at 515, 126 S. Ct. 1235 (internal quotation marks omitted).

**1245 We now apply this same approach to § 411(a).

B

Section 411(a) provides:

"Except for an action brought for a violation of the rights of the author under section 106A(a), and subject to the provisions of subsection (b), no civil action for infringement of the copyright in any United States work shall be instituted until preregistration or registration of the copyright claim has been made in accordance with this title. In any case, however, where the deposit, application, and fee required for registration have been delivered to the Copyright Office in proper form and registration has been refused, the applicant is entitled to institute a civil action for infringement if notice thereof, with a copy of the complaint, is served on the Register of Copyrights. The Register may, at his or her option, become a party to the action with respect to the issue of registrability of the copyright claim by entering an appearance within sixty days after such service, but the Register's failure to become a party shall not deprive the court of jurisdiction to determine that issue." (Footnote omitted).

We must consider whether § 411(a) "clearly states" that its registration requirement is "jurisdictional." *Arbaugh*, *supra*, at 515, 126 S. Ct. 1235. It does not. *Amicus* disagrees, pointing to the presence of the word "jurisdiction" in the last sentence of § 411(a) and contending that the use of the term there indicates the jurisdictional cast of § 411(a)'s first sentence as well. Brief for Court-Appointed *Amicus Curiae* in Support of Judgment Below 18 (hereinafter *Amicus* Brief). But this reference to "jurisdiction" cannot bear the weight that *amicus* places upon it. The sentence upon which *amicus* relies states:

"The Register[of Copyrights] may, at his or her option, become a party to the [copyright infringement] action with respect to *the issue of registrability of the copyright claim* by entering an appearance within sixty days after such service, but the

Register's failure to become a party shall not deprive the court of jurisdiction to determine *that issue.*" § 411(a)(emphasis added).

Congress added this sentence to the Act in 1976, 90 Stat. 2583, to clarify that a federal court can determine "the issue of registrability of the copyright claim" even if the Register does not appear in the infringement suit. That clarification was necessary because courts had interpreted § 411(a)'s precursor provision,[4] which imposed a similar registration requirement, as prohibiting copyright owners who had been *refused* registration by the Register of Copyrights from suing for infringement until the owners *first* sought mandamus against the Register. See *Vacheron & Constantin–Le Coultre Watches, Inc. v. Benrus Watch Co.*, 260 F. 2d 637, 640–641(C. A. 2 1958)(construing §411(a)'s precursor). The 1976 amendment made it clear that a federal court plainly has adjudicatory authority to determine "*that* issue,*" § 411(a)(emphasis added)—i.e., the issue of *registrability*—regardless of whether the Register is a party to the *infringement* suit. The word "jurisdiction," as used here, thus says nothing about whether a federal court has subject-matter jurisdiction to adjudicate claims for infringement of unregistered works.

Moreover, § 411(a)'s registration requirement, like Title VII's numerosity requirement, is located in a provision "separate" **1246 from those granting federal courts subject-matter jurisdiction over those respective claims. See *Arbaugh, supra,* at 514–515, 126 S. Ct. 1235. Federal district courts have subject-matter jurisdiction over copyright infringement actions based on 28 U. S. C. § § 1331 and 1338. But neither § 1331, which confers subject-matter jurisdiction over questions of federal law, nor § 1338(a), which is specific to copyright claims, conditions its jurisdictional grant on whether copyright holders have registered their works before suing for infringement. Cf. *Arbaugh*, 546 U. S., at 515, 126 S. Ct. 1235 ("Title VII's jurisdictional provision" does not "specif[y] any threshold ingredient akin to 28 U. S. C. § 1332's monetary floor").

Nor does any other factor suggest that 17 U. S. C. § 411(a)'s registration requirement can be read to "'speak in jurisdictional terms or refer in any way to the jurisdiction of the district courts.'" *Arbaugh, supra,* at 515, 126 S. Ct. 1235(quoting *Zipes*, 455 U. S., at 394, 102 S. Ct. 1127). First, and most significantly, § 411(a) expressly *allows* courts to adjudicate infringement claims involving unregistered works in three circumstances: where the work is not a U. S. work, where the infringement claim concerns rights of attribution and integrity under § 106A, or where the holder attempted to register the work and registration was refused. Separately, § 411(c) permits courts to adjudicate infringement actions over certain kinds of unregistered works where the author "declare[s] an intention to secure copyright in the work" and "makes registration for the work, if required by subsection(a), within three months after[the work's] first transmission." §§ 411(c)(1)-(2). It would be at least unusual to ascribe jurisdictional significance to a condition subject to these sorts of exceptions.[5]

That the numerosity requirement in *Arbaugh* could be considered an element of a Title VII claim, rather than a prerequisite to initiating a lawsuit, does not change this conclusion, as our decision in *Zipes* demonstrates. *Zipes* (upon which *Arbaugh* relied) held that Title VII's requirement that sex-discrimination claimants timely file a discrimination charge with the EEOC before filing a civil action in federal court was nonjurisdictional. See 455 U. S. , at 393, 102 S. Ct. 1127; 42 U. S. C. § 2000e-5(f)(1)(establishing specific time periods within which a discrimination claimant must file a lawsuit after filing a charge with the EEOC). A statutory condition that requires a party to take some action before filing a lawsuit is not automatically "a *jurisdictional* prerequisite to suit."*Zipes*, 455 U. S. , at 393, 102 S. Ct. 1127 (emphasis added). Rather, the jurisdictional analysis must focus on the "legal character" of the requirement, *id.* , at 395, 102 S. Ct. 1127, which we discerned by looking to the condition's text, context, and relevant historical treatment, *id.* , at 393-395, 102 S. Ct. 1127; see also *National Railroad Passenger Corporation v. Morgan*, 536 U. S. 101, 119-121, 122 S. Ct. 2061, 153 L. Ed. 2d 106 (2002). We similarly have treated as nonjurisdictional other types of threshold requirements that claimants **1247 must complete, or exhaust, before filing a lawsuit.[6]

The registration requirement in 17 U. S. C. § 411(a) fits in this mold. Section 411(a) imposes a precondition to filing a claim that is not clearly labeled jurisdictional, is not located in a jurisdiction-granting provision, and admits of congressionally authorized exceptions. See §§ 411(a)-(c). Section 411(a) thus imposes a type of precondition to suit that supports nonjurisdictional treatment under our precedents.

C

Amicus insists that our decision in *Bowles*, 551 U. S. 205, 127 S. Ct. 2360, 168 L. Ed. 2d 96, compels a conclusion contrary to the one we reach today. *Amicus* cites *Bowles* for the proposition that where Congress did not explicitly label a statutory condition as jurisdictional, a court nevertheless should treat it as such if that is how the condition consistently has been interpreted and if Congress has not disturbed that interpretation. *Amicus* Brief 26. Specifically, *amicus* relies on a footnote in *Bowles* to argue that here, as in *Bowles*, it would be improper to characterize the statutory condition as nonjurisdictional because doing so would override " ' a century's worth of precedent' " treating § 411(a)'s registration requirement as jurisdictional. *Amicus* Brief 26(quoting *Bowles*, *supra*, at 209, n. 2, 127 S. Ct. 2360). This argument focuses on the result in *Bowles*, rather than on the analysis we employed.

Bowles did not hold that any statutory condition devoid of an express jurisdictional label should be treated as jurisdictional simply because courts have long treated it as such. Nor did it hold that all statutory conditions imposing a time limit should be considered jurisdictional. [7] Rather, ⋆ ⋆ 1248 *Bowles* stands for the proposition that context, including this Court's interpretation of similar provisions in many years past, is relevant to whether a statute ranks a requirement as jurisdictional.

In *Bowles*, we considered 28 U. S. C. § 2107, which requires parties in a civil action to file a notice of appeal within 30 days of the judgment being appealed, and Rule 4 of the Federal Rules of Appellate Procedure, which "carries § 2107 into practice."551 U. S., at 208, 127 S. Ct. 2360. After analyzing § 2107's specific language and this Court's historical treatment of the type of limitation § 2107 imposes(*i. e.*, statutory deadlines for filing appeals), we concluded that Congress had ranked the statutory condition as jurisdictional. Our focus in *Bowles* on the historical treatment of statutory conditions for taking an appeal is thus consistent with the *Arbaugh* framework. Indeed, *Bowles* emphasized that this Court had long treated such conditions as jurisdictional, including in statutes *other* than § 2107, and specifically in statutes that predated the creation of the courts of appeals. See 551 U.

S. , at 209-210, and n. 2, 127 S. Ct. 2360.

Bowles therefore demonstrates that the relevant question here is not (as *amicus* puts it) whether § 411(a) itself has long been labeled jurisdictional, but whether the type of limitation that § 411(a) imposes is one that is properly ranked as jurisdictional absent an express designation. The statutory limitation in *Bowles* was of a type that we had long held *did* "speak in jurisdictional terms" even absent a "jurisdictional" label, and nothing about § 2107's text or context, or the historical treatment of that type of limitation, justified a departure from this view. That was not the case, however, for the types of conditions in *Zipes* and *Arbaugh*.

Here, that same analysis leads us to conclude that § 411(a) does not implicate the subject-matter jurisdiction of federal courts. Although § 411(a)'s historical treatment as "jurisdictional" is a factor in the analysis, it is not dispositive. The other factors discussed above demonstrate that § 411(a)'s registration requirement is more analogous to the nonjurisdictional conditions we considered in *Zipes* and *Arbaugh* than to the statutory time limit at issue in *Bowles*.[8] We thus conclude that § 411(a)'s registration requirement is nonjurisdictional, notwithstanding its prior jurisdictional treatment.[9]

III

Amicus argues that even if § 411(a) is nonjurisdictional, we should nonetheless affirm on estoppel grounds the Court of Appeals' judgment vacating the ＊＊ 1249 District Court's order approving the settlement and dismissing the case. According to *amicus*, petitioners asserted previously in these proceedings that copyright registration was jurisdictional, and this assertion should estop them from now asserting a right to waive objections to the authors' failure to register. *Amicus* urges us to prevent the parties "from 'playing fast and loose with the courts' by 'deliberately changing positions according to the exigencies of the moment.'" *Amicus* Brief 58(quoting *New Hampshire v. Maine*, 532 U. S. 742, 750, 121 S. Ct. 1808, 149 L. Ed. 2d 968(2001)).

We agree that some statements in the parties' submissions to the District Court and the Court of Appeals are in tension with their arguments here. But we decline to apply judicial estoppel. As we explained in *New Hampshire*, that doctrine typically applies when, among other things, a "party has succeeded in persuading a court to accept that party's earlier position, so that judicial acceptance of an inconsistent position in a later proceeding would create the perception that either the first or the second court was misled." *Ibid.* (internal quotation marks omitted).

Such circumstances do not exist here for two reasons. First, the parties made their prior statements when negotiating or defending the settlement agreement. We do not fault the parties' lawyers for invoking in the negotiations binding Circuit precedent that supported their clients' positions. Perhaps more importantly, in approving the settlement, the District Court did not adopt petitioners'interpretation of § 411(a) as jurisdictional. Second, when the Court of Appeals asked petitioners to brief whether § 411(a) restricted the District Court's subject-matter jurisdiction, they argued that it did not, and the Court of Appeals rejected their arguments. See App. to Reply Brief for Petitioners 3a – 5a, and n. 2. Accepting petitioners'arguments here thus cannot create "inconsistent court determinations" in their favor. *New Hampshire*, *supra*, at 751, 121 S. Ct. 1808 (internal quotation marks omitted). We therefore hold that the District Court had authority to adjudicate the parties' request to approve their settlement.

IV

Our holding that § 411(a) does not restrict a federal court's subject-matter jurisdiction precludes the need for us to address the parties' alternative arguments as to whether the District Court had authority to approve the settlement even under the Court of Appeals' erroneous reading of § 411. In concluding that the District Court had jurisdiction to approve the settlement, we express no opinion on the settlement's merits.

We also decline to address whether § 411(a)'s registration requirement is a mandatory precondition to suit that—like the threshold conditions in *Arizona v. California*, 530 U. S. 392, 412–413, 120 S. Ct. 2304, 147 L. Ed. 2d 374 (2000) (res judicata defense); *Day v. McDonough*, 547 U. S. 198, 205–206, 126 S. Ct. 1675, 164 L. Ed. 2d 376 (2006) (habeas statute of limitations); and *Hallstrom v. Tilla-*

mook County, 493 U. S. 20, 26, 31, 110 S. Ct. 304, 107 L. Ed. 2d 237(1989)(Resource Conservation and Recovery Act of 1976 notice provision)—district courts may or should enforce *sua sponte* by dismissing copyright infringement claims involving unregistered works.

……

We reverse the judgment of the Court of Appeals for the Second Circuit and remand this case for proceedings consistent with this opinion.

It is so ordered.

Justice SOTOMAYOR took no part in the consideration or decision of this case.

* * 1250 Justice GINSBURG, with whom Justice STEVENS and Justice BREYER join, concurring in part and concurring in the judgment.

I agree with the Court's characterization of 17 U. S. C. §411(a)(2006 ed. and Supp. II). That provision, which instructs authors to register their copyrights before commencing suit for infringement, "is a precondition to filing a claim that does not restrict a federal court's subject-matter jurisdiction." *Ante*, at 1241. I further agree that *Arbaugh v. Y & H Corp.*, 546 U. S. 500, 126 S. Ct. 1235, 163 L. Ed. 2d 1097(2006), is the controlling precedent, see *ante*, at 1244, and that *Bowles v. Russell*, 551 U. S. 205, 127 S. Ct. 2360, 168 L. Ed. 2d 96(2007), does not counsel otherwise. There is, however, undeniable tension between the two decisions. Aiming to stave off continuing controversy over what qualifies as "jurisdictional," and what does not, I set out my understanding of the Court's opinions in *Arbaugh* and *Bowles*, and the ground on which I would reconcile those rulings.

In *Arbaugh*, we held nonjurisdictional a prescription confining Title VII's coverage to employers with 15 or more employees, 42 U. S. C. § 2000e-2(a)(1). After observing that "the 15-employee threshold…'d[id] not speak in jurisdictional terms or refer in any way to the jurisdiction of the district courts,'" 546 U. S., at 515, 126 S. Ct. 1235(quoting *Zipes v. Trans World Airlines, Inc.*, 455 U. S. 385, 394, 102 S. Ct. 1127, 71 L. Ed. 2d 234(1982)), the *Arbaugh* opinion announced and applied a "readily administrable bright line":

"If the Legislature clearly states that a threshold limitation on a statute's scope shall count as jurisdictional, then courts and litigants will be duly instructed and will not be left to wrestle with the issue. But when Congress does not rank a statutory limitation on coverage as jurisdictional, courts should treat the restriction as nonjurisdictional in character. Applying that readily administrable bright line to this case, we hold that the threshold number of employees for application of Title VII is an element of a plaintiff's claim for relief, not a jurisdictional issue. " 546 U. S. , at 515-516, 126 S. Ct. 1235 (citation and footnote omitted).

As the above-quoted passage indicates, the unanimous *Arbaugh* Court anticipated that all federal courts would thereafter adhere to the "bright line" held dispositive that day.

Bowles moved in a different direction. A sharply divided Court there held "mandatory and jurisdictional" the time limits for filing a notice of appeal stated in 28 U. S. C. § 2107(a), (c). 551 U. S. , at 209, 127 S. Ct. 2360 (internal quotation marks omitted). *Bowles* mentioned *Arbaugh* only to distinguish it as involving a statute setting "an employee-numerosity requirement, not a time limit. " 551 U. S. , at 211, 127 S. Ct. 2360. Section 2107's time limits were "jurisdictional, " *Bowles* explained, because they were contained in a statute, not merely a rule, *id.* , at 210-213, 127 S. Ct. 2360, and because " [t] his Court ha [d] long held that the taking of an appeal within the prescribed time is ' mandatory and jurisdictional, ' " *id.* , at 209, 127 S. Ct. 2360. Fidelity to *Arbaugh* and similarly reasoned decisions, the dissent in *Bowles* observed, would have yielded the conclusion that statutory time limits "are only jurisdictional if Congress says so. " 551 U. S. , at 217, 127 S. Ct. 2360 (opinion of Souter, J.).

**1251 *Bowles* and *Arbaugh* can be reconciled without distorting either decision, however, on the ground that *Bowles* "rel [ied] on a long line of this Court's decisions left undisturbed by Congress. " *Union Pacific R. Co. v. Locomotive Engineers*, 558 U. S. 67, 82, 130 S. Ct. 584, 597, 175 L. Ed. 2d 428 (2009) (citing *Bowles*, 551 U. S. , at 209-211, 127 S. Ct. 2360). The same is true of our decision, subsequent to *Bowles*, in *John R. Sand & Gravel Co. v. United States*, 552 U. S. 130, 128 S. Ct. 750, 169 L. Ed. 2d 591 (2008). There the Court concluded, largely on *stare decisis* grounds, that the Court of Federal Claims statute of limitations requires *sua sponte* consideration of a lawsuit's timeliness. *Id.* , at 136, 128 S. Ct. 750 (" [P] etitioner can succeed only by convincing us that this Court has overturned, or that it should now overturn, its earlier precedent.").

Plainly read, *Arbaugh* and *Bowles* both point to the conclusion that § 411(a) is nonjurisdictional. Section 411(a) "does not speak in jurisdictional terms or refer in any way to the jurisdiction of the district courts." *Zipes*, 455 U. S., at 394, 102 S. Ct. 1127. *Arbaugh*'s "readily administrable bright line" is therefore controlling. 546 U. S., at 516, 126 S. Ct. 1235.

Bowles does not detract from that determination. *Amicus*, reading *Bowles* as I do, urges on its authority that we hold § 411(a) jurisdictional lest we disregard "'a century's worth of precedent.'" Brief for Court-Appointed *Amicus Curiae* in Support of Judgment Below 26(quoting *Bowles*, 551 U. S., at 209, n. 2, 127 S. Ct. 2360); see *ante*, at 1247. But in *Bowles* and *John R. Sand & Gravel Co.*, as just explained, we relied on longstanding decisions of *this Court* typing the relevant prescriptions "jurisdictional." *Bowles*, 551 U. S., at 209–210, 127 S. Ct. 2360(citing, inter alia, *Scarborough v. Pargoud*, 108 U. S. 567, 2 S. Ct. 877, 27 L. Ed. 824 (1883), and *United States v. Curry*, 6 How. 106, 12 L. Ed. 363(1848)); *John R. Sand & Gravel Co.*, 552 U. S., at 136, 128 S. Ct. 750. *Amicus* cites well over 200 opinions that characterize § 411(a) as jurisdictional, but not one is from this Court, and most are "'drive-by jurisdictional rulings' that should be accorded 'no precedential effect,'" *Arbaugh*, 546 U. S., at 511, 126 S. Ct. 1235(quoting *Steel Co. v. Citizens for Better Environment*, 523 U. S. 83, 91, 118 S. Ct. 1003, 140 L. Ed. 2d 210(1998)); see *Arbaugh*, 546 U. S., at 514–515, 126 S. Ct. 1235; *ante*, at 1243–1244.

……

For the reasons stated, I join the Court's judgment and concur in part in the Court's opinion.

Footnotes

1. Other sections of the Act—principally § §408–410—detail the registration process, and establish remedial incentives to encourage copyright holders to register their works, see, e. g., § 410(c); 17 U. S. C. § 412(2006 ed. and Supp. II).

2. See *La Resolana Architects*, *PA v. Clay Realtors Angel Fire*, 416 F. 3d 1195, 1200–1201(C. A. 10 2005); *Positive Black Talk Inc. v. Cash Money Records Inc.*, 394 F. 3d 357, 365(C. A. 5 2004); *Xoom, Inc. v. Imageline, Inc.*, 323 F. 3d 279, 283(C. A. 4 2003); *Murray Hill Publications*,

Inc. v. ABC Communications, Inc., 264 F. 3d 622, 630, and n. 1 (C. A. 6 2001); *Brewer-Giorgio v. Producers Video, Inc.*, 216 F. 3d 1281, 1285 (C. A. 11 2000); *Data Gen. Corp. v. Grumman Systems Support Corp.*, 36 F. 3d 1147, 1163 (C. A. 1 1994).

3. We appointed Deborah Jones Merritt to brief and argue the case, as amicus curiae, in support of the Court of Appeals' judgment. Ms. Merritt has ably discharged her assigned responsibilities.

4. See Act of Mar. 4, 1909, § 12, 35 Stat. 1078.

5. Cf. Zipes, 455 U. S., at 393–394, 397, 102 S. Ct. 1127 (relying on the fact that Congress had "approved" at least some cases awarding Title VII relief to claimants who had not complied with the statute's Equal Employment Opportunity Commission (EEOC) filing requirement in holding that the filing requirement was not a jurisdictional prerequisite to suit); *United States v. Cotton*, 535 U. S. 625, 630, 122 S. Ct. 1781, 152 L. Ed. 2d 860 (2002) ("[J]urisdiction" properly refers to a court's power to hear a case, a matter that "can never be forfeited or waived").

6. See *Jones v. Bock*, 549 U. S. 199, 211, 127 S. Ct. 910, 166 L. Ed. 2d 798 (2007) (treating the administrative exhaustion requirement of the Prison Litigation Reform Act of 1995 (PLRA)—which states that "[n]o action shall be brought with respect to prison conditions under section 1983 of this title, or any other Federal law, by a prisoner...until such administrative remedies as are available are exhausted," 42 U. S. C. § 1997e(a)—as an affirmative defense even though "[t]here is no question that exhaustion is mandatory under the PLRA and that unexhausted claims cannot be brought in court"); *Woodford v. Ngo*, 548 U. S. 81, 93, 126 S. Ct. 2378, 165 L. Ed. 2d 368 (2006) (same).

7. Bowles, for example, *distinguished Scarborough v. Principi*, 541 U. S. 401, 124 S. Ct. 1856, 158 L. Ed. 2d 674 (2004), which characterized as nonjurisdictional an express statutory time limit for initiating postjudgment proceedings for attorney's fees under the Equal Access to Justice Act. See 551 U. S., at 211, 127 S. Ct. 2360. As we explained, the time limit in Scarborough "concerned 'a mode of relief...ancillary to the judgment of a court' that already had plenary jurisdiction."551 U. S., at 211, 127 S. Ct. 2360 (quoting Scarborough, supra, at 413, 124 S. Ct. 1856; emphasis added). Bowles also distinguished *Kontrick v. Ryan*, 540 U. S. 443, 124 S. Ct. 906, 157 L. Ed. 2d 867 (2004), and *Eberhart v. United States*, 546 U. S. 12, 126 S. Ct. 403, 163 L. Ed. 2d 14 (2005) (per curiam), as cases in which the Court properly held that certain time limits were nonjurisdictional because they were imposed by rules that did not purport to have any jurisdictional significance. See 551 U. S., at 210–211, 127 S. Ct. 2360. Kontrick involved "time

constraints applicable to objections to discharge" in bankruptcy proceedings. 540 U. S. , at 453, 124 S. Ct. 906. In that case, we first examined 28 U. S. C. § 157(b)(2)(J), the statute "conferring jurisdiction over objections to discharge," and observed that it did not contain a timeliness requirement. Kontrick, 540 U. S. , at 453, 124 S. Ct. 906. Rather, the "time constraints applicable to objections to discharge" were contained in the Bankruptcy Rules, which expressly state that they "'shall not be construed to extend or limit the jurisdiction of the courts.'" See ibid. (quoting Fed. Rule Bkrtcy. Proc. 9030). Eberhart, in turn, treated as nonjurisdictional certain rules that the Court held "closely parallel[ed]" those in Kontrick. 546 U. S. , at 15, 126 S. Ct. 403.

8. This conclusion mirrors our holding in Zipes that Title VII's EEOC filing requirement was nonjurisdictional, even though some of our own decisions had characterized it as jurisdictional. See 455 U. S. , at 393, 102 S. Ct. 1127 (noting that "the legal character of the requirement was not at issue in those" earlier cases); see also *National Railroad Passenger Corporation v. Morgan*, 536 U. S. 101, 109, 121, 122 S. Ct. 2061, 153 L. Ed. 2d 106 (2002) (relying on the analysis in Zipes).

9. Amicus' remaining jurisdictional argument—that the policy goals underlying copyright registration support construing § 411(a)'s registration provisions as jurisdictional, see Amicus Brief 45—is similarly unavailing. We do not agree that a condition should be ranked as jurisdictional merely because it promotes important congressional objectives. See *Arbaugh v. Y & H Corp.*, 546 U. S. 500, 504, 515-516, 126 S. Ct. 1235, 163 L. Ed. 2d 1097 (2006) (holding that Title VII's numerosity requirement is nonjurisdictional even though it serves the important policy goal of "spar[ing] very small businesses from Title VII liability").

E. g. , *Eberhart v. United States*, 546 U. S. 12, 126 S. Ct. 403, 163 L. Ed. 2d 14 (2005) (per curiam); *Scarborough v. Principi*, 541 U. S. 401, 124 S. Ct. 1856, 158 L. Ed. 2d 674 (2004); *Kontrick v. Ryan*, 540 U. S. 443, 124 S. Ct. 906, 157 L. Ed. 2d 867 (2004).

劳伦斯·戈兰等（上诉人）

小埃里克·H. 霍尔德总检察长等

第 10-545 号
开庭日期：2011 年 10 月 5 日
裁决日期：2012 年 1 月 18 日

案情摘要与裁判要旨*

《保护文学艺术作品伯尔尼公约》（以下简称《伯尔尼公约》）于1886年生效，是规范国际版权关系的主要公约。《伯尔尼公约》的164❶个成员国同意提供最低限度的版权保护，并给予其他成员国作者本国国民待遇。本案的关键在于，《伯尔尼公约》第18条要求各成员国保护其他成员国作者的作品，除非该作品版权已在要求保护的国家或者起源国到期。美国一直执行的是另一种国际版权保护制度，在20世纪大部分时间里，只保护那些起源国给予美国作者互惠保护且作品在美国出版的外国作者。尽管有《伯尔尼公约》第18条的要求，美国在1989年加入《伯尔尼公约》时，并没有为在美国处于公有领域的外国作品提供保护，其中有许多作品从未在美国受到过保护。然而，1994年《与贸易有关的知识产权协定》要求世界贸易组织各成员执行《伯尔尼公约》前21条，违者将由世界贸易组织强令执行。

作为回应，国会将对美国作品的保护期限适用于来自《伯尔尼公约》成员国作者的现存作品。《乌拉圭回合协定法案》（URAA）第514条对在起源国受保护但在美国因以下三种原因之一不受保护的作品给予版权保护：（1）作品出版时美国并不保护来自起源国的作品；（2）属于美国所不保护的1972年以前固定的录音制品；（3）作者未办理美国法定版权

---

* 因篇幅所限，本判决书的原文和译文删除了少数意见法官的主张。——译者注
❶ 现有179个成员国。——译者注

劳伦斯·戈兰等（上诉人）诉小埃里克·H.霍尔德总检察长等

保护手续的作品。URAA 第 514 条保护的作品类型为：一旦起源国与美国维持互惠版权关系，或美国遵从《伯尔尼公约》移除版权保护手续，便应当保护的作品。由于之前美国版权保护中存在的障碍，第 514 条恢复保护的外国作品此前已进入公有领域。为缓和将外国作品重新置于受保护状态可能产生的冲击，URAA 第 514 条为颁布前已经利用相关外国作品的各方提供了过渡方案。

上诉人包括管弦乐队指挥、音乐家、出版商等人，在 URAA 第 514 条将作品从公有领域恢复至保护状态前，他们可以自由利用这些作品。他们坚持认为，国会通过第 514 条之举逾越了其在《宪法》版权条款下的权限，也冲破了《宪法》第一修正案的限制。地区法院批准了总检察长的简易决判申请。联邦第十巡回上诉法院维持了地区法院的部分判决，认为国会并未违反《宪法》版权条款，但认为第 514 条应遵从 *Eldred v. Ashcroft* 案进行《宪法》第一修正案审查。案件发回重审后，地区法院对上诉人提出的《宪法》第一修正案主张作出简易决判，认为第 514 条将部分公有领域作品恢复至保护状态未体现任何宣称的联邦利益。联邦第十巡回上诉法院推翻了这一裁决，认定第 514 条是美国政府为保护美国版权人海外利益这一重要目的而量身定做的。

联邦最高法院认为，国会通过 URAA 第 514 条之举没有逾越其在《宪法》版权条款下的权限，《宪法》第一修正案也并不禁止 URAA 第 514 条恢复作品版权保护。最终，联邦最高法院维持了联邦第十巡回上诉法院的裁决。

金斯伯格大法官发表了判决意见，罗伯茨首席大法官和斯卡利亚大法官、肯尼迪大法官、托马斯大法官和索托马约尔大法官赞同。布雷耶大法官发表了少数意见，阿利托大法官赞同。卡尔根大法官未参与对此案的讨论或裁决。

1886年生效的《伯尔尼公约》是规范国际版权关系的主要公约。作为《伯尔尼公约》所确立的国际版权秩序的后来者，美国于1989年加入了《伯尔尼公约》。为更好地执行该公约，同时作为美国对乌拉圭回合多边贸易谈判的部分回应，国会于1994年给予在外国受版权保护的作品与美国作品**878相同的保护期限。为此，国会拟定了URAA第514条，对于《伯尔尼公约》成员国的作品，在起源国受保护但在美国因以下三种原因之一而不受保护的作品给予版权保护：作品出版时美国并不保护来自起源国的作品；属于美国所不保护的1972年以前固定的录音制品；作者未办理美国法定的版权保护手续（国会不再将履行版权保护手续作为版权保护的先决条件）。

无论根据起源国的法律，还是美国的法律，只要外国作品过了版权保护期限，URAA都不会给予版权保护，从而使其进入公有领域。URAA第514条保护的作品类型为：一旦起源国与美国维持互惠版权关系，或美国遵从《伯尔尼公约》之规定移除版权保护手续，便是应当受保护的作品。然而，外国作者无法得到第514条颁布前他们所失去的版权保护。因此，与美国作者相比，外国作者获得的垄断性权利保护年限较短。由于在第514条颁布前美国版权保护中存在的障碍，被第514条恢复保护的外国作品此前已进入公有领域。为缓和将外国作品重新置于保护状态可能产生的冲击，第514条为在URAA颁布前已利用相关外国作品的各方提供了过渡条款。

上诉人包括管弦乐队指挥、音乐家、出版商等人，在第514条将作品从公有领域恢复至保护状态前，他们可以自由利用这些作品。他们坚持认为，《宪法》中的版权与专利条款（第1条8款8项）以及《宪法》第一修正案均宣告了第514条无效。根据最高位阶法律的规定，上诉人声称，无论出于何种原因，任何已进入公有领域的作品都必须永远留存于公有领域。

我们赞同联邦第十巡回上诉法院的裁决，认为国会制定第514条并未违反《宪法》对国会立法权限的限制。无论是《宪法》版权与专利条款，还是《宪法》第一修正案，在任何情况下，都不会让作品永远留存在公有领域。

◇ I ◇

A

伯尔尼联盟成员同意给予来自其他成员国的作者国民待遇（《伯尔尼公约》于1886年9月9日签订，1967年7月14日在斯德哥摩尔修订第1条、第5条1款，见《联合国条约系列》第828卷，第221、225页、第231-233页）。成员国国民以及在《伯尔尼公约》164个成员国之一出版作品的任何作者在全球多国享有版权保护（第2条6款、第3条）。此外，各国须为作者提供《伯尔尼公约》规定的最低限度保护。无论作者是否履行了成员国国内的法定保护手续，版权保护期限必须为作者终生加上死后至少50年（第5条2款、第7条1款）。而且，与本案相关的是，除非一件作品的版权保护在主张保护的国家或者起源国到期，否则外国必须给予作品版权保护（第18条1、2款）。

**879美国一直执行的是另一种国际版权保护制度。在1891年前，外国作品完全被排除在版权保护之外。在20世纪大部分时间里，受到保护的只有那些起源国给予美国作者互惠保护且作品在美国出版的外国作者（见1891年3月3日法案第3条、第13条，《美国制定法大全》第26卷，第1107、1110页；帕特里，"美国和国际版权法"，《休斯敦法律评论》2003年第40卷，起始页749，引证页750）。对国内外作者来说，能否获得保护取决于是否办理了通知、登记和续展等手续。

1989年，美国加入了《伯尔尼公约》这个多边、无手续要求的国际版权体系。最初，国会遵守公约的态度是"最低限度标准"。参见1988年《众议院报告》第100-609号（以下简称1988年《伯尔尼公约实施法案》众议院报告）第7页。1988年《伯尔尼公约实施法案》（BCIA，《美国制定法大全》第102卷，第2853页）仅就《伯尔尼公约》条款明确要求的内容对美国版权法进行了修改（1988年《伯尔尼公约实施法案》众议院报告第7页）。尽管《伯尔尼公约》要求成员国——包括"新加入伯尔尼联盟的成员国"——保护在起源国受保护的外国作品（《伯尔尼公约》第18条1款和4款,见《联合国条约系列》第828卷,第251页),但1988年《伯尔尼公约实施法案》对"美国公有领域的任何作品"不提供保护(《伯尔尼公约实施法案》第12条,《美国制定法大全》第102卷,第2860页)。1988年《伯尔尼公约实施法案》表示,保护未来外国作品就已经符合《伯尔尼公约》第18条的要求(见《伯尔尼公约实施法案》第2条3款,《美国制定法大全》第102卷,第2853页:"本法案所做的修订,以及本法案颁布之日现存的法律,满足了美国遵从《伯尔尼公约》的义务……")。然而,国会表示,它并没有明确拒绝对现存外国作品的"追溯性"保护;相反,它搁置了《伯尔尼公约》的实施问题,将其推迟到"有可能对宪法、商业和消费者等因素进行更为彻底的审查之后"(1988年《伯尔尼公约实施法案》众议院报告第51、52页)。

**880 美国采取的最低限度保护做法并不被《伯尔尼公约》其他成员国所认同。在进行《北美自由贸易协定》(NAFTA)谈判时,墨西哥当局就抱怨美国拒绝遵从《伯尔尼公约》第18条之规定,不保护墨西哥国内的版权作品。参见1991年第102届国会第1次会议(众议院司法委员会知识产权和司法行政小组委员会关于知识产权和国际问题听证会上美国版权局局长拉尔夫·阿曼的声明),见会议记录第168页。版权局局长还报告了来自土耳其、埃及和奥地利的"质疑"(同上)。对于在美国依然受保护但在其他国家处于公有领域的美国作品,泰国和俄罗斯采取了回避态度,直至美国同意为他们国家作者的作品提供互惠保护[URAA联合听证会美国贸易代表办公室(USTR)总法律顾问艾瑞·夏皮罗的声明,见会议记录第137页;(同上)雪拉·珀尔穆特教授的声明,见会议记录第208页;(同上)美国唱片业协会(RIAA)杰森·伯尔曼的声明,见会议记录第291页]。

然而,《伯尔尼公约》并未提供有效的执行机制。它虽考虑了在**881国际法院解决争端(第33条1款),但并没有具体规定对于不遵从第18条者的制裁措施,并且还允许各成员国在任何时候声明自己"不受公约争端解决条款的约束"(《伯尔尼公约》第33条2、3款,《联合国条约系列》第828卷,第277页)。1994年之前未发生因执行《伯尔尼公约》而引发的诉讼活动就不足为奇了[丹尼尔·热尔韦,《与贸易有关的知识产权协定》,第213页、注释134(2008年第三版)]。美国贸易代表告诉国会,尽管"伯尔尼联盟的一些成员国不赞成（我们）对于第18条的解读",但《伯尔尼公约》"没有提供一个有意义的争端解决机制"[URAA联合听证会（艾瑞·夏皮罗的声明），见会议记录第137页]。这一缺陷意味着，国会"可以自由采取最低限度保护方法并规避第18条"的规定（卡普，"关于《伯尔尼公约》第18条与美国追溯保护伯尔尼成员国及其他作品研究"最终报告，哥伦比亚-VLA法与艺术期刊，1996年第20卷，第157、172页）。

1994年情况发生了变化。乌拉圭回合多边贸易谈判催生了世界贸易组织和《与贸易有关的知识产权协定》，美国均已批准加入。《与贸易有关的知识产权协定》要求世界贸易组织各成员执行《伯尔尼公约》前21条，违者将由世界贸易组织强令执行（《与贸易有关的知识产权协定》第9条1款、《国际法律资料》第33卷，第1197、1201页：要求遵守除《伯尔尼公约》第6条之二"精神权利"外的所有规定）。世界贸易组织强化了公约的执行力——不遵守世界贸易组织裁决的成员可能遭受关税或跨部门报复。参见热尔韦，第213页；威廉·帕特里，《版权》第7卷，第24.1节，第24-8页至第24-9页（2011年版）。世界贸易组织的执法程序大大增加了美国的贸易伙伴质疑美国不充分遵从《伯尔尼公约》的风险。参见URAA联合听证会（艾瑞·夏皮罗的声明），会议记录第137页："其他世界贸易组织成员很可能会根据（世界贸易组织）程序质疑美国目前执行《伯尔尼公约》第18条的状况。"

国会对于乌拉圭协议的回应，平息了所有质疑美国遵从第18条状况的声音。URAA第514条[《美国制定法大全》第108卷，第4976条，编于《美国法典》第17卷第104A条和第109条（a）款]将版权保护扩展到在起源国受保护，但＊＊882因为以下三个原因之一而无权在美国享有排他性权利的作品：在作品出版时，起源国和美国之间缺乏互惠版权关系；美国不保护1972年以前固定的录音制品这一客体；未遵从美国法定的版权保护手续（例如，未提供版权状态信息，或者未登记和续展版权）。见《美国法典》第104A条（h）款（6）项之（B）-（C）。

无论是在美国还是在起源国，因版权保护期限到期而进入公有领域的作品，将不再受第514条的进一步保护（同上）。依据URAA第514条"恢复"保护的作品,"如果该作品从未进入公有领域,则在该作品本应被授予的版权期限内剩余的保护期限仍然有效……"[《美国法典》第104A条(a)款(1)项之(B)]。恢复版权保护的举措有望将外国作品与美国作品平等对待;假设一名外国作者和一名国内作者同一天死亡,那么他们的作品未来将同时进入公有领域[见《美国法典》第302条(a)款:版权保护通常在作者死亡后第70年到期]。然而,如果恢复保护的作品在美国一开始就受到保护,那么在URAA第514条颁布之前,这些作品本应享有的排他性权利期间不会得到补偿。因此,它们的保护期限总是短于类似的美国作品。

国会并没有忽略URAA对公有领域的干涉。＊＊883第514条对于在恢复保护之前发生的任何利用外国作品的行为并不追究任何责任。此外,在第514条颁布后的一年内,任何人都可以自由复制或者利用恢复版权保护的作品[见《美国法典》第17卷第104A条(h)款(2)项之(A)]。由于担心第514条与《宪法》第五修正案征收条款的兼容性问题,国会增加了对"信赖使用者"的额外保护。所谓"信赖使用者",是指在URAA颁布之前就已使用或获得当时处于公有领域的外国作品者[见《美国法典》第17卷第104A条(h)款(3)(4)项]。信赖使用者可以继续利用恢复保护的作品,直到被恢复保护作品的版权人在恢复后两年内向美国版权局通告其执行版权的意愿,或者直接通告信赖使用者[第104A条(c)款、(d)款(2)项(A)目之(i)和(B)目之(i)]。在此之后,信赖使用者可在一年宽限期内继续使用现有作品副本[第104A条(d)款(2)项(A)目之(ⅱ)和(B)目之(ⅱ)]。最后,在URAA颁布之前,任何人基于被恢复保护作品创作"演绎作品"的,在向版权人支付"合理补偿"后,可以无限期利用演绎作品。双方无法就补偿金额达成一致的,由地区法院法官确定[第104A条(d)款(3)项]。

B

2001年,上诉人提起诉讼,质疑第514条。他们坚持认为,国会通过的URAA逾越了其在《宪法》版权条款下的权限,并突破了《宪法》第一修正案的限制。地区法院批准了总检察长的简易决判申请,见 *Golan v.*

Gonzales 案，案号：Civ. 01-B-1854,2005 WL 914754（科罗拉多州地区法院，2005年4月20日）。在驳斥上诉人关于国会违反《宪法》版权条款下的权限时，地区法院称，历史上，国会"对将可受版权保护的作品从公有领域移出的决定很少反悔"（同上，第14页）。法院随后拒绝背离"通过执行版权来进行私人审查并不牵涉《宪法》第一修正案的既定规则"（同上，第17页）。

联邦第十巡回上诉法院部分维持了一审判决 [*Golan v. Gonzales* 案，《联邦上诉法院判例汇编·第三辑》第501卷，起始页1179（2007年裁决）]。与地区法院一样，联邦第十巡回上诉法院认为，公有领域并非国会无力"双向穿越"的"禁地"[同上，第1187页（省略文内引号）]。但是关于第514条，上诉法院遵循联邦最高法院对 *Eldred v. Ashcroft* 案 [《美国判例汇编》第537卷，起始页186；《最高法院判例汇编》第123卷，起始页769；《美国判例汇编律师版·第二辑》第154卷，起始页683（2003年裁决）] 判决的解读，认为需要进一步进行《宪法》第一修正案的审查（《联邦上诉法院判例汇编·第三辑》第501卷，引证页1187）。该措施"改变了版权保护的传统版图"，上诉法院特别指出一旦作品进入公有领域就不会再离开的"基本原则"[同上（引用＊＊884 *Eldred* 案，《美国判例汇编》第537卷，引证页221；《最高法院判例汇编》第123卷，起始页769）]。上诉法院将案件发回地区法院，指示地区法院根据上诉法院的意见，重新裁判URAA是否有逾越《宪法》第一修正案的嫌疑。

案件发回后，地区法院论证的出发点是无可争议的：第514条并非以内容为基础来规范言论，因此，如果第514条"系为重要的政府利益而量身定做，那就应得到支持"。参见《联邦地区法院判例汇编·第二辑》第611卷，起始页1165，引证页1170-1171（科罗拉多地区法院，2009年裁决）（引用 *Ward v. Rock Against Racism* 案，《美国判例汇编》第491卷，起始页781，引证页791；《最高法院判例汇编》第109卷，起始页2746；《美国判例汇编律师版·第二辑》第105卷，起始页661，1989年裁决）。地区法院判决认为，简易决判对于上诉人来说是恰当的，因为第514条对公有领域的压缩并未体现任何其所宣称的下述联邦利益，包括遵从《伯尔尼公约》，确保美国作者在国外获得更多保护，或是补救外国作者在美国因作品未受保护而遭遇的不公正待遇（《联邦法院判例汇编补遗·第二辑》第611卷，引证页1172-1177）。

联邦第十巡回上诉法院推翻了这一判决。有鉴于国会对于外交事务的远见，上诉法院认为，第514条经得起《宪法》第一修正案的审查。具体而言，上诉法院认定，这部法律是政府为保护美国版权人海外利益而量身定做的。参见《联邦上诉法院判例汇编·第三辑》第609卷，起始页1076（2010年裁决）。

我们批准了调卷令状申请，以考虑上诉人对于第514条是否违反《宪法》版权条款和《宪法》第一修正案的质疑［《美国判例汇编》第562卷——，《最高法院判例汇编》第131卷，起始页1600；《美国判例汇编律师版·第二辑》第179卷，起始页516（2011年裁决）］，现维持原判。

II

我们首先讨论上诉人关于根据《宪法》版权条款国会无权制定URAA第514条的主张。《宪法》规定，"国会有权……为促进科学进步……通过授予作者有限时间内……利用其作品的垄断权"（《宪法》第1条8款8项）。上诉人认为，《宪法》授予国会的这一立法权限，无论如何都不可能将版权保护延伸至因为任何原因已进入公有领域的作品。我们在《宪法》版权条款条文、国会立法的历史实践或者我们的先例中都看不到这一限制。

A

《宪法》版权条款文本并不排斥赋予公有领域的作品版权保护［专题论丛：国会权力与《宪法》版权条款的固有限制，《哥伦比亚法律与艺术评论》，第30卷，起始页259，引证页266（2007年出版）］。上诉人的相反论点主要源自《宪法》将版权保护期限限制在"有限时间"内。他们主张，"将作品从公有领域移除"意味着将固定、可预测的期限变成了可以随时重置或复活的期限，即便是已经过了保护期限。这"违反了'有限时间'限制"（上诉人陈述第22页）。

劳伦斯·戈兰等（上诉人）诉小埃里克·H.霍尔德总检察长等

我们在 Eldred 案中主要就上诉人关于有限时间的争论作出了终审裁决。在那一案件中，我们主要讨论了国会将现有的版权期限延长 20 年是否违反了《宪法》版权条款的问题。参见《美国判例汇编》第 537 卷，引证页 192-193；《最高法院判例汇编》第 123 卷，起始页 769：支持《版权期限延长法案》（CTEA）。在本案中，我们裁定国会是在《宪法》允许的范围内行事，并拒绝从版权条款中推断是否存在"保护期限一旦设定就永远'固定''不得调整'"的明确要求（同上，第 199 页）。我们注意到，"'有限'一词并没有传达如此狭窄的意思"（同上）。相反，该词最好理解为"限制在一定范围内""有节制的"或者"有约束的"［同上（省略文内引号）］。本案上诉人 **885 的解读方式与 Eldred 案最高法院拒绝接受的解读十分相似，同样不具有说服力。

第 514 条赋予被恢复保护作品的保护期限与《版权期限延长法案》延长后的作品保护期限一样长。就 Eldred 案而言，本案上诉人并未争论国会授予美国作者的保护期限——作者终生加上死后 70 年——是无限制的。参见《美国法典》第 17 卷第 302 条（a）款。上诉人也没有解释为什么相同的保护期限一旦适用于外国作品就不再是同样"有约束的"和"受限制的"。参见 Eldred 案，《美国判例汇编》第 537 卷，引证页 199；《最高法院判例汇编》第 123 卷，起始页 769。事实上，如前所述（见前文第 878 页、第 882-883 页），恢复保护的外国作品的版权保护期限比美国作者的作品保护期限要短。

在上诉人看来，区别在于，对于公有领域的作品而言，有限的保护期限已经过去。那么，曾经被排除在美国版权保护之外的外国作品的有限保护期限是几年呢？当然是"0"，上诉人回应说（上诉人陈述第 22 页：所涉作品"得到了一个具体保护期限……有时明确设置为零"；"在这段时间结束时"，它们"进入了公有领域"。口头辩论笔录第 52 页：通过"拒绝为一件作品提供任何保护"，国会将"保护期限设置为零"，从而"告诉我们保护期限终止之时"）。这一论点没有任何意义，因为一段"有限时间"的垄断性权利必须有始方能有终。

按照这一逻辑，上诉人坚称，政府的立场将会允许国会在作品第一个保护期届满后再设立第二个"有限的"保护期，之后再设立第三个，以此类推。上诉人因此认为，只要国会立法分期确定版权保护期限，就可能会引入永久的版权保护期限。但正如 Eldred 案，上诉人假设的国会立法中的不当行为与本案毫无关联（见《美国判例汇编》第 537 卷，引证页 198-200、209-210；《最高法院判例汇编》第 123 卷，起始页 769）。国会只是将美国和其他《伯尔尼公约》成员国放在相同保护水平上，进而向被美国冷落的外国作者提供公正的待遇，人们无法指责国会在悄悄考虑建立永久的版权保护体系。

B

纵观国会立法的历史实践，可以确认，《宪法》版权条款允许美国完全遵从《伯尔尼公约》。毫无疑问，联邦版权立法一般不会涉及公有领域的作品。上诉人称，第 514 条对于公有领域的侵扰，使他们的诉讼有别于 Eldred 案。上诉人指出，国会制定的《版权期限延长法案》将作品的保护期限在届满前延长了，遵循了"始终如一的国会立法操作"（《美国判例汇编》第 537 卷，引证页 200；《最高法院判例汇编》第 123 卷，起始页 769）。但他们认为，没有类似的历史实践支持第 514 条。

然而，国会有时认为有必要去保护一些曾经可以被自由获取的作品。例如，1790 年《版权法案》对许多以前在公有领域的作品进行了保护。参见 1790 年 5 月 31 日法案（以下简称"1970 年法案"）第 1 条，《美国制定法大全》第 1 卷，第 124 页：涵盖"已经在合众国各州印刷的任何地图、图表或书籍"。在该法案启动统一的国家版权体系之前，有三个州没有提供任何版权立法保护。在那些提供了部分版权保护的州里，有七个州不在＊＊886 保护地图上，八个州不保护以前出版的书籍，所有十个州都拒绝保护未办理版权手续的作品。因此，似乎第一届国会也并不认为公有领域完全不可以干涉。我们认识到，"1790 年第一部版权法案和 1802 年法案的起草者……与宪法的形成处于同一时代，他们中间有很多人是起草宪法的制宪会议代表，他们对宪法的解读本身具有很大的分量"。参见 Burrow-Giles Lithographic Co. v. Sarony 案，《美国判例汇编》第 111 卷，起始页 53，引证页 57；《最高法院判例汇编》第 4 卷，起始页 279；《美国判例汇编律师版·第二辑》第 28 卷，起始页 349（1884 年裁决）。

劳伦斯·戈兰等（上诉人）诉小埃里克·H.霍尔德总检察长等

  随后的行动也证实，国会并未将《宪法》版权条款理解为排除对现存作品的保护。一些私法案恢复了以前处于公有领域的作品的版权。参见1849年2月19日（《科森法案》），《美国制定法大全》第9卷，第57章，第763页；1874年6月23日（《赫尔穆特法案》），《美国制定法大全》第18卷，第534章，第618页；1898年2月17日（《琼斯法案》），《美国制定法大全》第30卷，第29章，第1396页。这些私法案在法庭上未引起过争议。

  相比之下，类似的专利法案在诉讼中得到了法院的支持。1808年，国会通过了一项私法案，恢复了对奥利弗·埃文斯磨坊的专利保护。当埃文斯起诉侵权时，巡回上诉法院的首任首席法官马歇尔［*Evans v. Jordan*案，《联邦判例》第8卷，起始页872（第4564号）（弗吉尼亚州，1813年裁决）］和随后的本法院布什罗德·华盛顿大法官［*Evans v. Jordan*案，克兰奇《美国判例汇编》第9卷，起始页199；《美国判例汇编律师版》第3卷，起始页704（1815年裁决）］，均支持恢复专利的有效性。在专利期满后，法院表示，"公众并不享有利用埃文斯发现的一般权利"，因此被告不可以继续使用他在专利期满后至法案通过期间建造的机器设备［同上，第202页。另见*Blanchard v. Sprague*案，《联邦判例》第3卷，起始页648页，引证页650（第1518号）（马萨诸塞联邦上诉法院，1839年裁决）（斯托里法官）："我从来没有怀疑过国会拥有'向一项已公开使用并深受大家喜爱的发明……授予专利权'这一宪法上的权力"］。

  在*McClurg v. Kingsland*案中，本法院再次支持国会恢复专利＊＊887至保护状态的做法。参见*McClurg v. Kingsland*案，霍华德《美国判例汇编》第1卷，起始页202；《美国判例汇编律师版》第11卷，起始页102（1843年裁决）。在这一案件里，我们执行了1839年的一项修正案，该修正案认可了一项发明的专利权，尽管发明人的雇主之前已使用了该发明。如果没有这种特别许可，雇主的使用将意味着该发明无法获得专利，进而未经发明者同意也就可以自由利用该发明（同上，第206-209页）。

  国会还通过了一些概括性法案，对失去保护的作品和发明授予版权和专利权。如果发明人"由于疏忽、意外或者过失"未能履行法定手续，致使原专利权"无效或者无法实施的"，1832年的一项法案授予该发明人一项新专利（1832 年 7 月 3 日法案第 3 条，《美国制定法大全》第 4 卷，第 559 页）。1893 年的一项措施同样允许那些没有及时交存作品的作者获得《版权法案》规定的"所有权利和特权"，前提是他们在 1893 年 3 月 1 日之前缴纳规定的保证金（1893 年 3 月 3 日法案第 215 条，《美国制定法大全》第 27 卷，第 743 页）。1919 年和 1941 年，国会授权总统发布公告，对在第一次世界大战和第二次世界大战期间落入公有领域的外国作品给予保护（见 1919 年 12 月 18 日法案第 11 条，《美国制定法大全》第 41 卷，第 368 页；1941 年 9 月 25 日法案第 421 条，《美国制定法大全》第 55 卷，第 732 页）。

上诉人提及了 Graham v. John Deere Co. of Kansas City 案［《美国判例汇编》第 383 卷，起始页 1；《最高法院判例汇编》第 86 卷，起始页 684；《美国判例汇编律师版·第二辑》第 15 卷，起始页 545（1966 年裁决）］的附带说明，希望我们回顾这段历史。在 Graham v. John Deere Co. of Kansas City 案中，我们指出，"如果授予专利的效果表现为从公有领域攫取现有知识，或限制对于已提供材料的自由获取，则国会不得授权颁发专利权"（同上，《美国判例汇编》第 383 卷，引证页 6；《最高法院判例汇编》第 86 卷，起始页 684；见下文第 907 页）。但正如我们在 Eldred 案中所解释的，这段话并没有提到《宪法》对国会在版权和专利立法上的限制。相反，它"涉及一项发明获得专利保护的资格问题"（《美国判例汇编》第 537 卷，引证页 202，注释 7；《最高法院判例汇编》第 123 卷，起始页 769）。

的确，建立联邦版权制度和应对全球战争所带来的侵扰，让国会面临着非同寻常的局面。然而，《与贸易有关的知识产权协定》要求美国完全遵从《伯尔尼公约》，也是一个重大事件［见上，第 880-881 页；比较 Eldred 案，《美国判例汇编》第 537 卷，引证页 259、264-265；《最高法院判例汇编》第 123 卷，起始页 769（布雷耶大法官在此案中的少数意见）：认可美国遵从《伯尔尼公约》所做的努力对促进国际统一版权制度的重要性］。鉴于我们认为国会拥有权限，我们不会再去揣测国会在不干扰公有领域和完全遵从《伯尔尼公约》之间会作出怎样的政治选择（对比同上，Eldred 案，《美国判例汇编》第 537 卷，引证页 212-213；《最高法院判例汇编》第 123 卷，起始页 769）。

劳伦斯·戈兰等（上诉人）诉小埃里克·H.霍尔德总检察长等

C

上诉人关于《宪法》版权和专利条款的最终论点涉及其原始措辞。国会有权通过确立版权和专利保护制度来"促进科学＊＊888和实用技艺的进步"（美国《宪法》第1条8款8项）。也许对于当代读者来说，与直觉相反的是，国会的版权立法权限与科学的进步联系在一起，专利立法权限与实用技艺的进步密切相关［见 Graham 案，《美国判例汇编》第383卷，引证页5与注释1；《最高法院判例汇编》第86卷，起始页684；Evans 案，《联邦判例》第8卷，引证页873（马歇尔法官的观点）］。

上诉人承认，"科学的进步"泛指"知识和学问的创造和传播"（上诉人陈述第21页；对应下文第899-900页）。然而，他们认为，除非联邦立法"刺激……新作品的产生"，否则达不到《宪法》版权条款的目的（上诉人陈述第24页；对应下文第899-900页、第903、908页）。由于第514条仅涉及现存作品，上诉人强烈认为，它"没有提供有效的激励措施来鼓励创作新作品"，因此是无效的（反答辩状第4页）。

然而，创作至少一项新作品并非国会促进知识和学问的唯一途径。在 Eldred 案中，我们驳斥了一个与上诉人近乎相同的论调。Eldred 案的上诉人强烈认为，"《版权期限延长法案》对现有版权保护期限的扩展绝对无法'促进科学的进步'……因为它并不会刺激新作品的产生"（《美国判例汇编》第537卷，引证页211-212；《最高法院判例汇编》第123卷，起始页769）。针对这一论点，我们的回应是，《宪法》版权条款并不要求每个单独的版权法条文都能够促进新作品的产生。相反，我们解释道，《宪法》版权条款"授权国会自由决定建立整体上服务于该条款所设定目标的知识产权体系"（同上，第222页；《最高法院判例汇编》第123卷，起始页769）。我们认为，这些允许的目标超出了创作新作品的范畴［同上，第205-206页；《最高法院判例汇编》第123卷，起始页769：驳斥了"促进科学进步的唯一途径是激励新作品的创作"这一观点（引用珀尔穆特的话，来自"参与国际版权体系，以促进科学和实用技艺的进步"，《洛约拉（洛杉矶）法律评论》2002年第36卷，第323、332页）］。

即使没有前面这些判例，上诉人的争辩也毫无意义。《宪法》版权条款文本中没有任何内容将"科学的进步"局限于"鼓励创作作品"（同上，第324页、注释5）。此外，《宪法》颁布以来的证据表明，相较于创作，鼓励现存作品的传播也被认为是促进科学进步的恰当手段［见纳克巴，"解读版权神话"，《律师行业·第二辑》2002年第6卷，第37、44页："《宪法》起草时的版权保护范围"瞄准的是"出版，而非创作"，"与版权必须促进创作活动才能有效地主张不一致"（省略文内引号）］。事实上，在1976年以前，国会一直将"联邦版权与出版捆绑在一起，因此主要鼓励＊＊889的不是创作作品"，而是传播作品（见上，第324页、注释5）。我们的裁决相应地承认"版权保护为创作**和传播思想**提供经济激励"［*Harper & Row, Publishers, Inc. v. Nation Enterprises*案，《美国判例汇编》第471卷，起始页539，引证页558；《最高法院判例汇编》第105卷，起始页2218；《美国判例汇编律师版·第二辑》第85卷，起始页588（1985年裁决）（黑体字强调后加）。另见*Eldred*案，《美国判例汇编》第537卷，引证页206；《最高法院判例汇编》第123卷，起始页769］。

考虑到这一背景，第514条完全落入《宪法》版权条款授予国会的立法权限范围。国会有理由确信，遵从《伯尔尼公约》可以"促进知识的传播"（上诉人陈述第4页）。一个完善的国际版权体系将有助于鼓励现存和未来作品的传播［URAA联合听证会会议记录第189页（珀尔穆特教授的声明）］。国会有理由相信，完全遵从《伯尔尼公约》有利于扩大美国作者的海外市场，在国外强化对美国作品的保护而免受盗版［《参议院报告》1994年第103-412号，第224、225页；URAA联合听证会会议记录第291页（美国唱片业协会伯尔曼的声明）；同上，第244、247页（国际知识产权联盟史密斯的声明）］，从而惠及美国本土版权密集型产业的发展，并在创造过程中吸纳更多投资。

刺激新作品的创作无疑是促进知识和学问传播的重要手段。然而，我们认为，这并不是国会"促进科学的进步"的唯一手段（珀尔穆特，见上，第332页：如果激励创作是促进科学进步的唯一路径，那么美国将"失去一切灵活性"）。国会认定，严格遵守《伯尔尼公约》有助于实现《宪法》版权条款设定的目标，本法院没有理由质疑国会作出的理性判断。

劳伦斯·戈兰等（上诉人）诉小埃里克·H.霍尔德总检察长等

III

A

我们接下来解释为什么《宪法》第一修正案并不会阻止第514条恢复版权保护。为此，我们首先总结一下具有开拓性意义的 Eldred 案裁决中的相关部分。Eldred 案上诉人和本案上诉人一样，都认为国会不仅仅是违反了《宪法》版权条款的"有限时间"规定，Eldred 案上诉人还单独指责国会违反了《宪法》第一修正案对言论自由的保障。在 Eldred 案中，我们认为《版权期限延长法案》将版权期限延长了20年未违反这两项规定。

关于第一修正案，我们认识到，对于言论表达施加某些限制是每一项版权保护固有的和预设的效果。＊＊890 鉴于"《宪法》版权条款和《宪法》第一修正案前后通过的时间比较接近"（《美国判例汇编》第537卷，引证页219；《最高法院判例汇编》第123卷，起始页769）。我们注意到，制定宪法者认为版权保护不仅是对表达性作品利用方式的限制，他们还将版权视为"言论自由的发动机，通过确立一种可以市场化利用表达的权利，版权提供了一种创作和传播思想的经济激励机制"［同上，引用 Harper & Row 案，《美国判例汇编》第471卷，引证页558；《最高法院判例汇编》第105卷，起始页2218（省略文内引号）。同上，《美国判例汇编》第471卷，引证页546；《最高法院判例汇编》第105卷，起始页2218："版权制度所授予的权利旨在确保知识贡献者的劳动得到合理的回报"］。

然后，我们描述了版权保护的"传统轮廓"："思想/表达二分法"和"合理使用"抗辩。在我们的法律体系中，两者都被认为是"《宪法》第一修正案内在的调节机制"（Eldred 案，《美国判例汇编》第537卷，引证页219；《最高法院判例汇编》第123卷，起始页769。见 Harper & Row 案，《美国判例汇编》第471卷，引证页560；《最高法院判例汇编》第105卷，起始页2218：对第一修正案言论自由的保障"体现在版权法案区分受版权保护的表达和不受版权保护的事实和思想"上，也体现在合理使用抗辩所保障的"学术和评论自由"上）。

思想/表达二分法成文于《美国法典》第17卷第102条（b）款："在任何情况下，版权都不保护受版权保护的作品中描述、解释、展示或包含的……任何思想、程序、过程、系统、操作方法、概念、原则或者发现。""由于这种思想/表达之区分，受版权保护的作品中的每一个思想、理论和事实在作品发表时立即可供公众自由利用"，只有作者的表达能获得版权保护［Eldred案，《美国判例汇编》第537卷，引证页219；《最高法院判例汇编》第123卷，起始页769。见Harper & Row案，《美国判例汇编》第471卷，引证页556；《最高法院判例汇编》第105卷，起始页2218："思想/表达二分法允许自由交流事实，同时仍然保护作者的表达，由此在《宪法》第一修正案和《版权法案》之间确立了明确的平衡"（省略文内引号）］。

版权保护的"传统轮廓"之二，即合理使用，成文于《美国法典》第17卷第107条："为批评、评论、新闻报道、教学（包括课堂内使用的多份副本）、学术或研究等目的，可以合理使用受版权保护的作品，包括为上述使用目的制作副本……，不构成版权侵权。"对垄断权的这一限制"允许公众不仅可以利用版权作品中的事实和思想，而且在某些情况下还可以利用作者的表达"［Eldred案，《美国判例汇编》第537卷，引证页219；《最高法院判例汇编》第123卷，起始页769；同上，第220页，《最高法院判例汇编》第123卷，起始页769："合理使用抗辩为学术和评论提供了相当大的空间，……甚至包括模仿在内"（省略内部引号）］。

鉴于版权法"保护言论自由的目的和措施"（同上，第219页；《最高法院判例汇编》第123卷，起始页769），我们在Eldred案中得出结论：没有必要再应上诉人的要求进行更严格的《宪法》第一修正案审查。我们在这里得出了相同的结论：第514条没有干扰＊＊891"思想/表达二分法"和"合理使用"抗辩。此外，国会还采取措施来舒缓从国内版权体系向国际版权体系的过渡，包括：推迟了实施日期，并且缓和了因恢复保护外国作品对在第514条生效前已利用相关作品的"信赖使用者"的冲击［见前面有关《美国法典》第17卷第104A条（c）（d）和（h）款的分析，第882—883页。另见Eldred案，《美国判例汇编》第537卷，引证页220；《最高法院判例汇编》第123卷，起始页769：描述了某些用户支付额外补偿以及免予追责情形，以减轻《版权期限延长法案》带来的不利影响］。

B

上诉人试图将他们的质疑与 *Eldred* 案中遭法院拒绝的质疑区分开。上诉人表示，他们享有的《宪法》第一修正案所保护的更高层级利益面临挑战，因为他们对已进入公共领域的作品享有"既定权利"，在这一点上，他们不同于 *Eldred* 案上诉人。他们认为，依据版权法"内在保护措施"所享有的有限权利根本无法比拟他们在第 514 条颁布之前所享有的无限权利。上诉人还说，第 514 条"前所未有"地侵入公有领域，也不具备支持 *Eldred* 案中争议的延长保护期限的历史渊源（上诉人陈述第 42-43 页）。

不管怎么说，这些争论都源于我们之前讨论并驳斥过的论点，即《宪法》基本上不允许国会立法干涉公有领域。本案上诉人试图打着《宪法》第一修正案的旗号，来实现他们根据《宪法》版权条款无法实现的目标：按照他们对《宪法》版权条款的理解，公有领域神圣不可侵犯；他们在阅读《宪法》第一修正案认为国会触及公有领域时，就需要对国会的手段和目的进行强化司法审查。我们已经解释（见上文第 884-887 页），《宪法》版权条款的文本和立法的历史记录并不能确定"作品一旦进入公有领域"，国会就不能再允许任何人——"即使是创作者——对其进行版权保护"（《联邦法院判例汇编·第三辑》第 501 卷，引证页 1184）。无论是历史证据、国会立法实践，还是本法院裁决，都不能表明《宪法》第一修正案赋予之前处于公有领域的作品版权保护为不正常现象。我们强调，无论是本案中的质疑，还是 *Eldred* 案中提出的质疑，都无法断言国会违反了《宪法》第一修正案所禁止的一般行为。例如，现在并未出现＊＊892 版权法保护作者观点的情况。

联邦第十巡回上诉法院的初步意见认为，相比较 *Eldred* 案的上诉人，本案上诉人关于第 514 条违反第一修正案的主张更强有力——*Eldred* 案上诉人从未"不受限制地获取任何争议作品"（《联邦法院判例汇编·第三辑》第 501 卷，引证页 1193。另同上，引证页 1194："一旦争议作品成为任何人都可以自由复制的作品，上诉人就对表达享有第一修正案上的既定权利，因此第 514 条对上诉人权利的干涉应接受第一修正案的审查"）。正如上诉人在法庭上所说，国会不由分说便撤销了他们利用公有领域中"属于他们"

的外国作品的权利（上诉人陈述第44-45页）。

对版权律师来说，"既定权利"这一提法可能听起来刚好相反：版权权利一般自获得保护之初就由作者或权利人享有（参见如《美国法典》第17卷第201条（a）款："受保护作品的版权……首先属于作者……"）。保护期限一旦结束，作品就不再重新赋予任何人，即会进入公有领域（参见如《伯尔尼公约》第18条1款；《联合国条约系列》第828卷，第251页："本公约适用于所有未进入公有领域的作品"）。任何人均可自由地获取公有领域中的作品，但版权保护期届满后，任何人均无法获得曾受保护作品的版权。

国会多次调整版权法案，以保护法案范畴以外的作品。例如，1891年，国会将版权保护延伸至外国作品，由此开创了新局面（1891年3月3日法案第13条；《美国制定法大全》第26卷，第1110页）；1856年将版权保护延伸至戏剧作品（1856年8月18日法案；《美国制定法大全》第11卷，第138页）；1865年将版权保护延伸至照片和底片（1865年3月3日法案第1条；《美国制定法大全》第13卷，第540页）；1912年将版权保护延伸至电影（1912年8月24日法案；《美国制定法大全》第37卷，第488页）；1972年将版权保护延伸至固定下来的录音制品（1971年10月15日法案；《美国制定法大全》第85卷，第391页）；以及1990年《建筑作品版权保护法案》将版权保护延伸至建筑作品（《美国制定法大全》第104卷，第5133页）。如上所述，国会也曾多次保护以前处于公有领域、公众可自由获取的作品（参见前文，第885-887页）。如果国会可以赋予上述作品版权保护而不用冒《宪法》第一修正案严格审查的风险，那么国会恢复保护那些因美国未遵从《伯尔尼公约》而提前进入公有领域的作品，又会违反什么言论自由原则呢？

我们还认为，第514条并没有完全禁止公众获取作品。上诉人抗议称，合理使用和思想/表达二分法"显然不足以保护第514条从上诉人或……公众那里夺走的言论和表达自由"——"为任何目的、不受限制地表演、复制、教学和分发整个作品"（上诉人陈述第46-47页）。上诉人称，"演奏肖斯塔科维奇交响曲的几小节，无法替代演奏整个作品"（同上，第47页）。

**893但国会并没有如此捆束上诉人。与 Eldred 案一样，这里的问题

劳伦斯·戈兰等（上诉人）诉小埃里克·H.霍尔德总检察长等

在于，未来用户如果想按照自己的意愿来利用某些作者的表达，要么付费，要么必须将利用控制在"合理使用"范围内。普罗科菲耶夫的《彼得与狼》曾经可以免费表演，在第514条颁布后，则须到市场上付费购买表演权。当然，普罗科菲耶夫同时期的美国作曲家的音乐也在这一市场上交易，例如，科普兰和伯恩斯坦的作品虽然受版权保护，但仍是美国音乐会节目单中的常客。

我们加入《伯尔尼公约》之前，国内和部分国外作品受到美国法律和双边国际协议的保护，而其他外国作品则因人为原因（因为不用交版税）可以以较低价格获得。通过全面实施《伯尔尼公约》，国会确保大部分作品，无论是本国还是外国，都将受到相同法律制度的规范。国会所回应的并非一个全新问题：同类的扭曲现象在1891年前发生频率更高，损害了国内外作者的利益。1891年以前，外国作品被完全排除在美国版权保护范围外。参见坎佩尔曼《美国与国际版权》，《美国国际法杂志》1947年第41卷，第406、413页："如果花25美分就能买到一本斯科特或狄更斯的小说，美国读者不太会愿意花一美元来阅读库珀或霍桑的小说。"第514条顺应了统一版权制度的趋势，将外国作品放于如果现行版权保护制度于外国作品创作和首次出版时就生效的情形。曾经被剥夺版权保护的作者，不再承受当初版权被剥夺的影响。第514条予以他们的，仅是在正常版权期限届满前他们应得的劳动利益。

与上诉人不同，少数意见法官反复提到了所谓"孤儿作品"的问题（见下文，第904-907、911-912页）。我们倒乐于承认，用户想要利用受版权保护的作品时，会面临确认或查找孤儿作品版权人的困难（见美国版权局2006年"关于孤儿作品的报告"第21-40页）。但正如少数意见所承认的（见下文，第906页），这一困难并非根据第514条恢复版权保护的作品所独有。比如，该问题同样困扰着尝试对美国书籍进行编目的美国图书馆（见下文，第905页。另见美国图书馆协会等作为法庭之友提交的意见摘要第22页：第514条"加剧"而非造成孤儿作品的问题；美国版权局，见前，第41-44页：将孤儿作品的问题归因于国会自1976年《版权法案》起取消了版权保护手续要求）。

＊＊894 该问题也不应由司法机关来解决，而应由立法机关来解决〔比

较 Authors Guild v. Google,Inc. 案,《联邦地区法院判例汇编新·第二辑》第770卷,起始页666,引证页677-678(纽约州南区联邦地区法院,2011年裁决):拒绝确认"谷歌图书馆"集体诉讼和解方案,主要是因为"国会比法院更适合建立无人认领书籍的利用机制"(引用 Eldred 案,《美国判例汇编》第537卷,引证页212;《最高法院判例汇编》第123卷,起始页769)]。实际上,少数意见提出的一系列政策和逻辑问题是不言而喻的(见下文,第905页)。尽管"经历了长期的努力"[见 Authors Guild v. Google,Inc. 案,《联邦地区法院判例汇编新·第二辑》第770卷,引证页678(引用玛丽伯斯·彼得斯的陈述)],国会仍未能像其他《伯尔尼公约》成员国那样颁布改善孤儿作品现状的立法。例如,1985年《加拿大版权法案》(985年加拿大修正法规,第C-42章第77条:授权版权委员会负责许可经用户投入适当努力后仍无法找到版权人的孤儿作品)。迄今为止,尚无人建议在执行《伯尔尼公约》过程中解决孤儿作品问题,目前都只是向国会建议宏观立法,少数意见法官引述了这些宏观立法[见下文第911-912页;美国版权局,《大众数字化中法律问题》第25-29页(2011年):讨论近期的立法工作]。我们对《伯尔尼公约》的坚定支持也许会推动国会制定此类立法。但是,对抗《伯尔尼公约》的规定,绝不是解决国会如何对待孤儿作品这一普遍问题的必要或适当的做法。

IV

国会判定,只有全力参与《伯尔尼公约》这一国际版权保护主导体系,才能最好地维护美国的利益,具体包括:确保做履行国际公约义务的典范、保障美国作者海外的利益,以及纠正过去针对外国作者的不公正做法。第514条所体现的判断恰好在各政府部门应有的职权范围内。当然,我们的职责是判断国会采取的行动是否违反《宪法》,而非明智与否。基于以上分析,我们很欣慰地看到没有出现所述情形。因此,维持联邦第十巡回上诉法院的判决!

Lawrence GOLAN, et al., Petitioners v.

Eric H. HOLDER, Jr., Attorney General, et al.

No. 10-545

Argued Oct. 5, 2011.

Decided Jan. 18, 2012.

https://www.supremecourt.gov/opinions/11pdf/10-545.pdf

The Berne Convention for the Protection of Literary and Artistic Works(Berne Convention or Berne), which took effect in 1886, is the principal accord governing international copyright relations. Latecomer to the international copyright regime launched by Berne, the United States joined the Convention in 1989. To perfect U. S. implementation of Berne, and as part of our response to the Uruguay Round of multilateral trade negotiations, Congress, in 1994, gave works enjoying copyright protection abroad the same full term of **878 protection available to U. S. works. Congress did so in § 514 of the Uruguay Round Agreements Act(URAA), which grants copyright protection to preexisting works of Berne member countries, protected in their country of origin, but lacking protection in the United States for any of three reasons: The United States did not protect works from the country of origin at the time of publication; the United States did not protect sound recordings fixed before 1972; or the author had failed to comply with U. S. statutory formalities(formalities Congress no longer requires as prerequisites to copyright protection).

The URAA accords no protection to a foreign work after its full copyright term has expired, causing it to fall into the public domain, whether under the laws of the country of origin or of this country. Works encompassed by § 514 are granted the protection they would have enjoyed had the United States maintained copyright relations with the author's country or removed formalities incompatible with Berne. Foreign authors, however, gain no credit for the protection they lacked in years prior to § 514's enactment. They therefore enjoy fewer total years of exclusivity than do their U. S. counterparts. As a consequence of the barriers to U. S. copyright protection prior to the enactment of § 514, foreign works "restored" to protection by the measure had entered the public domain in this country. To cushion the impact of their placement in protected status, Congress included in § 514 ameliorating accommodations for parties who had exploited affected works before the URAA was enacted.

Petitioners include orchestra conductors, musicians, publishers, and others who formerly enjoyed free access to works § 514 removed from the public domain. They maintain that the Constitution's Copyright and Patent Clause, Art. I, § 8, cl. 8, and First Amendment both decree the invalidity of § 514. Under those prescriptions of our highest law, petitioners assert, a work that has entered the public domain, for whatever reason, must forever remain there.

In accord with the judgment of the Tenth Circuit, we conclude that § 514 does not transgress constitutional limitations on Congress' authority. Neither the Copyright and Patent Clause nor the First Amendment, we hold, makes the public domain, in any and all cases, a territory that works may never exit.

A

Members of the Berne Union agree to treat authors from other member countries as well as they treat their own. Berne Convention, Sept. 9, 1886, as revised at Stockholm on July 14, 1967, Art. 1, 5(1), 828 U. N. T. S. 221, 225, 231 – 233. Nationals of a member country, as well as any author who publishes in one of Berne's 164 member states, thus enjoy copyright protection in nations across the globe. Art. 2(6), 3. Each country, moreover, must afford at least the minimum level of protection specified by Berne. The copyright term must span the author's lifetime, plus at least 50 additional years, whether or not the author has complied with a member state's legal formalities. Art. 5(2), 7(1). And, as relevant here, a work must be protected abroad unless its copyright term has expired in either the country where protection is claimed or the country of origin. Art. 18(1)–(2).

* * 879 A different system of transnational copyright protection long prevailed in this country. Until 1891, foreign works were categorically excluded from Copyright Act protection. Throughout most of the 20th century, the only eligible foreign authors were those whose countries granted reciprocal rights to U. S. authors and whose works were printed in the United States. See Act of Mar. 3, 1891, § 3, 13, 26 Stat. 1107, 1110; Patry, The United States and International Copyright Law, 40 Houston L. Rev. 749, 750 (2003). For domestic and foreign authors alike, protection hinged on compliance with notice, registration, and renewal formalities.

The United States became party to Berne's multilateral, formality–free copyright regime in 1989. Initially, Congress adopted a "minimalist approach" to compliance with the Convention. H. R. Rep. No. 100–609, p. 7 (1988) (hereinafter BCIA House Report). The Berne Convention Implementation Act of 1988

(BCIA), 102 Stat. 2853, made "only those changes to American copyright law that [were] clearly required under the treaty's provisions," BCIA House Report, at 7. Despite Berne's instruction that member countries—including "new accessions to the Union"—protect foreign works under copyright in the country of origin, Art. 18 (1) and (4), 828 U. N. T. S., at 251, the BCIA accorded no protection for "any work that is in the public domain in the United States," § 12, 102 Stat. 2860. Protection of future foreign works, the BCIA indicated, satisfied Article 18. See § 2 (3), 102 Stat. 2853 ("The amendments made by this Act, together with the law as it exists on the date of the enactment of this Act, satisfy the obligations of the United States in adhering to the Berne Convention..."). Congress indicated, however, that it had not definitively rejected "retroactive" protection for preexisting foreign works; instead it had punted on this issue of Berne's implementation, deferring consideration until "a more thorough examination of Constitutional, commercial, and consumer considerations is possible." BCIA House Report, at 51, 52.

**880 The minimalist approach essayed by the United States did not sit well with other Berne members. While negotiations were ongoing over the North American Free Trade Agreement (NAFTA), Mexican authorities complained about the United States' refusal to grant protection, in accord with Article 18, to Mexican works that remained under copyright domestically. See Intellectual Property and International Issues, Hearings before the Subcommittee on Intellectual Property and Judicial Administration, House Committee on the Judiciary, 102d Cong., 1st Sess., 168 (1991) (statement of Ralph Oman, U. S. Register of Copyrights). The Register of Copyrights also reported "questions" from Turkey, Egypt, and Austria. *Ibid.* Thailand and Russia balked at protecting U. S. works, copyrighted here but in those countries' public domains, until the United States reciprocated with respect to their authors' works. URAA Joint Hearing 137 (statement of Ira S. Shapiro, General Counsel, Office of the U. S. Trade Representative (USTR)); *id.*, at 208 (statement of Professor Shira Perlmutter); *id.*, at 291 (statement of Jason S. Berman, Recording Industry Association of America (RIAA)).

Berne, however, did not provide a potent enforcement mechanism. The Convention contemplates dispute resolution **881 before the International Court of Justice. Art. 33(1). But it specifies no sanctions for noncompliance and allows parties, at any time, to declare themselves "not...bound" by the Convention's dispute resolution provision. Art. 33(2)-(3) 828 U. N. T. S., at 277. Unsurprisingly, no enforcement actions were launched before 1994. D. Gervais, The TRIPS Agreement 213, and n. 134(3d ed. 2008). Although "several Berne Union Members disagreed with [our] interpretation of Article 18," the USTR told Congress, the Berne Convention did "not provide a meaningful dispute resolution process." URAA Joint Hearing 137(statement of Shapiro). This shortcoming left Congress "free to adopt a minimalist approach and evade Article 18." Karp, Final Report, Berne Article 18 Study on Retroactive United States Copyright Protection for Berne and other Works, 20 Colum. -VLA J. L. & Arts 157, 172(1996).

The landscape changed in 1994. The Uruguay round of multilateral trade negotiations produced the World Trade Organization(WTO) and the Agreement on Trade-Related Aspects of Intellectual Property Rights(TRIPS). The United States joined both. TRIPS mandates, on pain of WTO enforcement, implementation of Berne's first 21 articles. TRIPS, Art. 9. 1, 33 I. L. M. 1197, 1201(requiring adherence to all but the "moral rights" provisions of Article 6*bis*). The WTO gave teeth to the Convention's requirements: Noncompliance with a WTO ruling could subject member countries to tariffs or cross-sector retaliation. See Gervais, *supra*, at 213; 7 W. Patry, Copyright § 24:1, pp. 24-8 to 24-9(2011). The specter of WTO enforcement proceedings bolstered the credibility of our trading partners' threats to challenge the United States for inadequate compliance with Article 18. See URAA Joint Hearing 137(statement of Shapiro, USTR) ("It is likely that other WTO members would challenge the current U. S. implementation of Berne Article 18 under [WTO] procedures.").

Congress' response to the Uruguay agreements put to rest any questions concerning U. S. compliance with Article 18. Section 514 of the URAA, 108 Stat. 4976 (codified at 17 U. S. C. § 104A, 109(a)), extended copyright to works that garnered protection in their countries of origin, BUT * * 882 had no right to exclusivity in the united states for any of three reasons: lack of copyright relations between the country of origin and the United States at the time of publication; lack of subject-matter protection for sound recordings fixed before 1972; and failure to comply with U. S. statutory formalities(e. g., failure to provide notice of copyright status, or to register and renew a copyright). See § 104A(h)(6)(B)-(C).

Works that have fallen into the public domain after the expiration of a full copyright term—either in the United States or the country of origin—receive no further protection under § 514. *Ibid.* Copyrights "restored" under URAA § 514 "subsist for the remainder of the term of copyright that the work would have otherwise been granted…if the work never entered the public domain." § 104A(a)(1)(B). Prospectively, restoration places foreign works on an equal footing with their U.S. counterparts; assuming a foreign and domestic author died the same day, their works will enter the public domain simultaneously. See § 302(a)(copyrights generally expire 70 years after the author's death). Restored works, however, receive no compensatory time for the period of exclusivity they would have enjoyed before § 514's enactment, had they been protected at the outset in the United States. Their total term, therefore, falls short of that available to similarly situated U.S. works.

The URAA's disturbance of the public domain hardly escaped Congress' attention. * *883 Section 514 imposed no liability for any use of foreign works occurring before restoration. In addition, anyone remained free to copy and use restored works for one year following § 514's enactment. See 17 U.S.C. § 104A(h)(2)(A). Concerns about § 514's compatibility with the Fifth Amendment's Takings Clause led Congress to include additional protections for "reliance parties"—those who had, before the URAA's enactment, used or acquired a foreign work then in the public domain. See § 104A(h)(3)-(4). Reliance parties may continue to exploit a restored work until the owner of the restored copyright gives notice of intent to enforce—either by filing with the U.S. Copyright Office within two years of restoration, or by actually notifying the reliance party. § 104A(c),(d)(2)(A)(i), and(B)(i). After that, reliance parties may continue to exploit existing copies for a grace period of one year. § 104A(d)(2)(A)(ii), and(B)(ii). Finally, anyone who, before the URAA's enactment, created a "derivative work" based on a restored work may indefinitely exploit the derivation upon payment to the copyright holder of "reasonable compensation," to be set by a district judge if the parties cannot agree. § 104A(d)(3).

B

In 2001, petitioners filed this lawsuit challenging § 514. They maintain that Congress, when it passed the URAA, exceeded its authority under the Copyright Clause and transgressed First Amendment limitations. The District Court granted the Attorney General's motion for summary judgment. *Golan v. Gonzales*, No. Civ. 01-B-1854, 2005 WL 914754 (D. Colo., Apr. 20, 2005). In rejecting petitioners' Copyright Clause argument, the court stated that Congress "has historically demonstrated little compunction about removing copyrightable materials from the public domain." *Id.*, at *14. The court next declined to part from "the settled rule that private censorship via copyright enforcement does not implicate First Amendment concerns." *Id.*, at *17.

The Court of Appeals for the Tenth Circuit affirmed in part. *Golan v. Gonzales*, 501 F. 3d 1179 (2007). The public domain, it agreed, was not a "threshold that Congress" was powerless to "traverse in both directions." *Id.*, at 1187 (internal quotations marks omitted). But § 514, as the Court of Appeals read our decision in *Eldred v. Ashcroft*, 537 U. S. 186, 123 S. Ct. 769, 154 L. Ed. 2d 683 (2003), required further First Amendment inspection, 501 F. 3d, at 1187. The measure "'altered the traditional contours of copyright protection,'" the court said—specifically, the "bedrock principle" that once works enter the public domain, they do not leave. *Ibid.* (quoting ⋆ ⋆884 *Eldred*, 537 U. S., at 221, 123 S. Ct. 769). The case was remanded with an instruction to the District Court to address the First Amendment claim in light of the Tenth Circuit's opinion.

On remand, the District Court's starting premise was uncontested: Section 514 does not regulate speech on the basis of its content; therefore the law would be upheld if "narrowly tailored to serve a significant government interest." 611 F. Supp. 2d 1165, 1170–1171 (D. Colo. 2009) (quoting *Ward v. Rock Against Racism*, 491 U. S. 781, 791, 109 S. Ct. 2746, 105 L. Ed. 2d 661 (1989)). Summary judgment was due petitioners, the court concluded, because § 514's constriction of the public domain was not justified by any of the asserted federal interests: compliance with Berne, securing greater protection for U. S. authors abroad, or remediation of the inequitable treatment suffered by foreign authors whose works lacked protection in the United States. 611 F. Supp. 2d, at 1172–1177.

The Tenth Circuit reversed. Deferring to Congress'predictive judgments in matters relating to foreign affairs, the appellate court held that § 514 survived First Amendment scrutiny. Specifically, the court determined that the law was narrowly tailored to fit the important government aim of protecting U. S. copyright holders' interests abroad. 609 F. 3d 1076(2010).

We granted certiorari to consider petitioners'challenge to § 514 under both the Copyright Clause and the First Amendment, 562 U. S. ——, 131 S. Ct. 1600, 179 L. Ed. 2d 516(2011), and now affirm.

II

We first address petitioners' argument that Congress lacked authority, under the Copyright Clause, to enact § 514. The Constitution states that "Congress shall have Power…[t]o promote the Progress of Science…by securing for limited Times to Authors…the exclusive Right to their…Writings." Art. I, § 8, cl. 8. Petitioners find in this grant of authority an impenetrable barrier to the extension of copyright protection to authors whose writings, for whatever reason, are in the public domain. We see no such barrier in the text of the Copyright Clause, historical practice, or our precedents.

A

The text of the Copyright Clause does not exclude application of copyright protection to works in the public domain. Symposium, Congressional Power and Limitations Inherent in the Copyright Clause, 30 Colum. J. L. & Arts 259, 266(2007). Petitioners'contrary argument relies primarily on the Constitution's confinement of a copyright's lifespan to a "limited Tim[e]." "Removing works from the public domain," they contend, "violates the 'limited[t]imes' restriction by turning a fixed and predictable period into one that can be reset or resurrected at any time, even after it expires." Brief for Petitioners 22.

Our decision in *Eldred* is largely dispositive of petitioners' limited-time argument. There we addressed the question whether Congress violated the Copyright

Clause when it extended, by 20 years, the terms of existing copyrights. 537 U. S. , at 192–193, 123 S. Ct. 769 (upholding Copyright Term Extension Act (CTEA)). Ruling that Congress acted within constitutional bounds, we declined to infer from the text of the Copyright Clause "the command that a time prescription, once set, becomes forever 'fixed' or 'inalterable.'" *Id.* , at 199, 123 S. Ct. 769. "The word 'limited,'" we observed, "does not convey a meaning so constricted." *Ibid.* Rather, the term is best understood to mean "confine[d] within certain bounds," "restrain[ed]," or "circumscribed." *Ibid.* (internal quotation marks omitted). The construction petitioners ✶ ✶ 885 tender closely resembles the definition rejected in *Eldred* and is similarly infirm.

The terms afforded works restored by § 514 are no less "limited" than those the CTEA lengthened. In light of *Eldred*, petitioners do not here contend that the term Congress has granted U. S. authors—their lifetimes, plus 70 years—is unlimited. See 17 U. S. C. § 302(a). Nor do petitioners explain why terms of the same duration, as applied to foreign works, are not equally "circumscribed" and "confined." See *Eldred*, 537 U. S. , at 199, 123 S. Ct. 769. Indeed, as earlier noted, see *supra*, at 878, 882–883, the copyrights of restored foreign works typically last for fewer years than those of their domestic counterparts.

The difference, petitioners say, is that the limited time had already passed for works in the public domain. What was that limited term for foreign works once excluded from U. S. copyright protection? Exactly "zero," petitioners respond. Brief for Petitioners 22 (works in question "received a specific term of protection...sometimes expressly set to zero"; "at the end of that period," they "entered the public domain"); Tr. of Oral Arg. 52 (by "refusing to provide any protection for a work," Congress "set[s] the term at zero," and thereby "tell[s] us when the end has come"). We find scant sense in this argument, for surely a "limited time" of exclusivity must begin before it may end.

Carried to its logical conclusion, petitioners persist, the Government's position would allow Congress to institute a second "limited" term after the first expires, a third after that, and so on. Thus, as long as Congress legislated in installments, perpetual copyright terms would be achievable. As in *Eldred*, the hypothetical legislative misbehavior petitioners posit is far afield from the case before us. See 537 U.

S. , at 198-200,209-210,123 S. Ct. 769. In aligning the United States with other nations bound by the Berne Convention, and thereby according equitable treatment to once disfavored foreign authors, Congress can hardly be charged with a design to move stealthily toward a regime of perpetual copyrights.

B

Historical practice corroborates our reading of the Copyright Clause to permit full U. S. compliance with Berne. Undoubtedly, federal copyright legislation generally has not affected works in the public domain. Section 514's disturbance of that domain, petitioners argue, distinguishes their suit from Eldred's. In adopting the CTEA, petitioners note, Congress acted in accord with "an unbroken congressional practice" of granting pre-expiration term extensions, 537 U. S. , at 200, 123 S. Ct. 769. No comparable practice, they maintain, supports § 514.

On occasion, however, Congress has seen fit to protect works once freely available. Notably, the Copyright Act of 1790 granted protection to many works previously in the public domain. Act of May 31, 1790 (1790 Act), § 1, 1 Stat. 124 (covering "any map, chart, book, or books already printed within these United States"). Before the Act launched a uniform national system, three States provided no statutory copyright protection at all. Of those that did afford some protection, seven failed to * * 886 protect maps; eight did not cover previously published books; and all ten denied protection to works that failed to comply with formalities. The First Congress, it thus appears, did not view the public domain as inviolate. As we have recognized, the "construction placed upon the Constitution by[the drafters of] the first[copyright] act of 1790 and the act of 1802…men who were contemporary with[the Constitution's] formation, many of whom were members of the convention which framed it, is of itself entitled to very great weight." *Burrow-Giles Lithographic Co. v. Sarony*, 111 U. S. 53,57,4 S. Ct. 279,28 L. Ed. 349(1884).

Subsequent actions confirm that Congress has not understood the Copyright Clause to preclude protection for existing works. Several private bills restored the copyrights of works that previously had been in the public domain. See Act of Feb. 19,1849(Corson Act) ,ch. 57,9 Stat. 763; Act of June 23,1874(Helmuth Act) , ch. 534,18 Stat. 618; Act of Feb. 17,1898 (Jones Act) ,ch. 29,30 Stat. 1396.

These bills were unchallenged in court.

Analogous patent statutes, however, were upheld in litigation. In 1808, Congress passed a private bill restoring patent protection to Oliver Evans' flour mill. When Evans sued for infringement, first Chief Justice Marshall in the Circuit Court, *Evans v. Jordan*, 8 F. Cas. 872 (No. 4,564) (Va. 1813), and then Justice Bushrod Washington for this Court, *Evans v. Jordan*, 9 Cranch 199, 3 L. Ed. 704 (1815), upheld the restored patent's validity. After the patent's expiration, the Court said, "a general right to use [Evans'] discovery was not so vested in the public" as to allow the defendant to continue using the machinery, which he had constructed between the patent's expiration and the bill's passage. *Id.* , at 202. See also *Blanchard v. Sprague*, 3 F. Cas. 648, 650 (No. 1,518) (C. C. D. Mass. 1839) (Story, J.) ("I never have entertained any doubt of the constitutional authority of congress" to "give a patent for an invention, which...was in public use and enjoyed by the community at the time of the passage of the act.").

This Court again upheld Congress' restoration of an invention to protected status in **887 *McClurg v. Kingsland*, 1 How. 202, 11 L. Ed. 102 (1843). There we enforced an 1839 amendment that recognized a patent on an invention despite its prior use by the inventor's employer. Absent such dispensation, the employer's use would have rendered the invention unpatentable, and therefore open to exploitation without the inventor's leave. *Id.* , at 206–209.

Congress has also passed generally applicable legislation granting patents and copyrights to inventions and works that had lost protection. An 1832 statute authorized a new patent for any inventor whose failure, "by inadvertence, accident, or mistake," to comply with statutory formalities rendered the original patent "invalid or inoperative." Act of July 3, § 3, 4 Stat. 559. An 1893 measure similarly allowed authors who had not timely deposited their work to receive "all the rights and privileges" the Copyright Act affords, if they made the required deposit by March 1, 1893. Act of Mar. 3, ch. 215, 27 Stat. 743. And in 1919 and 1941, Congress authorized the President to issue proclamations granting protection to foreign works that had fallen into the public domain during World Wars I and II. See Act of Dec. 18, 1919, ch. 11, 41 Stat. 368; Act of Sept. 25, 1941, ch. 421, 55 Stat. 732.

Pointing to dictum in *Graham v. John Deere Co. of Kansas City*, 383 U. S. 1,

86 S. Ct. 684, 15 L. Ed. 2d 545(1966), petitioners would have us look past this history. In *Graham*, we stated that "Congress may not authorize the issuance of patents whose effects are to remove existent knowledge from the public domain, or to restrict free access to materials already available."*Id.*, at 6, 86 S. Ct. 684; *post*, at 907. But as we explained in *Eldred*, this passage did not speak to the constitutional limits on Congress' copyright and patent authority. Rather, it "addressed an invention's very eligibility for patent protection."537 U. S., at 202, n. 7, 123 S. Ct. 769.

Installing a federal copyright system and ameliorating the interruptions of global war, it is true, presented Congress with extraordinary situations. Yet the TRIPS accord, leading the United States to comply in full measure with Berne, was also a signal event. See *supra*, at 880-881; cf. *Eldred*, 537 U. S., at 259, 264-265, 123 S. Ct. 769(BREYER, J., dissenting)(acknowledging importance of international uniformity advanced by U. S. efforts to conform to the Berne Convention). Given the authority we hold Congress has, we will not second-guess the political choice Congress made between leaving the public domain untouched and embracing Berne unstintingly. Cf. *id.*, at 212-213, 123 S. Ct. 769.

C

Petitioners' ultimate argument as to the Copyright and Patent Clause concerns its initial words. Congress is empowered to "promote the Progress of Science＊＊888 and useful Arts" by enacting systems of copyright and patent protection. U. S. Const., Art. I, § 8, cl. 8. Perhaps counterintuitively for the contemporary reader, Congress' copyright authority is tied to the progress of science; its patent authority, to the progress of the useful arts. See *Graham*, 383 U. S., at 5, and n. 1, 86 S. Ct. 684; *Evans*, 8 F. Cas., at 873(Marshall, J.).

The "Progress of Science," petitioners acknowledge, refers broadly to "the creation and spread of knowledge and learning."Brief for Petitioners 21; accord *post*, at 899-900. They nevertheless argue that federal legislation cannot serve the Clause's aim unless the legislation "spur[s]the creation of...new works."Brief for Petitioners 24; accord *post*, at 899-900, 903, 908. Because § 514 deals solely with works already created, petitioners urge, it "provides no plausible incentive to create new works" and is therefore invalid. Reply Brief 4.

The creation of at least one new work, however, is not the sole way Congress may promote knowledge and learning. In *Eldred*, we rejected an argument nearly identical to the one petitioners rehearse. The *Eldred* petitioners urged that the "CTEA's extension of existing copyrights categorically fails to 'promote the Progress of Science,'...because it does not stimulate the creation of new works."537 U. S., at 211-212, 123 S. Ct. 769. In response to this argument, we held that the Copyright Clause does not demand that each copyright provision, examined discretely, operate to induce new works. Rather, we explained, the Clause "empowers Congress to determine the intellectual property regimes that, overall, in that body's judgment, will serve the ends of the Clause."*Id.*, at 222, 123 S. Ct. 769. And those permissible ends, we held, extended beyond the creation of new works. See *id.*, at 205-206, 123 S. Ct. 769(rejecting the notion that " 'the only way to promote the progress of science[is]to provide incentives to create new works' "(quoting Perlmutter, Participation in the International Copyright System as a Means to Promote the Progress of Science and Useful Arts, 36 Loyola(LA)L. Rev. 323, 332(2002))).

Even were we writing on a clean slate, petitioners' argument would be unavailing. Nothing in the text of the Copyright Clause confines the "Progress of Science" exclusively to "incentives for creation."*Id.*, at 324, n. 5(internal quotation marks omitted). Evidence from the founding, moreover, suggests that inducing *dissemination*—as opposed to creation—was viewed as an appropriate means to promote science. See Nachbar, Constructing Copyright's Mythology, 6 Green Bag 2d 37, 44 (2002)("The scope of copyright protection existing at the time of the framing," trained as it was on "publication, not creation,""is inconsistent with claims that copyright must promote creative activity in order to be valid."(internal quotation marks omitted)). Until 1976, in fact, Congress made "federal copyright contingent on publication[,][thereby] providing incentives ⋆ ⋆ 889 not primarily for creation," but for dissemination. Perlmutter, *supra*, at 324, n. 5. Our decisions correspondingly recognize that "copyright supplies the economic incentive to create *and disseminate* ideas."*Harper & Row, Publishers, Inc. v. Nation Enterprises*, 471 U. S. 539, 558, 105 S. Ct. 2218, 85 L. Ed. 2d 588(1985)(emphasis added). See also *Eldred*, 537 U. S., at 206, 123 S. Ct. 769.

Considered against this backdrop, § 514 falls comfortably within Congress' authority under the Copyright Clause. Congress rationally could have concluded that adherence to Berne "promotes the diffusion of knowledge," Brief for Petitioners 4. A well-functioning international copyright system would likely encourage the dissemination of existing and future works. See URAA Joint Hearing 189(statement of Professor Perlmutter). Full compliance with Berne, Congress had reason to believe, would expand the foreign markets available to U. S. authors and invigorate protection against piracy of U. S. works abroad, S. Rep. No. 103−412, pp. 224, 225 (1994); URAA Joint Hearing 291(statement of Berman, RIAA); *id.*, at 244, 247(statement of Smith, IIPA), thereby benefiting copyright-intensive industries stateside and inducing greater investment in the creative process.

The provision of incentives for the creation of new works is surely an essential means to advance the spread of knowledge and learning. We hold, however, that it is not the sole means Congress may use "[t]o promote the Progress of Science." See Perlmutter, *supra*, at 332(United States would "lose all flexibility" were the provision of incentives to create the exclusive way to promote the progress of science). Congress determined that exemplary adherence to Berne would serve the objectives of the Copyright Clause. We have no warrant to reject the rational judgment Congress made.

III

A

We next explain why the First Amendment does not inhibit the restoration authorized by § 514. To do so, we first recapitulate the relevant part of our path-marking decision in *Eldred*. The petitioners in *Eldred*, like those here, argued that Congress had violated not only the "limited Times" prescription of the Copyright Clause. In addition, and independently, the *Eldred* petitioners charged, Congress had offended the First Amendment's freedom of expression guarantee. The CTEA's 20-year enlargement of a copyright's duration, we held in *Eldred*, offended neither provision.

Concerning the First Amendment, we recognized that some restriction on expression is the inherent and intended effect of every grant of copyright. * * 890 Noting that the "Copyright Clause and the First Amendment were adopted close in time," 537 U. S. , at 219, 123 S. Ct. 769, we observed that the Framers regarded copyright protection not simply as a limit on the manner in which expressive works may be used. They also saw copyright as an "engine of free expression[:] By establishing a marketable right to the use of one's expression, copyright supplies the economic incentive to create and disseminate ideas." *Ibid.* (quoting *Harper & Row*, 471 U. S. , at 558, 105 S. Ct. 2218 (internal quotation marks omitted)) ; see *id.* , at 546, 105 S. Ct. 2218 ("rights conferred by copyright are designed to assure contributors to the store of knowledge a fair return for their labors").

We then described the "traditional contours" of copyright protection, *i. e.* , the "idea/expression dichotomy" and the "fair use" defense. Both are recognized in our jurisprudence as "built-in First Amendment accommodations." *Eldred*, 537 U. S. , at 219, 123 S. Ct. 769; see *Harper & Row*, 471 U. S. , at 560, 105 S. Ct. 2218 (First Amendment protections are "embodied in the Copyright Act's distinction between copyrightable expression and uncopyrightable facts and ideas," and in the "latitude for scholarship and comment" safeguarded by the fair use defense).

The idea/expression dichotomy is codified at 17 U. S. C. § 102(b) : "In no case does copyright protec[t] …any idea, procedure, process, system, method of operation, concept, principle, or discovery … described, explained, illustrated, or embodied in[the copyrighted] work. " "Due to this[idea/expression] distinction, every idea, theory, and fact in a copyrighted work becomes instantly available for public exploitation at the moment of publication" ; the author's expression alone gains copyright protection. *Eldred*, 537 U. S. , at 219, 123 S. Ct. 769; see *Harper & Row*, 471 U. S. , at 556, 105 S. Ct. 2218("idea/expression dichotomy strike[s] a definitional balance between the First Amendment and the Copyright Act by permitting free communication of facts while still protecting an author's expression" (internal quotation marks omitted)).

The second "traditional contour," the fair use defense, is codified at 17 U. S. C. § 107: "[T]he fair use of a copyrighted work, including such use by reproduction in copies…, for purposes such as criticism, comment, news reporting, teaching(including multiple copies for classroom use) , scholarship, or research, is not an infringement of copyright." This limitation on exclusivity "allows the public to use not only facts and ideas contained in a copyrighted work, but also [the author's] expression itself in certain circumstances." *Eldred*, 537 U. S., at 219, 123 S. Ct. 769; see *id.*, at 220, 123 S. Ct. 769 ("fair use defense affords considerable latitude for scholarship and comment, ... even for parody" (internal quotation marks omitted)).

Given the "speech-protective purposes and safeguards" embraced by copyright law, see *id.*, at 219, 123 S. Ct. 769, we concluded in *Eldred* that there was no call for the heightened review petitioners sought in that case. We reach the same conclusion here. Section 514 leaves undisturbed * * 891 the "idea/expression" distinction and the "fair use" defense. Moreover, Congress adopted measures to ease the transition from a national scheme to an international copyright regime: It deferred the date from which enforcement runs, and it cushioned the impact of restoration on "reliance parties" who exploited foreign works denied protection before § 514 took effect. See *supra*, at 882–883 (describing 17 U. S. C. § 104A(c), (d), and (h)). See also *Eldred*, 537 U. S., at 220, 123 S. Ct. 769 (describing supplemental allowances and exemptions available to certain users to mitigate the CTEA's impact).

B

Petitioners attempt to distinguish their challenge from the one turned away in *Eldred*. First Amendment interests of a higher order are at stake here, petitioners say, because they—unlike their counterparts in *Eldred*—enjoyed "vested rights" in works that had already entered the public domain. The limited rights they retain under copyright law's "built-in safeguards" are, in their view, no substitute for the unlimited use they enjoyed before § 514's enactment. Nor, petitioners urge, does § 514's "unprecedented" foray into the public domain possess the historical pedigree that supported the term extension at issue in *Eldred*. Brief for Petitioners 42–43.

However spun, these contentions depend on an argument we considered and rejected above, namely, that the Constitution renders the public domain largely untouchable by Congress. Petitioners here attempt to achieve under the banner of the

First Amendment what they could not win under the Copyright Clause: On their view of the Copyright Clause, the public domain is inviolable; as they read the First Amendment, the public domain is policed through heightened judicial scrutiny of Congress'means and ends. As we have already shown, see *supra*, at 884–887, the text of the Copyright Clause and the historical record scarcely establish that "once a work enters the public domain," Congress cannot permit anyone— "not even the creator—[to] copyright it," 501 F. 3d, at 1184. And nothing in the historical record, congressional practice, or our own jurisprudence warrants exceptional First Amendment solicitude for copyrighted works that were once in the public domain. Neither this challenge nor that raised in *Eldred*, we stress, allege Congress transgressed a generally applicable First Amendment prohibition; we are not ✶ ✶ 892 faced, for example, with copyright protection that hinges on the author's viewpoint.

The Tenth Circuit's initial opinion determined that petitioners marshaled a stronger First Amendment challenge than did their predecessors in *Eldred*, who never "possessed unfettered access to any of the works at issue." 501 F. 3d, at 1193. See also *id*. , at 1194 ("[O]nce the works at issue became free for anyone to copy, [petitioners] had vested First Amendment interests in the expressions, [thus] § 514's interference with [petitioners'] rights is subject to First Amendment scrutiny."). As petitioners put it in this Court, Congress impermissibly revoked their right to exploit foreign works that "belonged to them" once the works were in the public domain. Brief for Petitioners 44–45.

To copyright lawyers, the "vested rights" formulation might sound exactly backwards: Rights typically vest at the *outset* of copyright protection, in an author or rightholder. See, *e. g*. , 17 U. S. C. § 201 (a) ("Copyright in a work protected… vests initially in the author…."). Once the term of protection ends, the works do not revest in any rightholder. Instead, the works simply lapse into the public domain. See, *e. g*. , Berne, Art. 18 (1) , 828 U. N. T. S. , at 251 ("This Convention shall apply to all works which…have not yet fallen into the public domain…."). Anyone has free access to the public domain, but no one, after the copyright term has expired, acquires ownership rights in the once-protected works.

Congress recurrently adjusts copyright law to protect categories of works once outside the law's compass. For example, Congress broke new ground when it ex-

tended copyright protection to foreign works in 1891, Act of Mar. 3, § 13, 26 Stat. 1110; to dramatic works in 1856, Act of Aug. 18, 11 Stat. 138; to photographs and photographic negatives in 1865, Act of Mar. 3, § 1, 13 Stat. 540; to motion pictures in 1912, Act of Aug. 24, 37 Stat. 488; to fixed sound recordings in 1972, Act of Oct. 15, 1971, 85 Stat. 391; and to architectural works in 1990, Architectural Works Copyright Protection Act, 104 Stat. 5133. And on several occasions, as recounted above, Congress protected works previously in the public domain, hence freely usable by the public. See *supra*, at 885–887. If Congress could grant protection to these works without hazarding heightened First Amendment scrutiny, then what free speech principle disarms it from protecting works prematurely cast into the public domain for reasons antithetical to the Berne Convention?

Section 514, we add, does not impose a blanket prohibition on public access. Petitioners protest that fair use and the idea/expression dichotomy "are plainly inadequate to protect the speech and expression rights that Section 514 took from petitioners, or...the public"—that is, "the unrestricted right to perform, copy, teach and distribute the *entire* work, for any reason." Brief for Petitioners 46–47. "Playing a few bars of a Shostakovich symphony," petitioners observe, "is no substitute for performing the entire work." *Id.*, at 47.

* * 893 But Congress has not put petitioners in this bind. The question here, as in *Eldred*, is whether would–be users must pay for their desired use of the author's expression, or else limit their exploitation to "fair use" of that work. Prokofiev's Peter and the Wolf could once be performed free of charge; after §514 the right to perform it must be obtained in the marketplace. This is the same marketplace, of course, that exists for the music of Prokofiev's U. S. contemporaries: works of Copland and Bernstein, for example, that enjoy copyright protection, but nevertheless appear regularly in the programs of U. S. concertgoers.

Before we joined Berne, domestic works and some foreign works were protected under U. S. statutes and bilateral international agreements, while other foreign works were available at an artificially low (because royalty-free) cost. By fully implementing Berne, Congress ensured that most works, whether foreign or domestic, would be governed by the same legal regime. The phenomenon to which Congress responded is not new: Distortions of the same order occurred with greater frequency—and to the detriment of both foreign and domestic authors—when, before 1891, foreign works were excluded entirely from U. S. copyright protection. See Kampelman, The United States and International Copyright, 41 Am. J. Int'l L. 406, 413 (1947) ("American readers were less inclined to read the novels of Cooper or Hawthorne for a dollar when they could buy a novel of Scott or Dickens for a quarter."). Section 514 continued the trend toward a harmonized copyright regime by placing foreign works in the position they would have occupied if the current regime had been in effect when those works were created and first published. Authors once deprived of protection are spared the continuing effects of that initial deprivation; § 514 gives them nothing more than the benefit of their labors during whatever time remains before the normal copyright term expires.

Unlike petitioners, the dissent makes much of the so-called "orphan works" problem. See *post*, at 904-907, 911-912. We readily acknowledge the difficulties would-be users of copyrightable materials may face in identifying or locating copyright owners. See generally U. S. Copyright Office, Report on Orphan Works 21-40 (2006). But as the dissent concedes, see *post*, at 906, this difficulty is hardly peculiar to works restored under § 514. It similarly afflicts, for instance, U. S. libraries that attempt to catalogue U. S. books. See *post*, at 905. See also Brief for American Library Association et al. as *Amici Curiae* 22(Section 514 "exacerbated," but did not create, the problem of orphan works); U. S. Copyright Office, *supra*, at 41-44(tracing orphan-works problem to Congress' elimination of formalities, commencing with the 1976 Copyright Act).

**894 Nor is this a matter appropriate for judicial, as opposed to legislative, resolution. Cf. *Authors Guild v. Google, Inc.*, 770 F. Supp. 2d 666, 677-678 (S. D. N. Y. 2011)(rejecting proposed "Google Books" class settlement because, *inter alia*, "the establishment of a mechanism for exploiting unclaimed books is a matter more suited for Congress than this Court"(citing *Eldred*, 537 U. S., at 212, 123 S. Ct. 769)). Indeed, the host of policy and logistical questions identified by the dissent speak for themselves. *Post*, at 905. Despite "longstanding efforts," see *Authors Guild*, 770 F. Supp. 2d, at 678(quoting statement of Marybeth Peters), Congress has not yet passed ameliorative orphan-works legislation of the sort enacted by other Berne members, see, *e. g.*, Canada Copyright Act, R. S. C., 1985, c. C

–42, § 77(authorizing Copyright Board to license use of orphan works by persons unable, after making reasonable efforts, to locate the copyright owner). Heretofore, no one has suggested that the orphan-works issue should be addressed through our implementation of Berne, rather than through overarching legislation of the sort proposed in Congress and cited by the dissent. See *post*, at 911–912; U. S. Copyright Office, Legal Issues in Mass Digitization 25–29(2011)(discussing recent legislative efforts). Our unstinting adherence to Berne may add impetus to calls for the enactment of such legislation. But resistance to Berne's prescriptions surely is not a necessary or proper response to the pervasive question, what should Congress do about orphan works.

IV

Congress determined that U. S. interests were best served by our full participation in the dominant system of international copyright protection. Those interests include ensuring exemplary compliance with our international obligations, securing greater protection for U. S. authors abroad, and remedying unequal treatment of foreign authors. The judgment § 514 expresses lies well within the ken of the political branches. It is our obligation, of course, to determine whether the action Congress took, wise or not, encounters any constitutional shoal. For the reasons stated, we are satisfied it does not. The judgment of the Court of Appeals for the Tenth Circuit is therefore *Affirmed*.

葆拉·佩特拉（上诉人）

米高梅电影公司等

第 12-1315 号
开庭日期：2014 年 1 月 21 日
裁决日期：2014 年 5 月 19 日

案情摘要与裁判要旨

美国《版权法案》为1978年以前发表的版权作品提供首期28年的保护,并可续展将保护期延长至67年。版权转让后,作者在续展时间到来前死亡的,只有在继承人将续展权转让给受让人后,受让人才能继续使用作品。

本案中,被控侵权的作品是根据拳击冠军杰克·拉莫塔(Jake LaMotta)的经历摄制而成的电影《愤怒的公牛》。杰克·拉莫塔同法兰克·佩特拉(Frank Petrella)一起,在一部剧本里讲述了他的故事。剧本于1963年获得了版权保护。1976年,两人转让了作品的版权和续展权,而后被上诉人米高梅电影公司(Metro-Goldwyn-Mayer, Inc.)的子公司联艺电影公司(以下统称"米高梅")获得上述权利。1980年,米高梅发行了电影《愤怒的公牛》,进行了版权登记,并在市场上推广电影至今。由于法兰克·佩特拉在作品首期版权保护期内死亡,所以续展权流转至其继承人。

上诉人(原审原告)葆拉·佩特拉(以下简称"佩特拉")为法兰克·佩特拉之女,于1991年办理了1963年剧本的续展手续,成为剧本唯一的所有者。7年后,佩特拉通知米高梅,称米高梅电影《愤怒的公牛》侵犯了她的版权,并威胁提起诉讼。约9年后的2009年1月6日,佩特拉提起侵权诉讼,针对在2006年1月6日之后发生的侵权行为寻求金钱赔偿和禁令救济。米高梅援引衡平法上的迟误抗辩,请求简易判决。米高梅认为,佩特拉拖延了18年才提起诉讼不合理,并损害了被告的利益。地区法院同意米高梅的请求,认为佩特拉因怠于起诉无法再主张权利。联邦第九巡回上诉法院维持了该裁决。联邦最高法院认为,《版权法案》的诉讼时效条款只允许原告在胜诉后获得起诉之日起前三年内的追溯性救济,这说明已经考虑到了迟误问题。据此,联邦最高法院判决认定,不得以怠于起诉为由,阻却佩特拉主张第507条(b)款规定的三年内的损害赔偿,遂撤销原判,发回重审。

金斯伯格法官发表了判决意见,斯卡里亚大法官、托马斯大法官、阿利托大法官、索托马约尔大法官和卡尔根大法官赞同。布雷耶大法官撰写了少数意见,罗伯茨首席大法官和肯尼迪大法官赞同该少数意见。

《版权法案》规定,"根据本法案,除非在赔偿请求权利产生之日起三年内提起民事诉讼,否则不得再提起"[《美国法典》第17卷第507条(b)款]。本案争议的问题是,衡平法上的迟延(无正当理由的、有害的延迟起诉)是否可以阻止在第507条(b)款规定的三年诉讼时效期间内提起的版权侵权诉讼的救济。无可争议的是,第507条(b)款禁止针对超过三年诉讼时效期间的侵权行为提供任何救济。然而,如果侵权诉讼仅寻求对诉讼时效期间内所发生侵权行为的救济,则法院不能随意对国会关于诉讼时效的决定置之不理。本法院认为,不能援引迟延来对抗三年诉讼时效期间内的损害赔偿请求。但对于衡平法上的救济,在特殊情况下,怠于起诉可以在一开始就阻止原告所请求的特定救济。在救济阶段,法官确定恰当的禁令救济以及评估"侵权人的获益时,可以一直考虑原告怠于起诉这一事实"[第507条(b)款]。[1]

在上诉人佩特拉提起的版权侵权诉讼中,没有就发生在第507条(b)款规定的三年诉讼时效期间之外的侵权行为寻求救济。尽管如此,下级法院认为,怠于起诉完全阻止了佩特拉的诉讼,但下级法院没有考虑佩特拉所诉侵权行为持续发生的事实。本法院认为,这一立场＊＊1968违反了第507条(b)款和本法院适用迟延规则的先例。

I

《版权法案》(《美国法典》第17卷第101条及其后各条)赋予独创性作品以版权保护[第102条(a)款]。版权法的四个方面需要本法院一开始予以解释。

第一点是版权保护的期限。根据《版权法案》的规定,版权"首先由作品的作者(们)享有",作者(们)可以将权利转让给第三方(第201条)。《版权法案》赋予版权人某些垄断性权利,包括复制和分发作品,以及制作和销售演绎作品的权利(第106条)。1978年前出版并受版权保护的作品(本案争议作品即属此类),首期保护期限为28年,并可续展将保护期限延长至67年(如本案作品)[第304条(a)款]。从1978年1

月1日起，作品保护期限为自创作之日起至作者死后70年止［第302条(a)款］。

第二点是版权的继承。对于在1978年以前旧制度下受版权保护的作品，首期保护期届满后可以续展，国会规定作者的继承人可继承续展权［见第304条（a）款（1）项（C）目之（ii）-（iv）］。本法院在 Stewart v. Abend 案［《美国判例汇编》第495卷，起始页207；《最高法院判例汇编》第110卷，起始页1750；《美国判例汇编律师版·第二辑》第109卷，起始页184（1990年裁决）］中认为，如果作者已将版权转让出去，但"在续展期到来之前死亡"，那么只有在作者的继承人将续展权转让给受让人后，受让人才能继续使用原作品制作演绎作品（同上，第221页；《最高法院判例汇编》第110卷，起始页1750）。[2]

第三点是救济措施。《版权法案》针对侵权行为提供了各种民事救济，既有衡平法救济，也有普通法救济（见第502条至第505条，同上所述，第2页，注释1）。法院可以"按其认为合理的条件"颁布禁令，以预防或阻止版权侵权［第502条（a）款］。根据版权人的选择，法院还可以裁决：(1) 按"版权人的实际损失加上侵权人的任何额外获益"支付赔偿金［第504条（a）款（1）项］，本案上诉人选择了此类标准；或者（2）特定范围内的法定赔偿［第504条（c）款］。

第四点，同时也是最重要的一点，诉讼时效。直到1957年，民事诉讼的法定时效才写入联邦版权法。此前，联邦法院参照类似的州诉讼时效法律来确定侵权案件的时效［见第1014号参议院报告，1957年第85届国会第1次会议，第2页（以下简称"参议院报告"）］。他们有时援引懈怠行为来缩短州法律规定的诉讼时效。如 Teamsters & Employers Welfare Trust of Ill. v. Gorman Bros. Ready Mix 案［《联邦上诉法院判例汇编·第三辑》第283卷，起始页877，引证页881（联邦第七巡回上诉法院2002年7月判决）］的判决书所述："如果国会并未制定诉讼时效方面的法案，那么（联邦）法院参照州法案中的时效条款，允许根据懈怠原则缩短时效，这并不算侵犯国会的特权，而只是在填补立法漏洞"（内部引证略）。1957年，国会解决了这个问题，填补了漏洞，为根据《版权法案》提起的民事诉讼规定了三年的诉讼时效［见1957年9月7日法案，《公法》第85-313期；《联邦立法大全》第 80 卷，第 633 页；《美国法典》第 17 卷第 115 条（b）款（1958 年版）］。前面已经提到，该条款内容如下："依照本法案提起民事诉讼的，＊＊1969 必须要在赔偿请求权利产生之日起三年内提起"[3]　［第507 条（b）款］。

版权方面的联邦诉讼时效规定旨在实现两个目的：（1）统一确定主张版权权利的时间；以及（2）防止出现利用不同州诉讼时效上的差异（一年到八年不等）选择法院的情况（参议院报告第 2 页；见第 2419 号众议院报告，1956 年第 84 届国第 2 次会议，第 2 页）。要想弄清楚《版权法案》中诉讼时效是如何工作的，就必须了解就版权侵权请求赔偿的权利何时产生。

一般来说，当"原告有完整现存的诉由"时，请求赔偿权利随之产生［*Bay Area Laundry and Dry Cleaning Pension Trust Fund v. Ferbar Corp. of Cal* 案，《美国判例汇编》第 522 卷，起始页 192 页，引证页 201；《最高法院判例汇编》第 118 卷，起始页 542；《美国判例汇编律师版·第二辑》第 139 卷，起始页 553（1997 年裁决）（内部引用标记省略）］。换句话说，诉讼时效通常从"原告可以提起诉讼并获得救济"时开始起算（同上）。因此，当侵权行为发生时，就会发生或"产生"版权请求赔偿的权利。[4]

一般认为，单独累计规则适用于版权法中的诉讼时效。[5] 根据该规则，被告连续实施侵权行为的，诉讼时效将根据每一次违法行为分开计算。侵权作品每被复制或分发一次，就产生一次新的违法行为。每次违法行为都会"累积"一个新的"赔偿主张"。[6] 简言之，每一个侵权行为都意味着一个新的诉讼时效的开始。参见 *Stone v. Williams* 案，《联邦上诉法院判例汇编·第二辑》第 970 卷，起始页 1043，引证页 1049（联邦第二巡回上诉法院 1992 年裁决）："每一个侵权行为都是一次单独的伤害，催生一个独立的救济主张。"

根据法案的三年诉讼时效规定，侵权行为发生之日起三年内可以起诉，但也仅限于三年内。侵权人对同一作品三年前的侵权行为不承担责任参见 M. Nimmer & D. Nimmer 著《版权法》第 3 卷，第 12.05 节［B］［1］［b］，第＊＊1970 12-150.4 页（2013 年版）："如果侵权行为发生在起诉前三年内，不得阻止该诉讼活动，即使是同一侵权人之前对同一作品的侵权行为因发生在三年以前而不被追究责任。"这样一来，当被告实施了（或被指控实施了)一系列独立的侵权行为时,版权人针对最近实施的行为(即三年时效期间内的行为)提起诉讼,一般不会超过第507条(b)款规定的诉讼时效,但针对以前相同或类似行为提起诉讼为时已晚。[7]

总之,国会规定了两个时间控制措施:一是版权保护期限,持续数十年,并可能持续保护到下一代;二是第507条(b)款的诉讼时效,只允许原告针对起诉之日起倒推三年这一段时间内的侵权行为寻求救济。

A

本案被控侵权的作品是广受好评的电影《愤怒的公牛》,该片系根据拳击冠军杰克·拉莫塔的生活改编。拉莫塔从拳击场退役后,和他的老朋友法兰克·佩特拉合作,把他自己的职业生涯故事讲述了出来。他们合作创作了三部版权作品,包括两部剧本,分别于1963年和1973年登记,还有一本图书,于1970年登记。本案涉及的是1963年登记版权的剧本。版权登记证书上写明法兰克·佩特拉是该作品唯一作者,但同时声明该剧本系与拉莫塔"合作完成"(见附录第164页)。

1976年,法兰克·佩特拉和拉莫塔将他们在这三部作品中的权利,包括续展权,转让给了沙特夫—温克勒制片有限公司。两年后,米高梅获得了基于图书和两部剧本制作电影的版权,双方声明这些权利是"独占的、永久的,包括版权的全部期限、续展和延期"(同上,第49页)。1980年,米高梅发行电影《愤怒的公牛》并登记了版权。该片由马丁·斯科塞斯执导＊＊1971,主演是劳勃·狄·尼诺,他因饰演拉莫塔而获得了奥斯卡最佳男主角奖。米高梅继续推销这部电影,并将其转录成DVD和蓝光碟片出售,这些电影存储介质在1980年是无法想象的。

法兰克·佩特拉1981年去世,当时剧本和图书尚在首期版权保护期内。正如本法院在 Stewart 案的判决中所确认的那样,法兰克·佩特拉的续展权由其继承人继承,该继承人续展版权的权利不受作者之前所做的任何权利转让的影响[见《美国判例汇编》第495卷,引证页220-221;《最高法院判例汇编》第 11 卷，起始页 1750（该案遵从了本法院更早的判决：*Miller Music Corp. v. Charles N. Daniels , Inc.* 案，《美国判例汇编》第 362 卷，起始页 373；《最高法院判例汇编》第 80 卷，起始页 792；《美国判例汇编律师版·第二辑》第 4 卷，起始页 804，1960 判决）]。

本案上诉人（原审原告）佩特拉，是法兰克·佩特拉的女儿。在了解本法院 *Stewart* 案的判决后，聘请了一名律师，于 1991 年为 1963 年登记的剧本办理了版权续展手续。

由于 1973 年登记的剧本和 1970 年登记的图书未按时续展，本案的侵权赔偿要求只针对 1963 年登记的剧本。佩特拉现在是该作品版权的唯一拥有者。[8]

1998 年，即在办理 1963 年登记剧本版权续展手续七年后，佩特拉的律师通知米高梅，称佩特拉已经获得了该剧本的版权。律师声称，利用任何演绎作品，包括《愤怒的公牛》，都侵犯了佩特拉现在所享有的版权。在此后的两年里，佩特拉通过律师和米高梅通信。米高梅在信中否定侵权指控的合法性，而佩特拉则多次威胁要采取法律行动。

B

大约九年后的 2009 年 1 月 6 日，佩特拉向美国加州中区联邦地区法院提起版权侵权诉讼，指控米高梅侵犯并且持续侵犯其对 1963 年剧本的版权，理由是米高梅使用、制作和发行的电影《愤怒的公牛》是 1963 年剧本的演绎作品。佩特拉的诉求包括金钱救济和禁令救济。鉴于《版权法案》中的诉讼时效条款要求"必须要在赔偿请求权利产生之日起三年内"提起诉讼[第 507 条（b）款]，故佩特拉寻求的救济是针对米高梅 2006 年 1 月 6 日后实施的侵权行为。她认识到不能就此日期之前的侵权行为获得救济。

米高梅以多项理由提出即决判决动议，其中包括衡平法上的迟误规则。米高梅认为，从 1991 年佩特拉办理版权续展作为其取得权利的基础到 2009 年提起诉讼，中间已经过了 18 年，因此这一诉讼是不合理的，且有损被告的利益（参见"加州中区联邦地区法院 CV 09-0072 号判决书"中支持被告即决判决动议的要点及依据节略）。

地区法院同意了米高梅的即决判决请求（见调卷令申请附录第

28a-48a)。但关于侵权赔偿主张的实体内容,地区法院后来认为,因为重要事实存有争议,排除即决判决的可能(同上,第34a-42a)。即便如此,地区法院认为,怠于起诉阻碍了佩特拉的起诉(同上,第42a-48a)。地区法院最终判决认为,**1972佩特拉没有正当理由拖延到2009年才提起诉讼,并判定米高梅的利益因佩特拉怠于起诉受损(同上,第42a-46a)。地区法院还特别解释道,米高梅表示其已遭受"预期利益损失",因为米高梅已经为电影投入了大量资金;此外,地区法院认可了米高梅提出的"证据性损害"主张,因为原告起诉时,作者法兰克·佩特拉已经去世,拉莫塔也已88岁高龄,且似乎已经失忆(同上,第44a-46a)。[9]

地区法院以原告怠于起诉为由驳回了原告的诉讼请求,联邦第九巡回上诉法院维持了该裁决[《联邦上诉法院判例汇编·第三辑》第695卷,起始页946(2012年裁决)]。基于自己的先例,上诉法院先是注意到,"如果被控非法行为的任何部分发生在诉讼时效期间之外,则法院可认定推定原告存在懈怠,既而不支持其诉讼请求"[同上,引证页951(内部引号省略)]。上诉法院指出,本案应适用此推定,因为"民事案件中版权主张的诉讼时效期间为三年"[同上,引用第507条(b)款]。并且佩特拉在许多年前就意识到她潜在的权利主张(米高梅也是如此)(同上,引证页952)。上诉法院还指出,"正如佩特拉所承认的那样,怠于起诉的真正原因是电影在她等待的这几年里并没有盈利"(同上,引证页953)。[10] 上诉法院同意地区法院的意见,认定米高梅已证明其遭受"预期利益损失":该公司认为其拥有电影《愤怒的公牛》的完全所有权和控制权,因而进行了大量投资(同上,引证页953-954)。[11]

弗莱彻法官之所以持赞同意见,只是因为他必须要遵循巡回上诉法院的先例(同上,引证页958)。他注意到,版权案件中的迟误规则"完全是司法创造物",很明显"与国会规定的三年诉讼时效期间相冲突"(同上)。

本法院批准了调卷令状申请,以解决各上诉法院在处理根据国会规定的三年追溯期内提起的版权侵权案件中适用迟误这一衡平法抗辩上的分歧[《美国判例汇编》第570卷——;《最高法院判例汇编》第134卷,起始页50;《美国判例汇编律师版·第二辑》第186卷,起始页962(2013年裁决)]。[12]

III

我们首先考虑是否能如联邦第九巡回上诉法院所认为的那样，根据《美国法典》第507条（b）款，＊＊1973援引迟误来对抗佩特拉寻求的普通法救济。我们认为，联邦第九巡回上诉法院犯了错误，未认识到版权诉讼时效期间第507条（b）款本身已考虑了延迟。如前所述（见上，第1969-1970页），原告胜诉后，只能针对提起诉讼时向前追溯三年期间的行为获得救济，无法从更早的侵权行为获得救济。被告三年之前的获利仍可以自己保留。鉴于此，根据第507条（b）款，佩特拉无法获得米高梅在三年诉讼时效期间之外（即2006年以前）的投资回报。只有忽视诉讼时效条款的这一特征，以及附随于第507条（b）款的单独累计规则（同上，第1968-1970页），上诉法院才会错误地认为在2006年1月6日之前实施的侵权行为，会妨碍针对该日之后发生侵权行为寻求的一切金钱救济或禁令救济（参见《联邦上诉法院判例汇编·第二辑》第695卷第951页；同上，第1971-1972页）。[13]

此外，如果在三年追溯期内出现侵权行为，法案允许被告证明为实现该期间获利而产生的"可扣除费用"，并从获利中扣除这些费用［第507条（b）款］。此外，被告还可以证明并扣除"非因版权作品而产生的其他获利"［第507条（b）款］。因此，被告可以保留经证实可归因于企业自己、与被侵权作品无关的收益［见 Sheldon v. Metro‑Goldwyn Pictures Corp. 案，《美国判例汇编》第309卷，起始页390，引证页402、407；《最高法院判例汇编》第60卷，起始页681；《美国判例汇编律师版》第84卷，起始页825（1940年裁决）：公正地分辨因被告侵权所产生的收益。另见下文，第1977-1979页：怠于起诉是确定适当救济范围时应考虑的一个因素］。

最后一点，但并非最不重要的一点，迟误是衡平法院发展起来的一种抗辩，它主要在立法机关没有规定特定诉讼时效限制的场景下来保障公平。参见 Dan B. Dobbs（以下简称 Dobbs）著，《救济法》第1卷，第2章第4节之（4），第104页（1993年第二版）："迟误……可能源于没有法定诉讼时效规定情形下的衡平法……这表明迟误应限于没有法定诉讼时效的情况。"1938年普通法和衡平法合并前后，本法院都曾告诫，不要援引迟误来拦截普通法救济参见 Holmberg v. Armbrecht 案，《美国判例汇编》第327卷，起始页392，引证页395、396；《最高法院判例汇编》第66卷，起始页582；《美国判例汇编律师版》第90卷，起始页743，（1946年裁决）：在普通法诉讼中，"如果国会明确限制行使它所创设权利的时间，这项权利就有终结之时"，但"传统上……，诉讼时效并不约束衡平法上的救济措施"。又见 Merck & Co. v. Reynolds 案，《美国判例汇编》第559卷，起始页633，引证页652；《最高法院判例汇编》第130卷，起始页1784；《美国判例汇编律师版》第176卷，起始页582，2010年裁决（引用自以下案件相关内容：United States v. Mack 案，《美国判例汇编》第295卷，起始页480，引证页489；《最高法院判例汇编》第55卷，起始页813；《美国判例汇编律师版》第79卷，起始页1559页，1935年裁决，声明"诉讼时效期间内不得以迟误来对抗普通法诉讼"）；County of Oneida v. Oneida Indian Nation of N. Y. 案，《美国判例汇编》第470卷，起始页226，引证页244页，注释16；《最高法院判例汇编》第105卷，起始页1245；《美国判例汇编律师版》第84卷，起始页169，1985年裁决：＊＊1974"在普通法诉讼中援引迟误进行抗辩的确很新颖。"[15]

我们一贯坚持认为，面对国会颁布的诉讼时效法律，不能援引迟误来阻止法律救济，所以少数意见法官认为我们"对现代诉讼的规则和操作重视不够"（见后文，第1985页）。诚然，自1938年以来，"只有一种诉讼形式——民事诉讼"（《联邦民事诉讼程序规则》第2条），但是"联邦统一规则出现之前就已经存在的实体和救济规则并没有改变"［C. Wright & A. Miller，《联邦惯例及程序》第4卷，第1043节，第177页（2002年第3版）］。Holmberg 案，Merck 案和 Oneida 案等就是例证。少数意见法官提供了多个引证（见下文第1979、1980-1981、1982-1983、1984-1985页），许多引证与目前的争议问题无关，其他引证也遮掩了具体的裁决内容。对比下文第1979、1984页与后文第1977-1978页对下述案件的描述（Chirco v. Crosswinds Communities, Inc. 案，《联邦上诉法院判例汇编·第三辑》第474卷，起始页227（联邦第六巡回上诉法院2007年裁决）；对比下文第1979、1984-1985页与后文第1975页，注释16［对下述案件的描述：National

Railroad Passenger Corporation v. Morgan 案,《美国判例汇编》第 536 卷,起始页 101;《最高法院判例汇编》第 122 卷,起始页 2061;《美国判例汇编律师版·第二辑》第 153 卷,起始页 106(2002 年裁决)];对比下文第 1983 页与后文第 1975 页,注释 16 [描述 *Patterson v. Hewitt* 案,《美国判例汇编》第 195 卷,起始页 309;《最高法院判例汇编》第 25 卷,起始页 35 页;《美国判例汇编律师版》第 49 卷,起始页 214(1904 年裁决)]。但很明显,少数意见法官并没有举出任何在联邦诉讼时效制定法规定的诉讼时效内援引迟误来对抗赔偿请求且获得本法院支持的案例。在这方面,版权案例根本就没有什么"不同"(见后文,第 1985 页)。

IV

我们现在转向米高梅关于目前迟误当下适用范围的主要论点,少数意见法官全部接受这些论点。

A

《联邦民事诉讼程序规则》第 8 条(c)款将迟误与诉讼时效规定一起列为肯定性抗辩,但两者又相互独立。因此,米高梅认为,迟误"可以在每一件民事诉讼中……被引述",以对抗一切形式的救济主张(口头辩论笔录第 43 页;见被上诉人答辩陈述第 40 页)。对于本法院的问题"如果一般的诉讼时效期间是六年,那么是否可以适用迟误抗辩",米高梅律师的回答是肯定的,认为视案件具体情况,有可能认定第五年提起的诉讼太晚(口头辩论笔录第 52 页;同上,第 41 页)。

米高梅对扩大迟误适用范围的期望,偏离了过往至今对迟误功能的理解——它的本质功能在于填补制定法空白,而非取代制定法。本法院判例从未表明迟误可以有如此大的功效。恰恰相反,**1975 我们从未允许运用迟误抗辩来完全对抗在联邦法律规定的诉讼时效期间内发生的不连续违法行为提出的赔偿主张。[16] 我们注意到,如果任由法官设定一个时间限制,而不是遵从国会制定法之规定,将与国会制定第 507 条(b)款时寻求实现的一致性相抵触（见上，第 1968-1969 页）。

B

米高梅认为，每一部涉及诉讼时效的联邦法案里都隐含着"衡平法上的诉讼时效中断规则"（*Holmberg* 案，《美国判例汇编》第 327 卷，引证页 397；《最高法院判例汇编》第 66 卷，起始页 582），并质问为什么不这么对待迟误（见被上诉人答辩陈述第 23-26 页；后文，第 1982-1983 页）。诉讼时效中断规则旨在适当情况下延长可提起民事诉讼的时间[17]，适用于有诉讼时效限制的情况。实际上，诉讼时效中断是依附于诉讼时效限制的解释规则的。参见 *Young v. United States* 案，《美国判例汇编》第 535 卷，起始页 43 页，引证页 49-50；《最高法院判例汇编》第 122 卷，起始页 1036；《美国判例汇编律师版·第二辑》第 152 卷，起始页 79（2002 年裁决）；*Johnson v. Railway Express Agency, Inc.* 案，《美国判例汇编》第 421 卷，起始页 454，引证页 464；《最高法院判例汇编》第 95 卷，起始页 1716；《美国判例汇编律师版·第二辑》第 44 卷，起始页 295（1975 年出版判决）。[18] 相比之下，迟误最初适用于在没有诉讼时效制定法规定的情况下指引权利主张，它很难被描述为解释法定诉讼时效的规则。本案就属于这个情况，因为《版权法案》第 507 条（b）款规定，从提起诉讼之日起算的三年以前的侵权行为触发诉讼，而迟误，正如联邦第九巡回上诉法院所理解、米高梅所提出的那样，使得被告最初实施的侵权行为推定触发诉讼（见《联邦上诉法院判例汇编·第三辑》第 695 卷，引证页 951 页；专家意见书第 16 页）。

C

米高梅坚持认为，必须应准予运用迟误抗辩来防止版权＊＊1976 人无所事事，冷眼旁观被控侵权人的投资结果（见被上诉人答辩陈述 48）。米高梅强调说，在本案中，"佩特拉承认她之所以怠于起诉，是因为这部电影债台高筑，亏损严重，可能永远无法收回投资"（同上，第 47 页，引自附录第 110 页）。联邦第九巡回上诉法院同样批评了佩特拉等到电影《愤怒的公牛》赚钱之后才起诉的做法[《联邦上诉法院判例汇编·第三辑》第695卷,引证页953页(省略内部引号)。见后文,第1980-1981页:指责原告观望涉嫌侵权的作品能否赚钱]。

然而,本法院认为,指望版权人去挑战每一个可起诉的侵权行为并不现实。而且,原告观望侵权人对作品使用的结果究竟是降低了作品价值,或是对作品没有影响,还是提升了作品价值,这本身也没有什么不妥。比如,围绕一本书或一部电影建立起来的粉丝网站,可能会使版权人受益[见吴,《合理使用》,《哥伦比亚法律与艺术评论》第31卷,起始页617,引证页619-620(2008年出版)]。即使侵权造成伤害,其危害性也可能会因为太小而不值得权利人去起诉。

如果规则真如米高梅所说的"要么尽快起诉,要么永远沉默",那么版权人就必须在侵权尚处于萌芽状态就要到联邦法院起诉,以免这些侵权行为最终变得严重。然而,第507条(b)款的三年诉讼时效期间,加上单独累计规则(见上文,第1968-1970页),避免了此类诉讼泛滥成灾。这允许版权人推迟诉讼,直至评估确定起诉是否划算。她虽然会错过三年诉讼时效期间之前的损害赔偿,但大多数情况下,预期获得禁令救济的权利保持不变。[19]

D

米高梅指出,版权人的不作为可能会引发对责任抗辩所需或有用的证据丢失的风险(见被上诉人答辩陈述37-38;见后文,第1979-1981页)。[20]然而,回想一下,国会规定了作者继承人可以继承行使续展权,针对1978年以前获得版权的作品,最早可以于创作并获得版权28年后行使续展权(如前文,第1967-1968页)。在那个时候,作者或许还有其他见证作品创作的证人都已经去世了(同上,第1970页)。国会一定已经意识到,时间的流逝和作者的离世可能会导致证据丢失或模糊,但尽管如此,国会还是决定给作者的家人"第二次获得合理报酬的机会"(Stewart案,《美国判例汇编》第495卷,引证页220;《最高法院判例汇编》第110卷,起始页1750)。

此外,版权案件的原告承担证明侵权的责任。参见威廉·帕特里,《版权》第3卷第9.4节，第9-18页（2013年版）（以下简称"帕特里"）："与其他民事诉讼一样，版权人负责初步证明案件。"但对比后文第1981页，忽略了原告证明侵权的责任以及被告不负担"证明其未侵权"的责任＊＊1977。因此，任何因证据丢失而造成的不便，在对被告产生不利的同时，也同样可能会影响原告。类似佩特拉的诉讼就属于此类情况，因为已故作者本来就可能会支持其继承人的诉求。

我们进一步指出，版权登记机制减少了对外部证据的依赖。尽管版权登记是"自愿的"，但在版权人起诉侵权之前，要求版权登记证书和作品原件都必须在版权局登记备案［第408条（b）款、411条（a）款］。那么，在诉讼中，登记证书、作品原件和涉嫌侵权的作品将成为关键证据。而裁决往往意味着事实调查者直接比较作品原件和涉嫌侵权的作品，即事实调查者运用"好眼力和常识"比较两部作品的"整体理念和总体感觉"［见 *Peter F. Gaito Architecture，LLC v. Simone Development Corp.* 案，《联邦上诉法院判例汇编·第三辑》第602卷，起始页57，引证页66（联邦第二巡回上诉法院2010年裁决）（省略内部引号）］。

E

最后，如果版权人就其不起诉的原因故意作出误导性陈述，且被控侵权人基于对版权人误导性陈述的信赖而使自己遭受损失，在此情况下，禁止反悔原则将完全阻却版权人的权利主张，清除了所有可能的救济措施（见帕特里，第6卷第20：58节，第20-110页与第20-112页）。[21] 禁止反悔原则适用场景比迟误更为严苛，两种抗辩事由的导向也不同。在普通法诉讼中，禁止反悔原则是一种长期被认可的抗辩事由［见 *Wehrman v. Conklin* 案，《美国判例汇编》第155卷，起始页314，引证页327；《最高法院判例汇编》第15卷，起始页129；《美国判例汇编律师版》第39卷，起始页167（1894年裁决）］，它的核心在于误导性陈述和由此导致的损失（见帕特里，第6卷第20：58节，第20-110页与第20-112页）。禁止反悔原则虽可能涉及怠于起诉，但怠于起诉并非禁止反悔抗辩的必备要素。对于迟误抗辩来说，及时性是关键因素。与米高梅据以完全推翻国会规定诉讼时效规定的迟误不同，禁止反悔原则并没有违背国会的诉讼时效规定，因为它是基于误导性的陈述，而不论误导性陈述作出的早晚。

弗莱彻法官指出，联邦第九巡回上诉法院"对迟误在版权案件中的理解和应用上犯了错误"，他呼吁重新考虑这一问题（《联邦上诉法院判例汇编·第三辑》第695卷，引证页959）。他认为，"首先应弄清楚……禁止反悔原则和迟误的区别"（同上）。我们对此持赞成意见。

V

下级法院未经开庭审理，就基于迟误规则处置了佩特拉的案件，未对她根据案件事实提出的任何权利主张作出裁决，并拒绝提供任何形式的救济。我们已经解释了，这种处置方式是错误的。国会立法中关于时间的条款，一方面确保作者能享有一段很长时间的版权保护，另一方面使作者有权自起诉之日前向前追溯三年内侵权行为的责任。这一套安排意味着已经没有多少空间来进一步限制版权人起诉的时间［见Dobbs，第1卷，第2.6（1）节，第152页］。当然，在特定情况下，原告怠于诉讼的后果可能会严重到从诉讼一开始原告就被限制了衡平法上的救济。

＊＊1978 *Chirco v. Crosswinds Communities , Inc.* 案［《联邦上诉法院判例汇编·第三辑》第474卷，起始页227（联邦第六巡回上诉法院2007年裁决）］就是例证。在那起案件中，被告被指控未经许可使用了原告受版权保护的建筑设计来设计和建造住宅。原告很早就知道被告的建筑项目，但一直未采取任何措施去阻止住宅开发，直至超过168套住宅建成，且其中109个单元已经有人入住（同上，第230页）。虽然原告是在第507条（b）款中规定的三年诉讼时效内提起诉讼，但地区法院依然同意了被告即决判决请求，以迟误为由，驳回了整个案件。上诉法院解释说，初审法院驳回整个案件的做法是站不住脚的，因为司法机关无权对国会在第507条（b）款确立的三年追溯期是否明智品头论足（同上，第235页）。然而，上诉法院维持了地区法院的裁决，也认为原告即使成功证明被告侵犯了受版权保护的建筑设计，也没有权利要求法院下令摧毁住宅项目。联邦第六巡回上诉法院认为，摧毁住宅项目这种救济是不公平的，原因有二：其一，原告

在被告动土前就知道被告的建设规划，但未采取措施来阻止该项目；其二，原告所请求的救济将给被告和善意第三方造成"不合理的困难"［同上，第236页。另见 New Era Publications Int'l v. Henry Holt & Co. 案，《联邦上诉法院判例汇编·第二辑》第873卷，起始页576，引证页584-585（联邦第二巡回上诉法院1989年裁决）：本案中，尽管版权人1986年就知晓包含侵权内容的图书将在美国出版，但直到1988年图书印刷、包装和装运后才寻求禁令救济；由于禁令救济意味着"销毁全部图书"，法院"转而允许原告退而主张损害赔偿"］。

　　总之，下级法院错误地认为迟误可以完全阻却佩特拉提起版权侵权诉讼主张。该诉讼是在《版权法案》第507条（b）款规定的诉讼时效范围内提起的，并且不存在 Chiroco 案和 New Era 案所涉及的那些特殊情况。在米高梅投资数百万美元重拍《愤怒的公牛》这部电影前，佩特拉就已经将她的版权主张告知米高梅。佩特拉寻求的衡平法救济，如归还不当收益以及禁止继续侵权的禁令，并不会导致电影"彻底毁灭"或任何与之接近的后果（见 New Era 案，《联邦上诉法院判例汇编·第二辑》第873卷，引证页584）。米高梅在三十多年前发行了电影《愤怒的公牛》，此后一直在市场上进行放映。允许佩特拉继续进行诉讼，仅仅会让米高梅在三十多年间赚取的一小部分收入面临风险，不会给善意第三方（如购买了《愤怒的公牛》电影拷贝的消费者）造成"不合理的困难"（对比 Chirco 案，《联邦上诉法院判例汇编·第三辑》第474卷，引证页235-236：摧毁住宅这一救济措施可能会导致购房家庭被从所购房屋驱离）。本案情况可能或可能并不（我们无需来决定）意味着要在救济阶段限制救济措施，但本案情况不足以让法院一开始就拒绝原告的权利主张。

　　如果佩特拉最终在案件事实上获胜，地区法院在确定恰当禁令救济和评估获利时，可以考虑其怠于起诉的事实（见上，第1967-1968页，第1972-1973页）。然而这样做时，法院应仔细审查米高梅声称的对佩特拉怠于起诉的信赖。[22] 审查时应具体考虑：米高梅提前知晓＊＊1979佩特拉的赔偿主张、米高梅通过寻求宣告性判决所获得的保护、米高梅的投资受单独累计规则保护的程度、法院"按其认为合理的条件"颁布禁令救济的权力［第502条（a）款］以及影响禁令救济或评估获利的任何其他考虑因素［见

Haas v. Leo Feist, Inc. 案,《联邦地区法院判例汇编》第 234 卷,起始页 105,引证页 107-108(纽约南区联邦地区法院 1916 年裁决):根据案件事实裁决版权侵权诉讼并颁布禁令救济,但注意到在计算获益时,可以考虑版权人在侵权人投入大量资金利用争议作品前的不作为。另见口头辩论笔录 23 页:政府认为,在确定衡平法救济时,法院有相当大的回旋余地。例如,可以允许米高梅在向佩特拉支付合理版税后,继续使用《愤怒的公牛》剧本的演绎作品]。无论在裁定禁令救济和计算米高梅获益方面可能需要进行何种调整,基于目前呈现的事实,米高梅都没有理由在不支付版税的情况下继续使用受版权保护的作品。

基于上述原因,本法院推翻联邦第九巡回上诉法院的判决,将案件发回,要求联邦第九巡回上诉法院遵从本意见重审本案。

兹裁决如上。

布雷耶大法官持少数意见,首席大法官和肯尼迪大法官对少数意见表示赞同。

法律制度中包含一些原则,能帮助法院避免可能出现的不公正现象。无论案情有多特殊,这些原则应严格适用于每一个案件。亚里士多德很久以前就注意到,"衡平法的本质在于,当法律因为其普适性而存在缺陷时,由衡平法予以修正"[《尼各马可伦理学》第 99 页(译者 D. Ross,编者 L. Brown,2009 年版)]。迟误就属于此类衡平法原则,它适用于原告"无正当理由怠于起诉"[National Railroad Passenger Corporation v. Morgan 案,《美国判例汇编》第 536 卷,起始页 101,引证页 121;《最高法院判例汇编》第 122 卷,起始页 2061;《美国判例汇编律师版·第二辑》第 153 卷,起始页 106(2002 年裁决)],并因此给被告造成"不合理的困难"[Chirco v. Crosswinds Communities, Inc. 案,《联邦上诉法院判例汇编·第三辑》第 474 卷,起始页 227,引证页 236(联邦第六巡回上诉法院 2007 年裁决)(着重标记删除)]的特殊案件,目的在于避免出现"不公正"现象[Galliher v. Cadwell 案,《美国判例汇编》第 145 卷,起始页 368,引证页 373;《最高法院判例汇编》第 12 卷,起始页 873;《美国判例汇编律师版》第 36 卷,起始页 738(1892 年裁决)]。汉德法官指出:

"版权人已充分注意到他人打算实施的侵权行为,但当潜在侵权人花费大笔金钱利用作品时版权人却无动于衷，直至版权人的如意算盘打响后才选择介入，这是不公的。"参见 Haas v. Leo Feist, Inc. 案，《联邦地区法院判例汇编》第 234 卷，起始页 105，引证页 108（纽约南区联邦地区法院 1916 年裁决）。

今天的裁决导致联邦法院无法解决这一不公正问题，恕我难以赞同。

在版权诉讼中允许适用迟误抗辩的场景并非难以想象。《版权法案》规定的三年时效期间看似短暂，但事实并非如此［《美国法典》第 17 卷第 507 条（b）款］。因为这是一个滚动的时效期间——权利人每主张一次权利（"单独累积"），时效都将重新起算［同上，第 1969 页；帕特里，《版权》第 6 卷第 20：23 节，第 20-44 页至第 20-46 页（2013 年版）］。如果被告连续制售侵权作品，原告可以每三年起诉一次，直到版权保护期限终止＊＊1980——这可能是在作者死后第 70 年［第 302 条（a）款：1978 年 1 月 1 日以后创作的作品，受保护至作者死后第 70 年；第 304 条（a）款：1978 年 1 月 1 日之前创作的作品，保护期为 28 年加 67 年的续展期限］。例如，如果一个作品在 20 年内未产生收益，但在投入开发费用后，在接下来的 30 年里开始赚取收益。原告可以在第 21 年起诉，此后每隔三年起诉一次。原告每次起诉，都将收获被告前三年内的收益，除非原被告在诉讼前后就赔偿数额协商达成协议。被告可以要求从获利中扣除自己的费用支出和任何"非因版权作品产生的收益"［第 504 条（a）款（1）项及第 504 条（b）款］。

推迟 20 年才起诉很容易被证明是不公正的。例如，假设原告故意等待证人死亡，而这些证人或许能证明原被告之间曾达成协议、允许被告复制版权作品，或者能证明原告作品实际上是从被告许可的较早受版权保护的材料中演绎而来。或者，假设原告推迟起诉是因为他不想与被告提前就许可费用讨价还价。他了解，如果自己延迟起诉，而被告投入时间、精力和资源来制造演绎产品，原告在协商确定许可条款内容时的话语权将会更大。又或者，假设原告一直等到他确定被告的赌注获得了回报，演绎作品已经并将持续盈利，且原告有机会获得比如 90% 纯利润流中 80% 的份额［注：原告可获赔的收益应扣除被告制作侵权作品产生的任何"可扣除费用"以及任何"非因版权作品产生的收益"［第 504 条（b）款］。或者，假设所有上述情况都同时存在。

此等怠于起诉的案例并非杜撰出来的。原告在权利主张产生很多年后才起诉，并且延迟起诉导致了不公正的后果，在下级法院并不鲜见［如 *Ory v. McDonald* 案，《联邦法院判例汇编补遗》第 141 卷，起始页 581，引证页 583（联邦第九巡回上诉法院 2005 年裁决），在第 1 页维持了加利福尼亚中区联邦地区法院 2003 年 5 月 "2003 WL22909286" 号判决：原告称 1960 年的一首歌曲侵犯了 1926 年歌曲《Muskarat Ramble》的 "副歌或连复段"，在歌曲发行三十多年后才起诉；*Danjaq LLC v. Sony C.* 案，《联邦上诉法院判例汇编·第三辑》第 263 卷，起始页 842，引证页 952-956（联邦第九巡回上诉法院 2001 年裁决）：原告称 7 部詹姆斯·邦德电影侵犯了一部电影剧本版权，在这些电影上映 19 到 36 年后才起诉，而 "詹姆斯·邦德电影创作过程中的许多关键人物都去世了"，并且 "许多相关记录丢失"；*Jackson v. Axton* 案，《联邦上诉法院判例汇编·第三辑》第 25 卷，起始页 884，引证页 889（联邦第九巡回上诉法院 1994 年裁决），因其他原因不再是先例；《美国判例汇编》第 510 卷，起始页 517；《最高法院判例汇编》第 114 卷，起始页 1023；《美国判例汇编律师版·第二辑》第 127 卷，起始页 455：原告主张其参与了创作了歌曲《Joy to the World》，但得知其权利主张 17 年后方起诉，彼时记忆已经模糊，载有歌词的原始文件丢失，录音室（连同唱片）不复存在，而被告已 "围绕该歌曲安排商业事务" 多年；*Newsome v. Brown* 案（纽约南区联邦地区法院 2005 年 3 月 16 日 "2005 WL 627639" 号判决第 8-9 页）：就歌曲《It's a Man's World》在权利主张产生之日起 40 年后才起诉，彼时原告记忆已经模糊，且一个关键证据被烧毁。又见 *Chirco* 案，《联邦上诉法院判例汇编·第三辑》第 474 卷，引证页 230-231、234-236：声称公寓楼设计侵犯了原告的设计，虽然仅过两年半（左右）就起诉，＊＊1981 但公寓建成且对外出售，已经有 109 个家庭入住］。

再来看看本案。上诉人声称米高梅电影《愤怒的公牛》侵犯了她父亲最初拥有的版权，而她继承了该版权，并于 1991 年续展了版权。她在续展版权 18 年后，直到 2009 年才提起诉讼。在这 18 年里，米高梅花了数百万美元制作不同电影版本并进行营销（见附录，调卷令申请附录第 13a）。米高梅还签订了许多许可协议，其中一些许可协议允许电视网络在 2015 年全年播放这部电影（同上，第 14a）。与此同时，三名关键证人要么已离世，要么无法作证,加大了米高梅证明它没有侵犯上诉人版权的难度[米高梅可以证明1963年的剧本实际上由另一本书演绎而来,即米高梅可根据一份无争议的许可协议拥有该书权利,或者根据一份1976年与杰克·拉莫塔签署的协议可证明米高梅获得了该剧本的许可,而杰克·拉莫塔与上诉人的父亲共同创作了该剧本(见上,第3a、5a;附录第128-129、257-258、266-267页)]。因此,我认为上诉法院以迟误为由驳回诉讼请求是合法的。

长时间的拖延并不一定意味着不公正,但根据具体情况,它会增加这种可能性。事实上,假设上述歌曲案例中的版权人或继承人,在面对作品消费需求突然上升或证人最终死亡时才提起诉讼,而此时已经距离其权利主张首次出现过去了50年,甚至60年。或者假设丢失的证据对被告为自己辩护至关重要。本法院认为,只要版权人提出的是金钱赔偿请求,无论原告拖延的时间有多长、由此造成的损害有多大,或者即便是允许诉讼继续会导致不公正后果,法院也不能适用迟误规则。

II

本案应适用但为什么没有适用迟误规则呢?来看一下多数意见法官给出的理由。第一,多数法官认为,三年的"版权诉讼时效期间条款……本身已考虑了延迟",因此不再需要像迟误这样的额外保护(同上,第1972页)。我认为有时的确如此,但我也担心有时也并非如此。诉讼时效限制了原告可以追诉获得的救济,多数意见法官的这一认识是正确的。它将原告可获得的金钱赔偿限定于起诉前三年内被告的获利,外加原告在此期间遭受的一切损失[出处同上;第507条(b)款]。因此,如果原告从1980年一直等到2001年才提起诉讼,她就不能获得被告于1980年至1998年所获得的收益。但她可以获得被告1998年到2001年所获得的收益,这可能正是净收入转为正数的时间区间。此后,她可以每三年起诉一次,直到版权保护期限到期,也许是在2060年。如果原告的起诉导致了我所描述的不公正情形,那么她能获赔1998年到2001年被告的获利,而且获赔期限会一直延续到版权保护期限结束,这恰恰就是迟误所要阻止的那种不公正结果。

第二，多数意见法官指出，原告能获赔的是被告的收益减去获得这些收益所产生的"可扣除费用"[同上，第1973页，引述第504条（b）款]。换句话说，多数意见法官确信《版权法案》能让被告从获利中减去其在开发或销售被控侵权作品环节产生的费用。但同样，这样的事实可能会阻止不公正结果的出现，有时候并不能阻止不公正结果的出现。＊＊1982原告急于起诉可能意味着被告已经收回了大部分费用，剩下的主要是收益。这可能意味着被告将一生几十年的时间都奉献给了作品的制作，以至于失去了未来收益流（即使他能收回成本），这就相当于以后不会再有任何形式的收入。在上述情况下，由于原告不必要地拖延起诉，而使被告拱手将收益转交给原告可能是不公正的。＊＊1982简言之，"可扣除费用"规定并不保护被告免受近100年前汉德法官影响深远的版权意见中强调的潜在不公正。也就是说，它不能阻止版权人（或其继承人）"在所称侵权人花费大量金钱"进行风险投资时按兵不动，而当侵权人成功时才会露面起诉，然后收割远比一开始通过谈判可能获得的许可费和特许权费多得多的获益（见 Haas 案，《联邦地区法院判例汇编》第234卷，引证页108；但对比同上，引证页108-109：原告将获得禁令救济，因为其中一名被告是"故意剽窃"，但由于原告急于起诉，判决支持的收益将减少）。

第三，多数意见法官认为，"任由法官设定时效限制，而不去遵从国会（在《版权法案》中）规定的时间限制"，将与"国会制定第507条（b）款时寻求实现的一致性相抵触"（同上，第1975页）。但是，多数意见法官凭什么认为国会制定第507条（b）款旨在"实现"的部分目的是取缔衡平法上的迟误抗辩？正如多数意见法官认识到的那样，国会在1957年统一了版权诉讼时效立法，这样，联邦法院在确定时效时，就无需再借用因地而异的州法律（同上，第1968-1969页）。在1957年的法案中，或者在版权立法的其他地方，没有任何内容表明国会也试图阻止适用迟误抗辩。《版权法案》对此只字未提，这与衡平法原则的适用是一致的，而不是冲突的。

第507条的立法历史表明，国会刻意选择不去"具体列举那些可以在民事版权诉讼中主张的公正考虑因素"，因为国会清楚"联邦地区法院一般都认可这些衡平法上的抗辩"[见第1014号参议院报告，1957年第85届国会第1次会议，第2-3页（引用众议院司法委员会的话）]。早在1957年以前，联邦法院就经常在版权案件中适用懈怠原则［见 *Callaghan v. Myers* 案，《美国判例汇编》第 128 卷，起始页 617，引证页 658-659；《最高法院判例汇编》第 9 卷，起始页 177；《美国判例汇编律师版》第 32 卷，起始页 547（1888 年裁决）：认为在版权诉讼中可以援引迟误抗辩。*Edwin L. Wiegand Co. v. Harold E. Trent Co.* 案，《联邦上诉法院判例汇编·第二辑》第 122 卷，起始页 920，引证页 925（联邦第三巡回上诉法院 1941 年裁决）：适用懈怠原则来阻击版权诉讼。*D. O. Haynes & Co. v. Druggists' Circular* 案，《联邦上诉法院判例汇编·第二辑》第 32 卷，起始页 215，引证页 216-218（联邦第二巡回上诉法院 1929 年裁决）：同上］。国会期待联邦法院延续这一做法。

此外，本法院一直认为，联邦法院在适用诉讼时效法律时，可以"遵循那些中止或限制诉讼时效期间的衡平法原则"，这是因为"起诉时限""要求"可以根据"确保公正的需要"调整［*Morgan* 案，《美国判例汇编》第 536 卷，引证页 121-122；《最高法院判例汇编》第 122 卷，起始页 2061（引用自 *Zipes v. Trans World Airlines, Inc.* 案，《美国判例汇编》第 455 卷，起始页 385，引证页 398；《最高法院判例汇编》第 102 卷，起始页 1127；《美国判例汇编律师版·第二辑》第 71 卷，起始页 234，1982 年裁决；此处添加强调标记）］。在很多场合，即便是诉讼时效法案中没有提及遵循衡平法原则，本法院也认为支持迟误抗辩也是这些法案的应有之义，下级法院亦是如此［如 *Morgan* 案，见前，引证页 121；《最高法院判例汇编》第 122 卷，起始页 2061：法院认为根据第七卷"雇员可以提出迟误抗辩"＊＊1983。*Bay Area Laundry and Dry Cleaning Pension Trust Fund v. Ferbar Corp. of Cal.* 案，《美国判例汇编》第 522 卷，起始页 192，引证页 205；《最高法院判例汇编》第 118 卷，起始页 542；《美国判例汇编律师版·第二辑》第 139 卷，起始页 553（1997 年裁决）：根据 1980 年《多雇主养老金计划修正法案》提起的诉讼也如此。*Abbott Laboratories v. Gardner* 案，《美国判例汇编》第 387 卷，起始页 136，引证页 155；《最高法院判例汇编》第 87 卷，起始页 1507；《美国判例汇编律师版·第二辑》第 18 卷，起始页 681（1967 年裁决）：根据《行政诉讼法》提起的寻求宣告性和禁令救济的诉讼也如此。*Patterson v. Hewitt* 案，《美国判例汇编》第 195 卷，起始页 309，引证页 319-320；《最高法院判例汇编》第 25 卷，起始页 35；《美国判例汇编律师版》第49卷，起始页214（1904年裁决）：在新墨西哥州法定诉讼时效期间内提起财产诉讼的情形也如此。Alsop v. Riker 案，《美国判例汇编》第155卷，起始页448，引证页460；《最高法院判例汇编》第15卷1，起始页162；《美国判例汇编律师版》第39卷，起始页218（1894年裁决）：法院认为，"法定诉讼时效限制暂不考虑"，合同诉讼因"迟误"而不得提起。Teamsters & Employers Welfare Trust of Ill. v. Gorman Bros. Ready Mix 案，《联邦上诉法院判例汇编·第三辑》第283卷，起始页877，引证页883（美国联邦第七巡回上诉法院2002年裁决）：在针对1974年《雇员退休收入保障法案》（ERISA）福利计划的诉讼中可适用迟误抗辩。Hot Wax, Inc. v. Turtle Wax, Inc. 案，《联邦上诉法院判例汇编·第三辑》第191卷，起始页813，引证页822-823（美国联邦第七巡回上诉法院1999年裁决）：在诉讼时效期间内提起的《兰哈姆法案》诉讼中可适用迟误抗辩]。除非国会另有指示，否则法院通常会认为衡平法规则与诉讼时效期间并行不悖，并且平等地适用于原告和被告。参见 Astoria Fed. Sav. & Loan Assn. v. Solimino 案，《美国判例汇编》第501卷，起始页104，引证页108；《最高法院判例汇编》第111卷，起始页2166；《美国判例汇编律师版·第二辑》第115卷，起始页96（1991年裁决）："应认识到国会是在拥抱普通法裁判原则的背景下立法"，并将普通法裁判原则吸纳到制定法中，"除非立法目的明显与之相反"（省略内部引号和印证）。Porter v. Warner Holding Co. 案，《美国判例汇编》第328卷，起始页395，引证页398；《最高法院判例汇编》第66卷，起始页1086；《美国判例汇编律师版》第90卷，起始页1332（1946年裁决）："除非制定法另有规定，地区法院拥有为正确和完整行使审判权利而利用一切固有的衡平法上的权力。"

　　本法院在今天却得出了不同的结论。当衡平法上的考虑有利于原告时（如衡平法上的时效中止），本法院将第507条（b）款的"沉默"理解为包含了可以延长起诉时间的衡平法规则；而当衡平法规则有利于被告时（如迟误），本法院又转而将第507条（b）款的"沉默"理解为排斥衡平法规则（同上，第1975-1976页，第1977-1978页）。我不明白以这种方式解读制定法中未明示内容的逻辑。

　　第四，多数意见法官以迟误"系由衡平法院发展而来"，且本法院曾告诚即使在 1938 年普通法与衡平法合并之后也不要援引迟误抗辩来阻止法律救济等来捍卫自己的裁判结果（同上，第 1973-1974 页）。多数意见法官引述了三个案例来支持这一主张，但没有一个案例是决定性的。在第一个案件 [*Holmberg v. Armbrecht* 案，《美国判例汇编》第 327 卷，起始页 392；《最高法院判例汇编》第 66 卷，起始页 582；《美国判例汇编律师版》第 90 卷，起始页 743（1946 年裁决）]，本法院称：

"如果国会明确规定行使其所设立的权利有时间限制，那么权利的行使就会有终结之时。

……

传统上来说，并且基于充分理由，诉讼时效规定并非旨在限制衡平法上的救济措施（同上，引证页 395-396；《最高法院判例汇编》第 66 卷，起始页 582"）。

然而，这一陈述恰是本法院提供的部分阐释，以说明一旦联邦法案中没有涉及诉讼时效的条款，在适用时应与"执行联邦立法层面创设的衡平法权利时遵循的公正这一历史原则"保持一致，而不是去遵循纽约州的诉讼时效法案（同上，引证页 395；《最高法院判例汇编》第 66 卷，起始页 582）。*Holmberg* 案与普通法诉讼能否适用迟误抗辩无关。*Holmberg* 案是"根据衡平法"提起的，本法院将 *Holmberg* 案发回，要求确定上诉人是否 **1984 "存在迟误情形"（同上，引证页 393、397；《最高法院判例汇编》第 66 卷，起始页 582）。

多数意见法官援引的第二个案例 [*Merck & Co. v. Reynolds* 案，《美国判例汇编》第 559 卷，起始页 633；《最高法院判例汇编》第 130 卷，起始页 1784；《美国判例汇编律师版·第二辑》第 176 卷，起始页 582（2010 年裁决）] 提供了一些额外支撑，但力度有限。在那起案件中，本法院引用了 1935 年的一个案例，主张"在诉讼时效期间内，迟误并非普通法上的抗辩"[同上，引证页 652；《最高法院判例汇编》第 130 卷，起始页 1784；引自 *United States v. Mack* 案，《美国判例汇编》第 295 卷，起始页 480，引证页 489；《最高法院判例汇编》第 55 卷，起始页 813；《美国判例汇编律师版》第 79 卷，起始页 1559（1935 年裁决）]。但 *Merck* 案涉及的是一项联邦证券法案，该法案中既包含自"发现"之日起两年的诉讼时效条款，也包含从"违反"之日起五年的除诉期间［同上，引证页638；《最高法院判例汇编》第130卷，起始页1784，引用《美国法典》第28卷第1658条（b）款］。鉴于除诉期间立法为诉讼设定了"最长期限限制"，且通常"与时效终止"和类似的衡平法原则相冲突，本法院在该案中认为，争议的两年时效期间不受"调查通知"规则或类似的延误的约束［*Lampf, Pleva, Lipkind, Prupis & Petigrow v. Gilbertson* 案，《美国判例汇编》第501卷，起始页350，引证页363；《最高法院判例汇编》第111卷，起始页2773；《美国判例汇编律师版·第二辑》第115卷，起始页321（1991年裁决）（省略内部引号和引用）。*Merck* 案，同上，引证页650–652；《最高法院判例汇编》第130卷，起始页1784］。*Merck* 案并没有表明，当原告寻求损害赔偿救济时，诉讼时效条款总是或通常违背衡平法原则。它只是在本法院于普通法和衡平法合并前裁决的案件中找到了对其结论的额外支持。和 *Merck* 案不同，本案中，诉讼时效条款没有伴随着一个必然的除诉期间条款。

在第三个案例，即 *County of Oneida v. Oneida Indian Nation of N. Y.* 案［《美国判例汇编》第470卷，起始页226；《最高法院判例汇编》第105卷，起始页1245；《美国判例汇编律师版·第二辑》第84卷，起始页169（1985年裁决）］的裁决书中，本法院在一个脚注提到，"在普通法诉讼中援引迟误进行抗辩的确很新颖"（同上，引证页245，注释16；《最高法院判例汇编》第105卷，起始页1245）。这一表述是在与印第安部落有关的特殊政策背景下作出的，法院紧接着讨论了这些特殊政策（出处同上）。但无论如何，*Oneida* 案并没有解决被告是否可以仰仗迟误抗辩，因为下级法院没有就此问题作出裁决（同上，引证页244–245；《最高法院判例汇编》第105卷，起始页1245）。

总之，在国会规定了诉讼时效限制的背景下，关于在寻求普通法救济的诉讼中是否应支持迟误抗辩的问题，本法院在 *Holmberg* 案、*Merck* 案或 *Oneida* 案的任何说法都没能确立一个明确统一的规则。相反，本法院不止一次指出，尽管有明确的诉讼时效，被告依然可以在损害赔偿诉讼中援引迟误抗辩（尽管在案件中并未有人援引过迟误抗辩）（见 *Morgan* 案，《美国判例汇编》第536卷，引证页116–119、121–122；《最高法院判例汇编》第122卷，起始页2061：对恶劣工作环境根据第七卷提出赔偿主张时可以援引迟误抗辩。Bay Area Laundry 案，《美国判例汇编》522 卷，引证页 205；《最高法院判例汇编》第 118 卷，起始页 542：在根据 MPPAA 提起的"退出责任评估"诉讼中可以援引迟误抗辩）。下级法院也在各类情况下作出了类似裁决，通常不仅认可迟误抗辩，而且还在审理的具体案件中支持迟误抗辩［如 Cayuga Indian Nation of N. Y. v. Pataki 案，《联邦上诉法院判例汇编·第三辑》第 413 卷，起始页 266，引证页 274-277（联邦第二巡回上诉法院 2005 年裁决）：在"占有土地主张权"诉讼中地区法院曾判决支持损害赔偿，但联邦第二巡回上诉法院认为此类案件，无论是普通法还是衡平法上的诉讼，都可以援引迟误抗辩，并以迟误为由驳回了诉讼。Teamsters 案，《联邦上诉法院判例汇编·第三辑》第 283 卷，引证页 881-883：根据《职工退休所得保障条例》主张利益的诉讼可以援引迟误抗辩，但本案不符合条件。Hot Wax 案，《联邦上诉法院判例汇编·第三辑》第 191 卷，引证页 822-827："地区法院将迟误规则适用于 Hot Wax 提出的《兰哈姆法案》索赔案件（要求损害赔偿）是适当的"。A. C. Aukerman Co. v. R. L. Chaides ＊＊1985 Constr. Co. 案，《联邦上诉法院判例汇编·第二辑》第 960 卷，起始页 1020，引证页 1030-1032、1045-1046（联邦巡回上诉法院 1992 年裁决）（全院庭审）：在主张损害赔偿的专利诉讼中可以援引迟误抗辩，并因迟误抗辩是否得到支持为由发回重审。Cornetta v. United States 案，《联邦上诉法院判例汇编·第二辑》第 851 卷，起始页 1372，引证页 1376-1383（联邦巡回上诉法院 1988 年裁决）（全院庭审）：同上，索要欠薪的案件］。即使我们只关注联邦版权诉讼，六个处理过此类问题的巡回上诉法院中有四个认为迟误可以阻止普通法救济的请求［见《联邦上诉法院判例汇编·第三辑》第 695 卷，起始页 946，引证页 956（联邦第九巡回上诉法院 2012 年裁决）：本案下级法院裁决，认为迟误可以阻止一切版权主张。Peter Letterese & Assocs. ,Inc. v. World Inst. of Scientology Enterprises, Int'l 案，《联邦上诉法院判例汇编·第三辑》第 533 卷，起始页 1287，引证页 1319-1322（联邦第十一巡回上诉法院 2008 年裁决）：迟误可以阻止版权案件中的追溯赔偿。Chirco 案，《联邦上诉法院判例汇编·第三辑》第 474 卷，引证页 234-236："'无论普通法还是衡平法诉讼'，都可以提出迟误抗辩"，并认为，尽管原告可以获得赔偿金以及禁令，但他们对额外衡平法救济的请求"有点像汉德法官在 Hass 案中警告的以及司法系统应该嗤之以鼻的不公正性"（引用自 Teamsters 案，同上，引证页 881）。Jacobsen v. Deseret Book Co. 案，《联邦上诉法院判例汇编·第三辑》第 287 卷，起始页 936，引证页 950-951（联邦第十巡回上诉法院 2002 年裁决）："少数案例"可以适用迟误规则，未区分所寻求的救济类型（引用省略）。但见 New Era Publications Int'l v. Henry Holt & Co. 案，《联邦上诉法院判例汇编·第二辑》第 873 卷，起始页 576，引证页 584-585（联邦第二巡回上诉法院 1989 年裁决）：根据《版权法案》，迟误可以阻止对禁令救济的主张，但不能阻止损害赔偿主张。Lyons Partnership, L. P. v. Morris Costumes, Inc. 案，《联邦上诉法院判例汇编·第三辑》第 243 卷，起始页 789，引证页 798-799 联邦第四巡回上诉法院 2001 年裁决）：在版权案件中完全没有适用迟误的可能］。

可能更重要的是，在允许将迟误抗辩适用于寻求衡平法救济的版权主张，而非寻求普通救济的版权主张时，多数意见法官对现代诉讼的规则和实践重视不够。

自 1938 年以来，国会和联邦诉讼规则用"民事诉讼"来取代曾经的"普通法诉讼"和"衡平法诉讼"（《联邦民事诉讼程序规则》第 2 条："有一种诉讼形式，即民事诉讼"）。联邦民事诉讼活动同时受到衡平法和普通法的保护［《联邦民事诉讼程序规则》第 8 条（c）款（1）项："在答辩时，一方当事人必须积极陈述无效或肯定性抗辩，包括：……禁止反悔……迟误……以及诉讼时效"］。因此，自 1938 年以来，在一些过去曾属于普通法的诉讼中，联邦法院常允许被告援引衡平法抗辩，包括迟误抗辩（同上，第 1984-1985 页，引用案例）。那为何要在版权案件中区别对待呢？事实上，多数意见法官承认像"收益"这种"返还收益型救济"（版权案件中经常被主张）很难划分为"衡平法"或"普通法"救济中的任何一类［同上，第 1967 页，注释 1（省略内部引号）］。那下级法院为什么还要进行这种令人不安且生硬的分类呢?

第五，多数意见法官认为，运用另一种原则——衡平法上的禁止反悔原则——可以实现迟误规则寻求的避免不公正现象的效果（见前，第 1977 页）。对此我表示怀疑。正如多数意见法官所认识到的，"两种抗辩事由的导向也不同"（同上）。禁止反悔原则的核心是原告的误导性陈述，被告基于对误导性陈述的信赖而给自身造成损失（帕特里，《版权》第6卷第20：58节，第20-110、20-112页）。迟误的要义在于原告不合理地拖延，由此对被告造成损失（同上，第20：54节，第20-96页）。如果由于时间的流逝，有利于被告的证据已经消失或被告继续投资演绎作品，原告何以作出一种误导性陈述以禁止其反悔呢？

总而言之，正如多数意见法官所说，迟误规则在基于＊＊1986诉讼时效的制度中可能只占据"立锥之地"［见前，第1977页，引自Dobbs，《救济法》第1卷，第2章第6节之（1），第152页（1993年第二版）］。但这一"立锥之地"是很重要的。在少数特殊的案件里，原告无端拖延起诉，进而给被告造成不公正的伤害，迟误规则可以指引法院作出公正的判决。我认为没有理由将迟误规则从版权领域抹除，尤其是在适用于损害赔偿的诉讼时效期间上。

因此，恕我直言，我持反对意见。

注释

［1］作为侵权救济措施，《版权法案》第502条规定了禁令，第503条规定了扣押和处置侵权物品，第504条规定了损害赔偿和收益，第505条规定了诉讼费和律师费。像其他返还收益型救济一样，获赔收益"不太容易被定性为普通法或衡平救济"，因为它"融合了两种制度中的权利和救济措施"［《返还责任和不当得利重述（三）》第4条，评论b，第28页（2010年出版）］。鉴于获赔收益救济措施的"多变性"（同上，评论c，第30页），我们在本案中将其视为衡平法救济。

［2］对于1978年以后的作品，继承人仍有机会重新获取作者拥有的权利［见M. Nimmer & D. Nimmer著《版权法》第3卷，第11.01［A］节，第11-4页（2013年版）（以下简称"Nimmer"）］。

［3］1976年，《版权法案》被全面修订，但其中的三年追溯时效规定在本质上没有改变（见1976年10月19日法案第101条，《美国制定法大全》第90卷，第2586页）。

［4］虽然我们还没有就这一问题作出过裁决，但九个联邦巡回上诉法院已经采用了"发现规则"以替代"伤害事件规则"。"发现规则"是指从

"原告发现或经过审慎注意应当发现构成索赔基础的伤害事件"开始计算时效期限[*William A. Graham Co. v. Haughey*案,《联邦上诉法院判例汇编·第三辑》第568卷,起始页425,引证页433(联邦第三巡回上诉法院2009年裁决)(省略内部引号)。另见帕特里,《版权》第6卷第20:19节,第20-28页(2013年版)(以下简称"帕特里"):"绝大多数法院在版权案件中使用发现侵权行为起算规则。"]

[5]如上,第20:23节,第20-44页;Nimmer,《版权法》第3卷,第12.05[B][1][b]节,第12-150.2与12-150.4页。另见*William A. Graham Co.*案,《联邦上诉法院判例汇编·第三辑》第568卷,引证页433;*Peter Letterese & Assoc., Inc. v. World Inst. of Scientology Enterprises, Int'l*案,《联邦上诉法院判例汇编·第三辑》第533卷,起始页1287,引证页1320,注39(联邦第十一巡回上诉法院2008年裁决);*Bridgeport Music, Inc. v. Rhyme Syndicate Music*案,《联邦上诉法院判例汇编·第三辑》第376卷,起始页615,引证页621(联邦第六巡回上诉法院2004年裁决);*Makedwde Publishing Co. v. Johnson*案,《联邦上诉法院判例汇编·第三辑》第37卷,起始页180,引证页182(联邦第五巡回上诉法院1994年裁决);*Roley v. New World Pictures, Ltd.*案,《联邦上诉法院判例汇编·第三辑》第19卷,起始页479,引证页481(联邦第九巡回上诉法院1994年裁决)。

[6]单独累积的损害不应与过去的侵权行为在今后继续造成的损害相混淆。对比*Klehr v. A. O. Smith Corp.*案[《美国判例汇编》第521卷,起始页179,引证页190;《最高法院判例汇编》第117卷,起始页1984;《美国判例汇编律师版·第二辑》第138卷,起始页373(1997年裁决):对于单独累积的损害,每个新的损害行为必须比"先前损害行为(对原告)造成的损害大"]与*Havens Realty Corp. v. Coleman*案[《美国判例汇编》第455卷,起始页363,引证页380-381;《最高法院判例汇编》第102卷,起始页1114;《美国判例汇编律师版·第二辑》第71卷,起始页214,(1982年裁决):"如果原告……质疑……持续到诉讼时效期间内的侵权行为,则在(诉讼时效期间),从声称该行为的最后一次发生时算起,提出诉讼是及时的。"(脚注略)]。

[7]这里举一个非版权案例来说明问题。在*Bay Area Laundry and Dry*

Cleaning Pension Trust Fund v. Ferbar Corp. of Cal. 案 [《美国判例汇编》第522卷，起始页192；《最高法院判例汇编》第118卷，起始页542；《联邦上诉法院判例汇编·第二辑》第139卷，起始页552（1997年裁决）] 中，一名雇主拖欠了一批未足额缴纳养老金账户的款项（如上，引证页198-199；《最高法院判例汇编》第118卷，起始页542）。受托人在雇主第一次拖欠付款刚满6年后提起诉讼，这时刚好超出适用的6年诉讼时效期限（如上，引证页198；《最高法院判例汇编》第118卷，起始页542）。由于该批次中的第一笔拖欠付款不在诉讼时效范围内，雇主辩称，随后的拖欠付款也过了期限（如上，引证页206，《最高法院判例汇编》第118卷，起始页542）。本法院驳回了这一论点。法院认为，由于"每一笔未付款都会产生一个单独的诉讼理由，且有6年的时效期限，因此剩余的索赔是及时的"[同上，对比 Klehr 案，《美国判例汇编》第521卷，引证页190；《最高法院判例汇编》第117卷，起始页1984：对于依据《勒索影响和腐败组织法案》提起的民事诉讼，原告可以对时效期间内的行为产生的损失提出赔偿要求，但不得使用"独立的、新的前提行为作为引导，以期对时效期间外发生的其他早期前提行为造成的伤害提出赔偿"。National Railroad Passenger Corporation v. Morgan 案，《美国判例汇编》第536卷，起始页101，引证页114-122；《最高法院判例汇编》第122卷，起始页2061；《联邦上诉法院判例汇编·第二辑》第153卷，起始页106（2002年裁决）：将独立的行为，即每次独立且可诉的行为，与"会产生累积效果的"行为进行区分，如根据1964年《民权法案》第七章提出的有害工作环境索赔（《美国法典》第42卷，第2000e条及之后条款）："与不连续行为形成鲜明对比的是，可能无法单独起诉一个单独的有害事件。"但是对比后文第1984页至1985页：无视 Morgan 小心区分的可独立起诉的行为和会产生累积效果的行为]。

[8] 佩特拉的律师代表弗兰克·佩特拉的继承人提交了续展申请。当佩特拉的母亲去世，佩特拉的哥哥将自己的权利转让给佩特拉时，佩特拉成了1963年剧本所有权利的唯一拥有者。

[9] 本法院提出，拉莫塔"多年前作为一名拳击手，头部遭受了无数次打击"，尽管他已经认识佩特拉40年了，但他"已经不认识佩特拉了"（调卷令申请附录第45a-46a）。

[10] 佩特拉在声明中称,米高梅于2001年告知其该片"财务赤字巨大""永远不会盈利",基于此,"米高梅不会继续向她发送财务报告"(附录第234页)。

[11] 上诉法院没有考虑米高梅是否提出证据损害主张[《联邦上诉法院判例汇编·第三辑》第695卷,起始页946,引证页953(联邦第九巡回上诉法院2012年裁决)]。

[12] 见 *Lyons Partnership L. P. v. Morris Costumes, Inc.* 案[《联邦上诉法院判例汇编·第三辑》第243卷,起始页789,引证页798(联邦第四巡回上诉法院2001年裁决):不论上诉人所寻求的救济措施是何,迟误抗辩不适用于版权侵权案件];*Peter Letterese* 案(《联邦上诉法院判例汇编·第三辑》第533卷,引证页1320:"在版权案件中有一个强有力的假设,即如果原告的诉讼是在诉讼时效结束之前提起的,则该诉讼是及时的。只有在极其特别的情况下,迟误抗辩才会被认可");*Chirco v. Crosswinds Communities, Inc.* 案[《联邦上诉法院判例汇编·第三辑》第474卷,起始页227,引证页233(联邦第六巡回上诉法院2007年裁决):在版权诉讼中,迟误只适用于"最有说服力的案例"];*Jacobsen v. Deseret Book Co.* 案[《联邦上诉法院判例汇编·第三辑》第287卷,起始页936,引证页950(联邦第十巡回上诉法院2002年裁决):法院一般应遵从三年时效法规,而不是根据案件中的迟误作出裁决"];*New Era Publications Int'l v. Henry Holt & Co.* 案[《联邦上诉法院判例汇编·第二辑》第873卷,起始页576,引证页584-585(联邦第二巡回上诉法院1989年裁决):"严重损害,加上……不合情理的迟误……意味着无权……获得禁令救济,(原告)只得退而求其次,主张损害赔偿救济。"对比后文第1979、1985-1986页:承认迟误的适用应是"特殊的",仅限于"少数特例"]。

[13] 假设佩特拉在案件实体上胜诉,上诉法院关于迟误的裁决将在事实上准许米高梅在版权漫长的有效期内免费使用《愤怒的公牛》的版权。对于米高梅来说,这种免费的、强制许可所带来的价值可能远远超过米高梅在这部电影上的投入。

[14] 见《联邦民事诉讼程序规则》第2条:"有一种诉讼形式,即民事诉讼。"第8条(c)款将迟误与诉讼时效规定一起列为肯定性抗辩。

[15] 与《版权法案》不同的是,规范商标的《兰哈姆法案》并不包含

时效条款，并明确规定允许使用"衡平法上的规则，包括迟误在内"进行抗辩 [《美国法典》第 15 卷第 1115 条（b）款 9 项]。但对比后文，第 1983、1984 页 [引用 Hot Wax, Inc. v. Turtle Wax, Inc. 案，《联邦上诉法院判例汇编·第三辑》第 191 卷，起始页 813（联邦第七巡回上诉法院 1999 年裁决），却没有注意到《兰哈姆法案》不包括时效条款]。《专利法案》规定，"上诉人不能针对侵权人在上诉前 6 年之前所实施的任何侵权行为进行追赔"（《美国法典》第 35 卷第 286 条）。该法案还规定，"在任何涉及专利有效性或侵权的诉讼中"，都可以提出"未侵权、不对侵权负责或不可执行"抗辩 [第 286 条（b）款（2012 版）]。部分基于第 282 条及其评注、立法历史和过往实践，联邦巡回上诉法院认为，迟误可以阻止在诉讼开始前产生的损害赔偿，但不能阻止禁令救济 [A. C. Aukerman Co. v. R. L. Chaides Constr. Co. 案，《联邦上诉法院判例汇编·第二辑》第 960 卷，起始页 1020，引证页 1029-1031，1039-1041（1992 年裁决）（全院庭审）]。我们还没有机会去评论联邦巡回上诉法院的立场。

[16] 米高梅假装不是这样，但它所举的案例并不具备米高梅所期待的分量。Morgan 案（如上所述，第 1970 页，注 7）显然是对米高梅最有利的案例，因为该案例在米高梅的答辩陈述中被引用了 13 次（见被上诉人答辩陈述第 8、9、14、16、18、19、25、31、34、35、36、40、47 页；见后第 1979、1982、1984、1985 页）然而，Morgan 案并没有暗示迟误可能会阻止对联邦法律规定的诉讼时效内发生的不连续非法行为的索赔。判决意见第 II-A 部分提到了单独累计规则，认为每一个不连续的侵权行为都意味着新的赔偿主张"，无论"过去的侵权行为"是否已由于超出联邦法律规定的诉讼时效而不能对其提出索赔（《美国判例汇编》第 536 卷，引证页 113；《最高法院判例汇编》第 122 卷，起始页 2061）。判决意见第 II-B 及 II-C 部分将单独累积的非法行为与有害工作环境索赔中的会产生累积效果的行为和延续许久的行为区分开来（如上，引证页 115-117、121；《最高法院判例汇编》第 122 卷，起始页 2061）。法院认为，可以援引迟误来限制持续违反原则被用来拯救过期权利主张的可能性，而不是限制诉讼时效期限内单独累积的权利主张。Bay Area Laundry 案及 Morgan 案（如后所述，第 1970 页，注 7）与米高梅案相似（另见后文第 1982、1983、1984 页）。但是，该意见认为，

只有在联邦法律要求"尽快"提起诉讼的背景下才考虑迟误［《美国法典》第29卷，第1399条（b）款（1）项。参见《美国判例汇编》第522卷，引证页205；《最高法院判例汇编》第118卷，起始页542］。米高梅认为 Patterson v. Hewitt 案［《美国判例汇编》第195卷，起始页309；《最高法院判例汇编》第25卷，起始页35；《联邦上诉法院判例汇编》第49卷，起始页214（1904年裁决）］与佩特拉案相似（见口头辩论笔录第32-22、53页）。Patterson v. Hewitt 案阻止了在联邦法律规定的诉讼时效期间产生的诉讼主张。在参考适用州法律时，联邦法院有时会适用迟误来实现进一步控制［见后文，第1968-1969页；Russell v. Todd 案，《美国判例汇编》第309卷，起始页280，引证页288，注1；《最高法院判例汇编》第60卷，起始页527；《美国判例汇编律师版》第84卷，起始页754（1940年裁决）："在适用当地的州法律前，迟误可以阻止衡平法救济"］。Patterson 案中并没有适用联邦诉讼时效规则。

［17］如一方年幼或精神障碍、被告不在管辖区域内、欺诈隐瞒等情况［见第1014号参议院报告，1957年第85届国会第1次会议，第2-3页，（以下简称"参议院报告"）］。

［18］少数意见所指的立法历史（见后，第1982页）谈到了"一般不适用时效法规的衡平法场景中"（参议院报告第3页），并没有提及迟误缩短了国会允许的诉讼时效期间。

［19］少数意见法官担心原告可能为了收益"每三年起诉一次……直到版权保护期限到期"（见后，第1981页；见后，第1979页）。该意见忽略了一点，即原告在证明其遭受侵权后，很可能会获得针对未来侵权行为的禁令救济，以阻止被告再重复实施侵权行为。

［20］如前所述（见上文，第1972页，注11），上诉法院没有解决证据损害是否存在的问题。

［21］尽管米高梅在应对佩特拉之诉的答辩中，分别提出了迟误和禁止反悔原则作为肯定性抗辩（参见"加州中区联邦地区法院CV 09-0072号判决书"中被告应原告之诉的答辩），但下级法院没有回应禁止反悔的抗辩。

［22］尽管在本案中信赖或不信赖可能很重要，但我们并不认为信赖在所有案例中都是调整禁令救济或获利据以参考的必要条件。

Paula PETRELLA, Petitioner v.

METRO-GOLDWYN-MAYER, INC., et al.

No. 12–1315.
Argued Jan. 21, 2014.
Decided May 19, 2014.
https://www.supremecourt.gov/opinions/13pdf/12-1315_f20h.pdf

The Copyright Act provides that "[n]o civil action shall be maintained under the [Act] unless it is commenced within three years after the claim accrued." 17 U. S. C. § 507(b). This case presents the question whether the equitable defense of laches (unreasonable, prejudicial delay in commencing suit) may bar relief on a copyright infringement claim brought within § 507(b)'s three-year limitations period. Section 507(b), it is undisputed, bars relief of any kind for conduct occurring prior to the three-year limitations period. To the extent that an infringement suit seeks relief solely for conduct occurring within the limitations period, however, courts are not at liberty to jettison Congress' judgment on the timeliness of suit. Laches, we hold, cannot be invoked to preclude adjudication of a claim for damages brought within the three-year window. As to equitable relief, in extraordinary circumstances, laches may bar at the very threshold the particular relief requested by the plaintiff. And a plaintiff's delay can always be brought to bear at the remedial stage, in determining appropriate injunctive relief, and in assessing the "profits of the infringer...attributable to the infringement." § 504(b). [1]

Petitioner Paula Petrella, in her suit for copyright infringement, sought no relief for conduct occurring outside § 507(b)'s three-year limitations period. Nevertheless, the courts below held that laches barred her suit in its entirety, without regard to the currency of the conduct of which Petrella complains. That position, ＊＊1968 we hold, is contrary to § 507(b) and this Court's precedent on the province of laches.

I

The Copyright Act (Act), 17 U. S. C. § 101 *et seq.*, grants copyright protection to original works of authorship. § 102(a). Four aspects of copyright law bear explanation at the outset.

First, the length of a copyright term. Under the Act, a copyright "vests initially in the author or authors of the work," who may transfer ownership to a third party. § 201. The Act confers on a copyright owner certain exclusive rights, including the rights to reproduce and distribute the work and to develop and market derivative works. § 106. Copyrighted works published before 1978—as was the work at issue—are protected for an initial period of 28 years, which may be—and in this case was—extended for a renewal period of up to 67 years. § 304(a). From and after January 1,1978, works are generally protected from the date of creation until 70 years after the author's death. § 302(a).

Second, copyright inheritance. For works copyrighted under the pre-1978 regime in which an initial period of protection may be followed by a renewal period, Congress provided that the author's heirs inherit the renewal rights. See § 304(a)(1)(C)(ii)-(iv). We held in *Stewart v. Abend*, 495 U. S. 207, 110 S. Ct. 1750, 109 L. Ed. 2d 184(1990), that if an author who has assigned her rights away "dies before the renewal period, then the assignee may continue to use the original work [to produce a derivative work] only if the author's successor transfers the renewal rights to the assignee." *Id.*, at 221, 110 S. Ct. 1750. [2]

Third, remedies. The Act provides a variety of civil remedies for infringement, both equitable and legal. See § § 502-505, described *supra*, at 2, n. 1. A court may issue an injunction "on such terms as it may deem reasonable to prevent or restrain infringement of a copyright." § 502(a). At the election of the copyright owner, a court may also award either(1) "the copyright owner's actual damages and any additional profits of the infringer," § 504(a)(1), which petitioner seeks in the instant case, or(2) statutory damages within a defined range, § 504(c).

Fourth, and most significant here, the statute of limitations. Until 1957, federal copyright law did not include a statute of limitations for civil suits. Federal courts therefore used analogous state statutes of limitations to determine the timeliness of infringement claims. See S. Rep. No. 1014, 85th Cong., 1st Sess., 2(1957)(hereinafter Senate Report). And they sometimes invoked laches to abridge the state-law prescription. As explained in *Teamsters & Employers Welfare Trust of Ill. v. Gorman Bros. Ready Mix*, 283 F. 3d 877, 881(C. A. 7 2002): "When Congress fails to enact a statute of limitations, a[federal] court that borrows a state statute of limitations but permits it to be abridged by the doctrine of laches is not invading congressional prerogatives. It is merely filling a legislative hole." (internal citation omitted). In 1957, Congress addressed the matter and filled the hole; it prescribed a three-year look-back limitations period for all civil claims arising under the Copyright Act. See Act of Sept. 7, 1957, Pub. L. 85-313, 71 Stat. 633, 17 U. S. C. § 115(b)(1958 ed.). The provision, as already noted, reads: "No civil action shall be maintained under the provisions of this **1969 title unless it is commenced within three years after the claim accrued." § 507(b). [3]

The federal limitations prescription governing copyright suits serves two purposes: (1) to render uniform and certain the time within which copyright claims could be pursued; and (2) to prevent the forum shopping invited by disparate state limitations periods, which ranged from one to eight years. Senate Report 2; see H. R. Rep. No. 2419, 84th Cong., 2d Sess., 2 (1956). To comprehend how the Copyright Act's limitations period works, one must understand when a copyright infringement claim accrues.

A claim ordinarily accrues "when [a] plaintiff has a complete and present cause of action." *Bay Area Laundry and Dry Cleaning Pension Trust Fund v. Ferbar Corp. of Cal.*, 522 U. S. 192, 201, 118 S. Ct. 542, 139 L. Ed. 2d 553 (1997) (internal quotation marks omitted). In other words, the limitations period generally begins to run at the point when "the plaintiff can file suit and obtain relief." *Ibid.* A copyright claim thus arises or "accrue[s]" when an infringing act occurs. [4]

It is widely recognized that the separate-accrual rule attends the copyright statute of limitations. [5] Under that rule, when a defendant commits successive violations, the statute of limitations runs separately from each violation. Each time an infringing work is reproduced or distributed, the infringer commits a new wrong. Each wrong gives rise to a discrete "claim" that "accrue[s]" at the time the wrong occurs. [6] In short, each infringing act starts a new limitations period. See *Stone v. Williams*, 970 F. 2d 1043, 1049 (C. A. 2 1992) ("Each act of infringement is a distinct harm giving rise to an independent claim for relief.").

Under the Act's three-year provision, an infringement is actionable within three years, and only three years, of its occurrence. And the infringer is insulated from liability for earlier infringements of the same work. See 3 M. Nimmer & D. Nimmer, Copyright § 12.05[B][1][b], p. **1970 12-150.4 (2013) ("If infringement occurred within three years prior to filing, the action will not be barred even if prior infringements by the same party as to the same work are barred because they occurred more than three years previously."). Thus, when a defendant has engaged (or is alleged to have engaged) in a series of discrete infringing acts, the copyright holder's suit ordinarily will be timely under § 507(b) with respect to more recent acts of infringement (i. e. , acts within the three-year window), but untimely with respect to prior acts of the same or similar kind. [7]

In sum, Congress provided two controlling time prescriptions: the copyright term, which endures for decades, and may pass from one generation to another; and § 507(b)'s limitations period, which allows plaintiffs during that lengthy term to gain retrospective relief running only three years back from the date the complaint was filed.

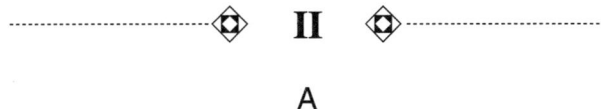

A

The allegedly infringing work in this case is the critically acclaimed motion picture Raging Bull, based on the life of boxing champion Jake LaMotta. After retiring from the ring, LaMotta worked with his longtime friend, Frank Petrella, to tell the story of the boxer's career. Their venture resulted in three copyrighted works: two screenplays, one registered in 1963, the other in 1973, and a book, registered in 1970. This case centers on the screenplay registered in 1963. The registration identified Frank Petrella as sole author, but also stated that the screenplay was written "in collaboration with" LaMotta. App. 164.

In 1976, Frank Petrella and LaMotta assigned their rights in the three works, including renewal rights, to Chartoff-Winkler Productions, Inc. Two years later, respondent United Artists Corporation, a subsidiary of respondent Metro-Goldwyn-Mayer, Inc. (collectively, MGM), acquired the motion picture rights to the book and both screenplays, rights stated by the parties to be "exclusiv[e] and forever, including all periods of copyright and renewals and extensions thereof. " Id. , at 49. In 1980, MGM released, and registered a copyright in, the film Raging Bull, directed ⋆ ⋆1971 by Martin Scorcese and starring Robert De Niro, who won a Best Actor Academy Award for his portrayal of LaMotta. MGM continues to market the film, and has converted it into formats unimagined in 1980, including DVD and Blu-ray.

Frank Petrella died in 1981, during the initial terms of the copyrights in the screenplays and book. As this Court's decision in *Stewart* confirmed, Frank

Petrella's renewal rights reverted to his heirs, who could renew the copyrights unburdened by any assignment previously made by the author. See 495 U. S., at 220–221, 110 S. Ct. 1750(relying on Court's earlier decision in *Miller Music Corp. v. Charles N. Daniels, Inc.*, 362 U. S. 373, 80 S. Ct. 792, 4 L. Ed. 2d 804(1960)).

Plaintiff below, petitioner here, Paula Petrella (Petrella) is Frank Petrella's daughter. Learning of this Court's decision in *Stewart*, Petrella engaged an attorney who, in 1991, renewed the copyright in the 1963 screenplay.

Because the copyrights in the 1973 screenplay and the 1970 book were not timely renewed, the infringement claims in this case rest exclusively on the screenplay registered in 1963. Petrella is now sole owner of the copyright in that work.[8]

In 1998, seven years after filing for renewal of the copyright in the 1963 screenplay, Petrella's attorney informed MGM that Petrella had obtained the copyright to that screenplay. Exploitation of any derivative work, including Raging Bull, the attorney asserted, infringed on the copyright now vested in Petrella. During the next two years, counsel for Petrella and MGM exchanged letters in which MGM denied the validity of the infringement claims, and Petrella repeatedly threatened to take legal action.

B

Some nine years later, on January 6, 2009, Petrella filed a copyright infringement suit in the United States District Court for the Central District of California. She alleged that MGM violated and continued to violate her copyright in the 1963 screenplay by using, producing, and distributing Raging Bull, a work she described as derivative of the 1963 screenplay. Petrella's complaint sought monetary and injunctive relief. Because the statute of limitations for copyright claims requires commencement of suit "within three years after the claim accrued," § 507(b), Petrella sought relief only for acts of infringement occurring on or after January 6, 2006. No relief, she recognizes, can be awarded for infringing acts prior to that date.

MGM moved for summary judgment on several grounds, among them, the equitable doctrine of laches. Petrella's 18 – year delay, from the 1991 renewal of the copyright on which she relied, until 2009, when she commenced suit, MGM maintained, was unreasonable and prejudicial to MGM. See Memorandum of Points and Authorities in Support of Defendants' Motion for Summary Judgment in No. CV 09–0072(CD Cal.).

The District Court granted MGM's motion. See App. to Pet. for Cert. 28a–48a. As to the merits of the infringement claims, the court found, disputed issues of material fact precluded summary adjudication. See *id.*, at 34a–42a. Even so, the court held, laches barred Petrella's complaint. *Id.*, at 42a–48a. Petrella had unreasonably delayed suit by not filing until 2009, the court concluded, and further determined ＊＊1972 that MGM was prejudiced by the delay. *Id.*, at 42a–46a. In particular, the court stated, MGM had shown "expectations-based prejudice," because the company had "made significant investments in exploiting the film"; in addition, the court accepted that MGM would encounter "evidentiary prejudice," because Frank Petrella had died and LaMotta, then aged 88, appeared to have sustained a loss of memory. *Id.*, at 44a–46a. [9]

The U. S. Court of Appeals for the Ninth Circuit affirmed the laches-based dismissal. 695 F. 3d 946(2012). Under Ninth Circuit precedent, the Court of Appeals first observed, "[i]f any part of the alleged wrongful conduct occurred outside of the limitations period, courts presume that the plaintiff's claims are barred by laches."*Id.*, at 951(internal quotation marks omitted). The presumption was applicable here, the court indicated, because "[t]he statute of limitations for copyright claims in civil cases is three years," *ibid.* (citing § 507(b)), and Petrella was aware of her potential claims many years earlier(as was MGM), *id.*, at 952. "[T]he true cause of Petrella's delay," the court suggested, "was, as [Petrella] admits, that 'the film hadn't made money'[in years she deferred suit]."*Id.*, at 953. [10] Agreeing with the District Court, the Ninth Circuit determined that MGM had established expectations-based prejudice: the company had made a large investment in Raging Bull, believing it had complete ownership and control of the film. *Id.*, at 953–954. [11]

Judge Fletcher concurred only because Circuit precedent obliged him to do so. *Id.*, at 958. Laches in copyright cases, he observed, is "entirely a judicial creation," one notably "in tension with Congress' [provision of a three-year limitations period]."*Ibid.*

We granted certiorari to resolve a conflict among the Circuits on the application of the equitable defense of laches to copyright infringement claims brought within the three-year look-back period prescribed by Congress.[12] 570 U. S. ----, 134 S. Ct. 50, 186 L. Ed. 2d 962(2013).

III

We consider first whether, as the Ninth Circuit held, laches may be invoked **1973 as a bar to Petrella's pursuit of legal remedies under 17 U. S. C. § 504 (b). The Ninth Circuit erred, we hold, in failing to recognize that the copyright statute of limitations, § 507(b), itself takes account of delay. As earlier observed, see *supra*, at 1969–1970, a successful plaintiff can gain retrospective relief only three years back from the time of suit. No recovery may be had for infringement in earlier years. Profits made in those years remain the defendant's to keep. Brought to bear here, § 507(b) directs that MGM's returns on its investment in Raging Bull in years outside the three-year window (years before 2006) cannot be reached by Petrella. Only by disregarding that feature of the statute, and the separate-accrual rule attending § 507(b), see *supra*, at 1968–1970, could the Court of Appeals presume that infringing acts occurring before January 6, 2006 bar all relief, monetary and injunctive, for infringement occurring on and after that date. See 695 F. 3d, at 951; *supra*, at 1971–1972.[13]

Moreover, if infringement within the three-year look-back period is shown, the Act allows the defendant to prove and offset against profits made in that period "deductible expenses" incurred in generating those profits. § 504(b). In addition, the defendant may prove and offset "elements of profit attributable to factors other than the copyrighted work." § 504(b). The defendant thus may retain the return on investment shown to be attributable to its own enterprise, as distinct from the value created by the infringed work. See *Sheldon v. Metro-Goldwyn Pictures Corp.*, 309 U. S. 390, 402, 407, 60 S. Ct. 681, 84 L. Ed. 825(1940) (equitably apportioning profits to account for independent contributions of infringing defendant). See also *infra*, at 1977–1979 (delay in commencing suit as a factor in determining contours of relief appropriately awarded).

Last, but hardly least, laches is a defense developed by courts of equity; its principal application was, and remains, to claims of an equitable cast for which the Legislature has provided no fixed time limitation. See 1 D. Dobbs, Law of Remedies § 2.4(4), p. 104(2d ed. 1993) (hereinafter Dobbs) ("laches...may have originated in equity because no statute of limitations applied,...suggest[ing] that laches should be limited to cases in which no statute of limitations applies"). Both before and after the merger of law and equity in 1938,[14] this Court has cautioned against invoking laches to bar legal relief.[10] See *Holmberg v. Armbrecht*, 327 U. S. 392, 395, 396, 66 S. Ct. 582, 90 L. Ed. 743(1946) (in actions at law, "[i]f Congress explicitly puts a limit upon the time for enforcing a right which it created, there is an end of the matter," but "[t]raditionally..., statutes of limitation are not controlling measures of equitable relief"); *Merck & Co. v. Reynolds*, 559 U. S. 633, 652, 130 S. Ct. 1784, 176 L. Ed. 2d 582(2010) (quoting, for its current relevance, statement in *United States v. Mack*, 295 U. S. 480, 489, 55 S. Ct. 813, 79 L. Ed. 1559(1935), that "[l]aches within the term of the statute of limitations is no defense[to an action] at law"); *County of Oneida v. Oneida Indian Nation of N. Y.*, 470 U. S. 226, 244, n. 16, 105 S. Ct. 1245, 84 L. Ed. 2d 169(1985) ("[A]pplication ✶ ✶ 1974 of the equitable defense of laches in an action at law would be novel indeed.")[15]

Because we adhere to the position that, in face of a statute of limitations enacted by Congress, laches cannot be invoked to bar legal relief, the dissent thinks we "plac[e] insufficient weight upon the rules and practice of modern litigation." *Post*, at 1985. True, there has been, since 1938, only "one form of action—the civil action." Fed. Rule Civ. Proc. 2. But " the substantive and remedial principles[applicable] prior to the advent of the federal rules[have] not changed."4 C. Wright & A. Miller, Federal Practice and Procedure § 1043, p. 177(3d ed. 2002). *Holmberg*, *Merck*, and *Oneida* so illustrate. The dissent presents multiple citations, see *post*, at 1979, 1980-1981, 1982-1983, 1984-1985, many of them far afield from the issue at hand, others obscuring what the cited decisions in fact ruled. Compare, *e. g.*, *post*, at 1979, 1984, with *infra*, at 1977 - 1978 (describing *Chirco v. Crosswinds Communities, Inc.*, 474 F. 3d 227(C. A. 6 2007)); *post*, at 1979, 1984-1985, with

125

infra, at 1975, n. 16 (describing *National Railroad Passenger Corporation v. Morgan*, 536 U. S. 101, 122 S. Ct. 2061, 153 L. Ed. 2d 106 (2002)); *post*, at 1983, with *infra*, at 1975, n. 16 (describing *Patterson v. Hewitt*, 195 U. S. 309, 25 S. Ct. 35, 49 L. Ed. 214 (1904)). Yet tellingly, the dissent has come up with no case in which this Court has approved the application of laches to bar a claim for damages brought within the time allowed by a federal statute of limitations. There is nothing at all "differen[t]," see *post*, at 1985, about copyright cases in this regard.

IV

We turn now to MGM's principal arguments regarding the contemporary scope of the laches defense, all of them embraced by the dissent.

A

Laches is listed among affirmative defenses, along with, but discrete from, the statute of limitations, in Federal Rule of Civil Procedure 8(c). Accordingly, MGM maintains, the plea is "available…in every civil action" to bar all forms of relief. Tr. of Oral Arg. 43; see Brief for Respondents 40. To the Court's question, could laches apply where there is an ordinary six-year statute of limitations, MGM's counsel responded yes, case-specific circumstances might warrant a ruling that a suit brought in year five came too late. Tr. of Oral Arg. 52; see *id.*, at 41.

The expansive role for laches MGM envisions careens away from understandings, past and present, of the essentially gap-filling, not legislation-overriding, office of laches. Nothing in this Court's precedent suggests a doctrine of such sweep. Quite **1975 the contrary, we have never applied laches to bar in their entirety claims for discrete wrongs occurring within a federally prescribed limitations period. [16] Inviting individual judges to set a time limit other than the one Congress prescribed, we note, would tug against the uniformity Congress sought to achieve when it enacted § 507(b). See *supra*, at 1968–1969.

B

MGM observes that equitable tolling "is read into every federal statute of limitation," *Holmberg*, 327 U. S., at 397, 66 S. Ct. 582, and asks why laches should not be treated similarly. See Brief for Respondents 23–26; *post*, at 1982–1983. Tolling, which lengthens the time for commencing a civil action in appropriate circumstances, [17] applies when there is a statute of limitations; it is, in effect, a rule of interpretation tied to that limit. See *Young v. United States*, 535 U. S. 43, 49–50, 122 S. Ct. 1036, 152 L. Ed. 2d 79 (2002); *Johnson v. Railway Express Agency, Inc.*, 421 U. S. 454, 464, 95 S. Ct. 1716, 44 L. Ed. 2d 295 (1975). [18] Laches, in contrast, originally served as a guide when no statute of limitations controlled the claim; it can scarcely be described as a rule for interpreting a statutory prescription. That is so here, because the statute, § 507(b), makes the starting trigger an infringing act committed three years back from the commencement of suit, while laches, as conceived by the Ninth Circuit and advanced by MGM, makes the presumptive trigger the defendant's *initial* infringing act. See 695 F. 3d, at 951; Brief for United States 16.

C

MGM insists that the defense of laches must be available to prevent a copyright ✶ ✶ 1976 owner from sitting still, doing nothing, waiting to see what the outcome of an alleged infringer's investment will be. See Brief for Respondents 48. In this case, MGM stresses, "[Petrella] *conceded* that she waited to file because 'the film was deeply in debt and in the red and would probably never recoup.' " *Id.*, at 47 (quoting from App. 110). The Ninth Circuit similarly faulted Petrella for waiting to sue until the film Raging Bull "made money." 695 F. 3d, at 953 (internal quotation marks omitted). See also *post*, at 1980–1981 (deploring plaintiffs who wait to see whether the allegedly infringing work makes money).

It is hardly incumbent on copyright owners, however, to challenge each and every actionable infringement. And there is nothing untoward about waiting to see whether an infringer's exploitation undercuts the value of the copyrighted work, has no effect on the original work, or even complements it. Fan sites prompted by a book or film, for example, may benefit the copyright owner. See Wu, Tolerated Use, 31 Colum. J. L. & Arts 617, 619–620 (2008). Even if an infringement is harmful, the harm may be too small to justify the cost of litigation.

If the rule were, as MGM urges, "sue soon, or forever hold your peace," copyright owners would have to mount a federal case fast to stop seemingly innocuous infringements, lest those infringements eventually grow in magnitude. Section 507 (b)'s three-year limitations period, however, coupled to the separate-accrual rule, see *supra*, at 1968–1970, avoids such litigation profusion. It allows a copyright owner to defer suit until she can estimate whether litigation is worth the candle. She will miss out on damages for periods prior to the three-year look-back, but her right to prospective injunctive relief should, in most cases, remain unaltered. [19]

D

MGM points to the danger that evidence needed or useful to defend against liability will be lost during a copyright owner's inaction. Brief for Respondents 37–38; see *post*, at 1979–1981. [20] Recall, however, that Congress provided for reversionary renewal rights exercisable by an author's heirs, rights that can be exercised, at the earliest for pre-1978 copyrights, 28 years after a work was written and copyrighted. See, *supra*, at 1967–1968. At that time, the author, and perhaps other witnesses to the creation of the work, will be dead. See *supra*, at 1970. Congress must have been aware that the passage of time and the author's death could cause a loss or dilution of evidence. Congress chose, nonetheless, to give the author's family "a second chance to obtain fair remuneration." *Stewart*, 495 U. S., at 220, 110 S. Ct. 1750.

[13] Moreover, a copyright plaintiff bears the burden of proving infringement. See 3 W. Patry, Copyright § 9.4, p. 9–18 (2013) (hereinafter Patry) ("As in other civil litigation, a copyright owner bears the burden of establishing a prima facie case."). But cf. *post*, at 1981 (overlooking plaintiff's burden to show infringement and the absence of any burden upon the defendant "to prove that it did not infringe" * * 1977). Any hindrance caused by the unavailability of evidence, therefore, is at least as likely to affect plaintiffs as it is to disadvantage defendants. That is so in cases of the kind Petrella is pursuing, for a deceased author most probably would have supported his heir's claim.

The registration mechanism, we further note, reduces the need for extrinsic evidence. Although registration is "permissive," both the certificate and the original work must be on file with the Copyright Office before a copyright owner can sue for infringement. §§ 408(b),411(a). Key evidence in the litigation, then, will be the certificate, the original work, and the allegedly infringing work. And the adjudication will often turn on the factfinder's direct comparison of the original and the infringing works, i. e. , on the factfinder's "good eyes and common sense" in comparing the two works' "total concept and overall feel." *Peter F. Gaito Architecture, LLC v. Simone Development Corp.* ,602 F. 3d 57,66(C. A. 2 2010) (internal quotation marks omitted).

E

Finally, when a copyright owner engages in intentionally misleading representations concerning his abstention from suit, and the alleged infringer detrimentally relies on the copyright owner's deception, the doctrine of estoppel may bar the copyright owner's claims completely, eliminating all potential remedies. See 6 Patry § 20:58, at 20–110 to 20–112. [21] The test for estoppel is more exacting than the test for laches, and the two defenses are differently oriented. The gravamen of estoppel, a defense long recognized as available in actions at law, see *Wehrman v. Conklin*, 155 U. S. 314, 327, 15 S. Ct. 129, 39 L. Ed. 167(1894), is misleading and consequent loss, see 6 Patry § 20:58, at 20–110 to 20–112. Delay may be involved, but is not an element of the defense. For laches, timeliness is the essential element. In contrast to laches, urged by MGM entirely to override the statute of limitations Congress prescribed, estoppel does not undermine Congress' prescription, for it rests on misleading, whether engaged in early on, or later in time.

Stating that the Ninth Circuit "ha[d] taken a wrong turn in its formulation and application of laches in copyright cases," Judge Fletcher called for fresh consideration of the issue. 695 F. 3d, at 959. "A recognition of the distinction between…estoppel and laches," he suggested, "would be a good place to start." *Ibid.* We agree.

The courts below summarily disposed of Petrella's case based on laches, preventing adjudication of any of her claims on the merits and foreclosing the possibility of any form of relief. That disposition, we have explained, was erroneous. Congress' time provisions secured to authors a copyright term of long duration, and a right to sue for infringement occurring no more than three years back from the time of suit. That regime leaves "little place" for a doctrine that would further limit the timeliness of a copyright owner's suit. See 1 Dobbs § 2.6(1), at 152. In extraordinary circumstances, however, the consequences of a delay in commencing suit may be of sufficient magnitude to warrant, at the very outset of the litigation, curtailment of the relief equitably awardable.

**1978 *Chirco v. Crosswinds Communities, Inc.*, 474 F. 3d 227(C. A. 6 2007), is illustrative. In that case, the defendants were alleged to have used without permission, in planning and building a housing development, the plaintiffs' copyrighted architectural design. Long aware of the defendants' project, the plaintiffs took no steps to halt the housing development until more than 168 units were built, 109 of which were occupied. *Id.*, at 230. Although the action was filed within § 507(b)'s three-year statute of limitations, the District Court granted summary judgment to the defendants, dismissing the entire case on grounds of laches. The trial court's rejection of the entire suit could not stand, the Court of Appeals explained, for it was not within the Judiciary's ken to debate the wisdom of § 507(b)'s three-year look-back prescription. *Id.*, at 235. Nevertheless, the Court of Appeals affirmed the District Court's judgment to this extent: The plaintiffs, even if they might succeed in proving infringement of their copyrighted design, would not be entitled to an order mandating destruction of the housing project. That relief would be inequitable, the Sixth Circuit held, for two reasons: the plaintiffs knew of the defendants' construction plans before the defendants broke ground, yet failed to take readily available measures to stop the project; and the requested relief would "work an *unjust* hardship" upon the defendants and innocent third parties. *Id.*, at 236. See also *New Era Publications Int'l v. Henry Holt & Co.*, 873 F. 2d 576, 584-585(C. A. 2 1989)(despite awareness since 1986 that book containing allegedly infringing material would be published in the United States, copyright owner did not seek a restraining order until 1988, after the book had been printed, packed, and shipped; as injunctive relief "would[have]result[ed]in the total destruction of the work," the court "relegat[ed plaintiff]to its damages remedy").

In sum, the courts below erred in treating laches as a complete bar to Petrella's copyright infringement suit. The action was commenced within the bounds of § 507(b), the Act's time-to-sue prescription, and does not present extraordinary circumstances of the kind involved in *Chirco* and *New Era*. Petrella notified MGM of her copyright claims *before* MGM invested millions of dollars in creating a new edition of Raging Bull. And the equitable relief Petrella seeks—e. g., disgorgement of unjust gains and an injunction against future infringement—would not result in "total destruction" of the film, or anything close to it. See *New Era*, 873 F. 2d, at 584. MGM released Raging Bull more than three decades ago and has marketed it continuously since then. Allowing Petrella's suit to go forward will put at risk only a fraction of the income MGM has earned during that period and will work no unjust hardship on innocent third parties, such as consumers who have purchased copies of Raging Bull. Cf. *Chirco*, 474 F. 3d, at 235-236 (destruction remedy would have ousted families from recently purchased homes). The circumstances here may or may not (we need not decide) warrant limiting relief at the remedial stage, but they are not sufficiently extraordinary to justify threshold dismissal.

Should Petrella ultimately prevail on the merits, the District Court, in determining appropriate injunctive relief and assessing profits, may take account of her delay in commencing suit. See *supra*, at 1967-1968, 1972-1973. In doing so, however, that court should closely examine MGM's alleged reliance on Petrella's delay.[22] This examination should take account of MGM's * * 1979 early knowledge of Petrella's claims, the protection MGM might have achieved through pursuit of a declaratory judgment action, the extent to which MGM's investment was protected by the separate-accrual rule, the court's authority to order injunctive relief "on such terms as it may deem reasonable," § 502(a), and any other considerations that would justify adjusting injunctive relief or profits. See *Haas v. Leo Feist, Inc.*, 234 F. 105, 107-108 (S. D. N. Y. 1916) (adjudicating copyright infringement suit on the merits and decreeing injunctive relief, but observing that, in awarding profits, account may be taken of copyright owner's inaction until infringer had spent large sums exploiting the work at issue). See also Tr. of Oral Arg. 23 (Government observation that, in fashioning equitable remedies, court has considerable leeway; it could, for example, allow MGM to continue using Raging Bull as a derivative work upon payment of a reasonable royalty to Petrella). Whatever adjustments may be in order in awarding injunctive relief, and in accounting for MGM's gains and profits, on the facts thus far presented, there is no evident basis for immunizing MGM's present and future uses of the copyrighted work, free from any obligation to pay royalties.

For the reasons stated, the judgment of the United States Court of Appeals for the Ninth Circuit is reversed, and the case is remanded for further proceedings consistent with this opinion.

It is so ordered.

Justice BREYER, with whom THE CHIEF JUSTICE, and Justice KENNEDY join, dissenting.

Legal systems contain doctrines that help courts avoid the unfairness that might arise were legal rules to apply strictly to every case no matter how unusual the circumstances. "[T]he nature of the equitable," Aristotle long ago observed, is "a correction of law where it is defective owing to its universality." Nicomachean Ethics 99(D. Ross transl. L. Brown ed. 2009). Laches is one such equitable doctrine. It applies in those extraordinary cases where the plaintiff "unreasonably delays in filing a suit," *National Railroad Passenger Corporation v. Morgan*, 536 U. S. 101, 121, 122 S. Ct. 2061, 153 L. Ed. 2d 106(2002), and, as a result, causes "unjust hardship" to the defendant, *Chirco v. Crosswinds Communities, Inc.*, 474 F. 3d 227, 236(C. A. 6 2007)(emphasis deleted). Its purpose is to avoid "inequity." *Galliher v. Cadwell*, 145 U. S. 368, 373, 12 S. Ct. 873, 36 L. Ed. 738(1892). And, as Learned Hand pointed out, it may well be

"inequitable for the owner of a copyright, with full notice of an intended infringement, to stand inactive while the proposed infringer spends large sums of money in its exploitation, and to intervene only when his speculation has proved a success." *Haas v. Leo Feist, Inc.*, 234 F. 105, 108(S. D. N. Y. 1916).

Today's decision disables federal courts from addressing that inequity. I respectfully dissent.

Circumstances warranting the application of laches in the context of copyright claims are not difficult to imagine. The 3-year limitations period under the Copyright Act may seem brief, but it is not. 17 U. S. C. § 507(b). That is because it is a rolling limitations period, which restarts upon each "separate accrual" of a claim. See *ante*, at 1969; 6 W. Patry, Copyright § 20:23, pp. 20-44 to 20-46 (2013). If a defendant reproduces or sells an infringing work on a continuing basis, a plaintiff can sue every 3 years until the copyright term expires—which may be up to 70 years * *1980 after the author's death. § 302(a) (works created after January 1, 1978, are protected until 70 years after the author's death); § 304(a) (works created before January 1, 1978, are protected for 28 years plus a 67-year renewal period). If, for example, a work earns no money for 20 years, but then, after development expenses have been incurred, it earns profits for the next 30, a plaintiff can sue in year 21 and at regular 3-year intervals thereafter. Each time the plaintiff will collect the defendant's profits earned during the prior three years, unless he settles for a lump sum along the way. The defendant will recoup no more than his outlays and any "elements of profit attributable to factors other than the copyrighted work." § § 504(a)(1), (b).

A 20-year delay in bringing suit could easily prove inequitable. Suppose, for example, the plaintiff has deliberately waited for the death of witnesses who might prove the existence of understandings about a license to reproduce the copyrighted work, or who might show that the plaintiff's work was in fact derived from older copyrighted materials that the defendant has licensed. Or, suppose the plaintiff has delayed in bringing suit because he wants to avoid bargaining with the defendant up front over a license. He knows that if he delays legal action, and the defendant invests time, effort, and resources into making the derivative product, the plaintiff will be in a much stronger position to obtain favorable licensing terms through settlement. Or, suppose the plaintiff has waited until he becomes certain that the defendant's production bet paid off, that the derivative work did and would continue to earn money, and that the plaintiff has a chance of obtaining, say, an 80% share of what is now a 90% pure profit stream. (N. B. The plaintiff's profits recovery will be reduced by any "deductible expenses" incurred by the defendant in producing the work, and by any "elements of profits attributable to factors other than the copyrighted work," § 504(b)). Or, suppose that all of these circumstances exist together.

Cases that present these kinds of delays are not imaginary. One can easily find examples from the lower courts where plaintiffs have brought claims years after they accrued and where delay-related inequity resulted. See, *e. g.*, *Ory v. McDonald*,

141 Fed. Appx. 581,583(C. A. 9 2005), aff'g 2003 WL 22909286, at ＊1(C. D. Cal. , Aug. 5,2003)(claim that a 1960's song infringed the "hook or riff" from the 1926 song "Muskrat Ramble," brought more than 30 years after the song was released); *Danjaq LLC v. Sony Corp.* , 263 F. 3d 942, 952 – 956(C. A. 9 2001) (claim that seven James Bond films infringed a copyright to a screenplay, brought 19 to 36 years after the films were released, and where "many of the key figures in the creation of the James Bond movies ha[d]died" and "many of the relevant records[went]missing"); *Jackson v. Axton*, 25 F. 3d 884, 889(C. A. 9 1994), overruled on other grounds, 510 U. S. 517, 114 S. Ct. 1023, 127 L. Ed. 2d 455(1994) (claim of coauthorship of the song "Joy to the World," brought 17 years after the plaintiff learned of his claim such that memories faded, the original paper containing the lyrics was lost, the recording studio(with its records)closed, and the defendant had "arranged his business affairs around the Song" for years); *Newsome v. Brown*, 2005 WL 627639, at ＊8 – ＊9(S. D. N. Y. , Mar. 16, 2005)(claim regarding the song "It's a Man's World," brought 40 years after first accrual, where the plaintiff's memory had faded and a key piece of evidence was destroyed by fire). See also *Chirco*, 474 F. 3d, at 230 – 231, 234 – 236(claim that condominium design infringed plaintiff's design, brought only 2. 5 years(or so)after claim accrued but after condominium was ＊＊1981 built, apartments were sold, and 109 families had moved in).

Consider, too, the present case. The petitioner claims the MGM film Raging Bull violated a copyright originally owned by her father, which she inherited and then renewed in 1991. She waited 18 years after renewing the copyright, until 2009, to bring suit. During those 18 years, MGM spent millions of dollars developing different editions of, and marketing, the film. See App. to Pet. for Cert. 13a. MGM also entered into numerous licensing agreements, some of which allowed television networks to broadcast the film through 2015. *Id.* , at 14a. Meanwhile, three key witness died or became unavailable, making it more difficult for MGM to prove that it did not infringe the petitioner's copyright(either because the 1963 screenplay was in fact derived from a different book, the rights to which MGM owned under a nonchallenged license, or because MGM held a license to the screenplay under a 1976 agreement that it signed with Jake LaMotta, who coauthored the screenplay with the petitioner's father, see *id.* at 3a, 5a; App. 128–129, 257–258, 266–267). Consequently, I believe the Court of Appeals acted lawfully in dismissing the suit due to laches.

Long delays do not automatically prove inequity, but, depending upon the circumstances, they raise that possibility. Indeed, suppose that that the copyright-holders in the song cases cited above, or their heirs, facing sudden revivals in demand or eventual deaths of witnesses, had brought their claims 50, or even 60 years after those claims first accrued. Or suppose that the loss of evidence was clearly critical to the defendants' abilities to prove their cases. The Court holds that insofar as a copyright claim seeks damages, a court cannot *ever* apply laches, irrespective of the length of the plaintiff's delay, the amount of the harm that it caused, or the inequity of permitting the action to go forward.

II

Why should laches not be available in an appropriate case? Consider the reasons the majority offers. First, the majority says that the 3-year "copyright statute of limitations...itself takes account of delay," and so additional safeguards like laches are not needed. *Ante*, at 1972. I agree that sometimes that is so. But I also fear that sometimes it is not. The majority correctly points out that the limitations period limits the retrospective relief a plaintiff can recover. It imposes a cap equal to the profits earned during the prior three years, in addition to any actual damages sustained during this time. *Ibid.* ; § 504(b). Thus, if the plaintiff waits from, say, 1980 until 2001 to bring suit, she cannot recover profits for the 1980 to 1998 period. But she can recover the defendant's profits from 1998 through 2001, which might be precisely when net revenues turned positive. And she can sue every three years thereafter until the copyright expires, perhaps in the year 2060. If the plaintiff's suit involves the type of inequitable circumstances I have described, her ability to recover profits from 1998 to 2001 and until the copyright expires could be just the kind of unfairness that laches is designed to prevent.

Second, the majority points out that the plaintiff can recover only the defendant's profits less " 'deductible expenses' incurred in generating those prof-

its."*Ante*,at 1973(quoting § 504(b)). In other words,the majority takes assurance from the fact that the Act enables the defendant to recoup his outlays in developing or selling the allegedly infringing work. Again,sometimes that fact will prevent inequitable results. But sometimes it will not. A ＊＊1982 plaintiff's delay may mean that the defendant has already recovered the majority of his expenses,and what is left is primarily profit. It may mean that the defendant has dedicated decades of his life to producing the work,such that the loss of a future profit stream(even if he can recover past expenses)is tantamount to the loss of any income in later years. And in circumstances such as those described,it could prove inequitable to give the profit to a plaintiff who has unnecessarily delayed in filing an action. ＊＊1982 Simply put,the "deductible expenses" provision does not protect the defendant from the potential inequity highlighted by Judge Hand nearly 100 years ago in his influential copyright opinion. That is,it does not stop a copyright–holder (or his heirs)from "stand[ing]inactive while the proposed infringer spends large sums of money" in a risky venture;appearing on the scene only when the venture has proved a success;and thereby collecting substantially more money than he could have obtained at the outset,had he bargained with the investor over a license and royalty fee. *Haas*,234 F.,at 108. But cf. *id.* ,at 108–109(plaintiff to receive injunctive relief since one of the defendants was a "deliberate pirate," but profit award to be potentially reduced in light of laches).

Third,the majority says that "[i]nviting individual judges to set a time limit other than the one Congress prescribed" in the Copyright Act would "tug against the uniformity Congress sought to achieve when it enacted § 507(b)."*Ante*,at 1975. But why does the majority believe that part of what Congress intended to "achieve" was the elimination of the equitable defense of laches? As the majority recognizes,Congress enacted a uniform statute of limitations for copyright claims in 1957 so that federal courts,in determining timeliness,no longer had to borrow from state law which varied from place to place. See *ante*,at 1968–1969. Nothing in the 1957 Act—or anywhere else in the text of the copyright statute—indicates that Congress also sought to bar the operation of laches. The Copyright Act is silent on the subject. And silence is consistent,not inconsistent,with the application of equitable doctrines.

For one thing, the legislative history for § 507 shows that Congress chose not to "specifically enumerat[e] certain equitable considerations which might be advanced in connection with civil copyright actions" because it understood that " '[f]ederal district courts, generally, recognize these equitable defenses anyway. ' "S. Rep. No. 1014, 85th Cong. , 1st Sess. , 2–3 (1957) (quoting the House Judiciary Committee). Courts prior to 1957 had often applied laches in federal copyright cases. See, e. g. , *Callaghan v. Myers*, 128 U. S. 617, 658–659, 9 S. Ct. 177, 32 L. Ed. 547 (1888) (assuming laches was an available defense in a copyright suit); *Edwin L. Wiegand Co. v. Harold E. Trent Co.* , 122 F. 2d 920, 925 (C. A. 3 1941) (applying laches to bar a copyright suit); *D. O. Haynes & Co. v. Druggists' Circular*, 32 F. 2d 215, 216–218 (C. A. 2 1929) (same). Congress expected they would continue to do so.

Furthermore, this Court has held that federal courts may "appl[y] equitable doctrines that may toll *or limit* the time period" for suit when applying a statute of limitations, because a statutory "filing period" is a "requirement" subject to adjustment " 'when equity so requires. ' "*Morgan*, 536 U. S. , at 121–122, 122 S. Ct. 2061 (quoting *Zipes v. Trans World Airlines, Inc.* , 455 U. S. 385, 398, 102 S. Ct. 1127, 71 L. Ed. 2d 234 (1982); emphasis added). This Court has read laches into statutes of limitations otherwise silent on the topic of equitable doctrines in a multitude of contexts, as have lower courts. See, e. g. , *Morgan*, *supra*, at 121, 122 S. Ct. 2061 ("an employer may raise a laches defense" under ⋆ ⋆ 1983 Title VII); *Bay Area Laundry and Dry Cleaning Pension Trust Fund v. Ferbar Corp. of Cal.* , 522 U. S. 192, 205, 118 S. Ct. 542, 139 L. Ed. 2d 553 (1997) (similar, in respect to suits under the Multiemployer Pension Plan Amendments Act of 1980 (MPPAA)); *Abbott Laboratories v. Gardner*, 387 U. S. 136, 155, 87 S. Ct. 1507, 18 L. Ed. 2d 681 (1967) (similar, in respect to an action for declaratory and injunctive relief under the Administrative Procedure Act; *Patterson v. Hewitt*, 195 U. S. 309, 319–320, 25 S. Ct. 35, 49 L. Ed. 214 (1904) (similar, in the case of a property action brought within New Mexico's statute of limitations); *Alsop v. Riker*, 155 U. S. 448, 460, 15 S. Ct. 162, 39 L. Ed. 218 (1894) (holding that "independently of the statute of limitations," the contract action was barred "because of laches"); *Teamsters & Employers Welfare Trust of Ill. v. Gorman Bros. Ready Mix*, 283 F. 3d 877,

883(C. A. 7 2002)(laches available "in a suit against an[Employee Retirement Income Security Act of 1974](ERISA)]plan for benefits"); *Hot Wax,Inc. v. Turtle Wax,Inc.* ,191 F. 3d 813,822-823(C. A. 7 1999)(laches available in a Lanham Act suit filed within the limitations period). Unless Congress indicates otherwise,courts normally assume that equitable rules continue to operate alongside limitations periods,and that equity applies both to plaintiffs and to defendants. See *Astoria Fed. Sav. & Loan Assn. v. Solimino*,501 U. S. 104,108,111 S. Ct. 2166,115 L. Ed. 2d 96(1991)("Congress is understood to legislate against a background of common-law adjudicatory principles" and to incorporate them " except when a statutory purpose to the contrary is evident"(internal quotation marks and citation omitted));*Porter v. Warner Holding Co.* ,328 U. S. 395,398,66 S. Ct. 1086,90 L. Ed. 1332(1946)("Unless otherwise provided by statute,all the inherent equitable powers of the District Court are available for the proper and complete exercise of that jurisdiction").

The Court today comes to a different conclusion. It reads § 507(b)'s silence as preserving doctrines that lengthen the period for suit when equitable considerations favor the plaintiff(*e. g.* ,equitable tolling),but as foreclosing a doctrine that would shorten the period when equity favors the defendant(*i. e.* ,laches). See *ante*,at 1975-1976,1977-1978. I do not understand the logic of reading a silent statute in this manner.

Fourth,the majority defends its rule by observing that laches was "developed by courts of equity," and that this Court has "cautioned against invoking laches to bar legal relief" even following the merger of law and equity in 1938. *Ante*,at 1973-1974. The majority refers to three cases that offer support for this proposition,but none is determinative. In the first,*Holmberg v. Armbrecht*,327 U. S. 392,66 S. Ct. 582,90 L. Ed. 743(1946),the Court said:

"If Congress explicitly puts a limit upon the time for enforcing a right which it created,there is an end of the matter.

…

"Traditionally and for good reasons,statutes of limitation are not controlling measures of equitable relief."*Id.* ,at 395-396,66 S. Ct. 582.

This statement,however,constituted part of the Court's explanation as to why a federal statute, silent about limitations, should be applied consistently with "historic principles of equity in the enforcement of federally-created equitable rights" rather than with New York's statute of limitations. *Id.*, at 395, 66 S. Ct. 582. The case had nothing to do with whether laches governs in actions at law. The lawsuit in *Holmberg* had been brought "in equity," and the Court remanded for a determination of whether the petitioners were * * 1984 "chargeable with laches." *Id.*, at 393, 397, 66 S. Ct. 582.

The second case the majority cites, *Merck & Co. v. Reynolds*, 559 U. S. 633, 130 S. Ct. 1784, 176 L. Ed. 2d 582 (2010), provides some additional support, but not much. There, the Court cited a 1935 case for the proposition that " '[l]aches within the term of the statute of limitations is no defense at law.' " *Id.*, at 652, 130 S. Ct. 1784 (quoting *United States v. Mack*, 295 U. S. 480, 489, 55 S. Ct. 813, 79 L. Ed. 1559 (1935)). But *Merck* concerned a federal securities statute that contained both a 2-year statute of limitations, running from the time of "discovery," and a 5-year statute of repose, running from the time of a "violation." *Id.*, at 638, 130 S. Ct. 1784 (citing 28 U. S. C. § 1658(b)). Given that repose statutes set "an outside limit" on suit and are generally "inconsistent with tolling" and similar equitable doctrines, the Court held that the 2-year limitations period at issue was not subject to an "inquiry notice" rule or, by analogy, to laches. *Lampf, Pleva, Lipkind, Prupis & Petigrow v. Gilbertson*, 501 U. S. 350, 363, 111 S. Ct. 2773, 115 L. Ed. 2d 321 (1991) (internal quotation marks and citation omitted); *Merck, supra*, at 650–652, 130 S. Ct. 1784. *Merck* did not suggest that statutes of limitations are always or normally inconsistent with equitable doctrines when plaintiffs seek damages. It simply found additional support for its conclusion in a case that this Court decided *before* the merger of law and equity. And here, unlike in *Merck*, the statute of limitations is not accompanied by a corollary statute of repose.

Third, in *County of Oneida v. Oneida Indian Nation of N. Y.*, 470 U. S. 226, 105 S. Ct. 1245, 84 L. Ed. 2d 169 (1985), the Court said in a footnote that "application of the equitable defense of laches in an action at law would be novel indeed." *Id.*, at 245, n. 16, 105 S. Ct. 1245. This statement was made in light of special policies related to Indian tribes, which the Court went on to discuss in the following sentences. *Ibid.* In any event, *Oneida* did not resolve whether laches was available to the defendants, for the lower court had not ruled on the issue. *Id.*, at 244–245, 105 S. Ct. 1245.

In sum, there is no reason to believe that the Court meant any of its statements in *Holmberg*, *Merck*, or *Oneida* to announce a general rule about the availability of laches in actions for legal relief, whenever Congress provides a statute of limitations. To the contrary, the Court has said more than once that a defendant could invoke laches in an action for damages (even though no assertion of the defense had actually been made in the case), despite a fixed statute of limitations. See *Morgan*, 536 U. S., at 116–119, 121–122, 122 S. Ct. 2061 (laches available in hostile work environment claims seeking damages under Title VII); *Bay Area Laundry*, 522 U. S., at 205, 118 S. Ct. 542 (laches available in actions for "withdrawal liability assessment[s]" under the MPPAA). Lower courts have come to similar holdings in a wide array of circumstances—often approving not only of the availability of the laches defense, but of its application to the case at hand. *E. g.*, *Cayuga Indian Nation of N. Y. v. Pataki*, 413 F. 3d 266, 274–277 (C. A. 2 2005) (laches available in a "possessory land claim" in which the District Court awarded damages, whether "characterized as an action at law or in equity," and dismissing the action due to laches); *Teamsters*, 283 F. 3d, at 881–883 (laches available in suits under ERISA for benefits, but not warranted in that case); *Hot Wax*, 191 F. 3d, at 822–827 ("[T]he application of the doctrine of laches to Hot Wax's Lanham Act claims [requesting damages] by the district court was proper"); *A. C. Aukerman Co. v. R. L. Chaides* * *1985 Constr. Co.*, 960 F. 2d 1020, 1030–1032, 1045–1046 (C. A. Fed. 1992) (en banc) (laches available in patent suit claiming damages, and remanding for whether the defense was successful); *Cornetta v. United States*, 851 F. 2d 1372, 1376–1383 (C. A. Fed. 1988) (en banc) (same, in suit seeking backpay). Even if we focus only upon federal copyright litigation, four of the six Circuits to have considered the matter have held that laches can bar claims for legal relief. See 695 F. 3d 946, 956 (C. A. 9 2012) (case below, barring all copyright claims due to laches); *Peter Letterese & Assocs., Inc. v. World Inst. of Scientology Enterprises, Int'l*, 533 F. 3d 1287, 1319–1322 (C. A. 11 2008) (laches can bar copyright claims for retrospective damages); *Chirco*, 474 F. 3d, at 234–236 ("laches can be argued 'regardless of whether the suit is at law or in equity,'" and holding that while the plaintiffs could obtain damages and an injunction, their request for additional equitable relief "smack[ed] of the inequity against which Judge Hand cautioned in *Haas* and which the judicial system should abhor" (quoting *Teamsters*, supra, at 881)); *Jacobsen v. Deseret Book Co.*, 287 F. 3d 936, 950–951 (C. A. 10 2002) (laches available in " 'rare cases,' " and failing to draw a distinction in the type of remedy sought (citation omitted). But see *New Era Publications Int'l v. Henry Holt & Co.*, 873 F. 2d 576, 584–585 (C. A. 2 1989) (laches can bar claims for injunctive relief, but not damages, under the Copyright Act); *Lyons Partnership, L. P. v. Morris Costumes, Inc.*, 243 F. 3d 789, 798–799 (C. A. 4 2001) (laches unavailable in copyright cases altogether).

Perhaps more importantly, in permitting laches to apply to copyright claims seeking equitable relief but not to those seeking legal relief, the majority places insufficient weight upon the rules and practice of modern litigation.

Since 1938, Congress and the Federal Rules have replaced what would once have been actions "at law" and actions "in equity" with the "civil action." Fed. Rule Civ. Proc. 2 ("There is one form of action—the civil action"). A federal civil action is subject to both equitable and legal defenses. Fed. Rule Civ. Proc. 8(c)(1) ("In responding to a pleading, a party must affirmatively state any avoidance or affirmative defense, including: ... estoppel ... laches ... [and] statute of limitations"). Accordingly, since 1938, federal courts have frequently allowed defendants to assert what were formerly equitable defenses—including laches—in what were formerly legal actions. See *supra*, at 1984–1985 (citing cases). Why should copyright be treated differently? Indeed, the majority concedes that " restitutional remedies" like "profits" (which are often claimed in copyright cases) defy clear classification as "equitable" or "legal." *Ante*, at 1967, n. 1 (internal quotation marks omitted). Why should lower courts have to make these uneasy and unnatural distinctions?

Fifth, the majority believes it can prevent the inequities that laches seeks to avoid through the use of a different doctrine, namely equitable estoppel. *Ante*, at 1977. I doubt that is so. As the majority recognizes, "the two defenses are differently oriented." *Ibid.* The "gravamen" of estoppel is a misleading representation by the plaintiff that the defendant relies on to his detriment. 6 Patry, Copyright § 20:

58, at 20-110 to 20-112. The gravamen of laches is the plaintiff's unreasonable delay, and the consequent prejudice to the defendant. *Id.*, § 20:54, at 20-96. Where due to the passage of time, evidence favorable to the defense has disappeared or the defendant has continued to invest in a derivative work, what misleading representation by the plaintiff is there to estop?

In sum, as the majority says, the doctrine of laches may occupy only a " 'little place' " in a regime based upon statutes of * * 1986 limitations. *Ante*, at 1977 (quoting 1 D. Dobbs, Law of Remedies § 2.6(1), p. 152(2d ed. 1993)). But that place is an important one. In those few and unusual cases where a plaintiff unreasonably delays in bringing suit and consequently causes inequitable harm to the defendant, the doctrine permits a court to bring about a fair result. I see no reason to erase the doctrine from copyright's lexicon, not even in respect to limitations periods applicable to damages actions.

Consequently, with respect, I dissent.

Footnotes

1. As infringement remedies, the Copyright Act provides for injunctions, § 502, impoundment and disposition of infringing articles, § 503, damages and profits, § 504, costs and attorney's fees, § 505. Like other restitutional remedies, recovery of profits "is not easily characterized as legal or equitable," for it is an "amalgamation of rights and remedies drawn from both systems." Restatement (Third) of Restitution and Unjust Enrichment § 4, Comment b, p. 28 (2010). Given the "protean character" of the profits-recovery remedy, see id., Comment c, at 30, we regard as appropriate its treatment as "equitable" in this case.

2. For post-1978 works, heirs still have an opportunity to recapture rights of the author. See 3 M. Nimmer & D. Nimmer, Copyright § 11.01[A], p. 11-4(2013) (hereinafter Nimmer).

3. The Copyright Act was pervasively revised in 1976, but the three-year look-back statute of limitations has remained materially unchanged. See Act of Oct. 19, 1976, § 101, 90 Stat. 2586.

4. Although we have not passed on the question, nine Courts of Appeals have adopted, as an alternative to the incident of injury rule, a "discovery rule," which starts the limitations period when "the plaintiff discovers, or with due diligence should have discovered, the injury that forms the basis for the claim." *William A. Graham Co. v. Haughey*, 568 F.3d 425, 433(C.A.3 2009) (internal quotation marks omitted). See also 6 W. Patry, Copyright § 20:19, p. 20-28(2013) (hereinafter Patry) ("The overwhelming majority of courts use discovery accrual in copyright ca-

ses.").

5. See generally id. , § 20:23, at 20-44; 3 Nimmer § 12. 05[B][1][b], at 12-150. 2 to 12-150. 4. See also, e. g. , William A. Graham Co. , 568 F. 3d, at 433; *Peter Letterese & Assoc. , Inc. v. World Inst. of Scientology Enterprises*, *Int'l*, 533 F. 3d 1287, 1320, n. 39 (C. A. 11 2008); *Bridgeport Music, Inc. v. Rhyme Syndicate Music*, 376 F. 3d 615, 621 (C. A. 6 2004); *Makedwde Publishing Co. v. Johnson*, 37 F. 3d 180, 182 (C. A. 5 1994); *Roley v. New World Pictures, Ltd.* , 19 F. 3d 479, 481 (C. A. 9 1994).

6. Separately accruing harm should not be confused with harm from past violations that are continuing. *Compare Klehr v. A. O. Smith Corp.* , 521 U. S. 179, 190, 117 S. Ct. 1984, 138 L. Ed. 2d 373 (1997) (for separately accruing harm, each new act must cause "harm[to the plaintiff] over and above the harm that the earlier acts caused"), with *Havens Realty Corp. v. Coleman*, 455 U. S. 363, 380-381, 102 S. Ct. 1114, 71 L. Ed. 2d 214 (1982) ("[W]here a plaintiff...challenges...an unlawful practice that continues into the limitations period, the complaint is timely when it is filed within[the limitations period, measured from] the last asserted occurrence of that practice. " (footnote omitted)).

7. A case arising outside of the copyright context is illustrative. In *Bay Area Laundry and Dry Cleaning Pension Trust Fund v. Ferbar Corp. of Cal.* , 522 U. S. 192, 118 S. Ct. 542, 139 L. Ed. 2d 553 (1997), an employer was delinquent in making a series of scheduled payments to an underfunded pension plan. See id. , at 198-199, 118 S. Ct. 542. The trustees filed suit just over six years after the first missed payment, barely outside of the applicable six-year statute of limitations. See id. , at 198, 118 S. Ct. 542. Because the first missed payment in the series fell outside the statute of limitations, the employer argued that the subsequent missed payments were also time barred. See id. , at 206, 118 S. Ct. 542. We rejected that argument. The remaining claims were timely, we held, because "each missed payment create[d] a separate cause of action with its own six-year limitations period. " Ibid. Cf. Klehr, 521 U. S. , at 190, 117 S. Ct. 1984 (for civil Racketeer Influenced and Corrupt Organizations Act claims, plaintiff may recover for acts occurring within the limitations period, but may not use an "independent, new predicate act as a bootstrap to recover for injuries caused by other earlier predicate acts that took place outside the limitations period"); *National Railroad Passenger Corporation v. Morgan*, 536 U. S. 101, 114-121, 122 S. Ct. 2061, 153 L. Ed. 2d 106 (2002) (distinguishing discrete acts, each independently actionable, from conduct "cumulative[in]effect," e. g. , hostile environment claims pursued under Title VII of the Civil Rights Act of 1964, 42 U. S. C. § 2000e et seq. ; "in direct contrast to dis-

crete acts, a single[instance of hostility] may not be actionable on its own"). But cf. post, at 1984 -1985(ignoring the distinction Morgan took care to draw between discrete acts independently actionable and conduct cumulative in effect).

8. Petrella's attorney filed the renewal application on behalf of Frank Petrella's heirs. When Petrella's mother died and her brother assigned his rights to her, Petrella became the sole owner of all rights in the 1963 screenplay.

9. LaMotta, the court noted, "ha[d] suffered myriad blows to his head as a fighter years ago," and "no longer recognize[d Petrella], even though he ha[d] known her for forty years." App. to Pet. for Cert. 45a-46a.

10. In her declaration, Petrella stated that MGM told her in 2001 that the film was in "a huge deficit financially," "would never show a profit," and, for that reason, "MGM would not continue to send[financial] statements[to her]." App. 234.

11. The Court of Appeals did not consider whether MGM had also shown evidentiary prejudice. 695 F. 3d 946, 953(C. A. 9 2012).

12. See *Lyons Partnership L. P. v. Morris Costumes, Inc.*, 243 F. 3d 789, 798(C. A. 4 2001) (laches defense unavailable in copyright infringement cases, regardless of remedy sought); Peter Letterese, 533 F. 3d, at 1320("[T]here is a strong presumption[in copyright cases] that a plaintiff's suit is timely if it is filed before the statute of limitations has run. Only in the most extraordinary circumstances will laches be recognized as a defense."); *Chirco v. Crosswinds Communities, Inc.*, 474 F. 3d 227, 233(C. A. 6 2007)(in copyright litigation, laches applies only to "the most compelling of cases"); *Jacobsen v. Deseret Book Co.*, 287 F. 3d 936, 950(C. A. 10 2002) ("Rather than deciding copyright cases on the issue of laches, courts should generally defer to the three-year statute of limitations."); *New Era Publications Int'l v. Henry Holt & Co.*, 873 F. 2d 576, 584-585(C. A. 2 1989)("severe prejudice, coupled with…unconscionable delay…mandates denial of…injunction for laches and relegation of[plaintiff] to its damages remedy"). Cf. post, at 1979, 1985-1986(acknowledging that application of laches should be "extraordinary," confined to "few and unusual cases").

13. Assuming Petrella had a winning case on the merits, the Court of Appeals' ruling on laches would effectively give MGM a cost-free license to exploit Raging Bull throughout the long term of the copyright. The value to MGM of such a free, compulsory license could exceed by far MGM's expenditures on the film.

14. See Fed. Rule Civ. Proc. 2("There is one form of action—the civil action."); Rule 8

(c)(listing among affirmative defenses both "laches" and "statute of limitations").

15. In contrast to the Copyright Act, the Lanham Act, which governs trademarks, contains no statute of limitations, and expressly provides for defensive use of "equitable principles, including laches."15 U. S. C. § 1115(b)(9). But cf. post, at 1983, 1984(citing *Hot Wax, Inc. v. Turtle Wax, Inc.*, 191 F. 3d 813(C. A. 7 1999), but failing to observe that Lanham Act contains no statute of limitations). The Patent Act states: "[N]o recovery shall be had for any infringement committed more than six years prior to the filing of the complaint."35 U. S. C. § 286. The Act also provides that "[n]oninfringement, absence of liability for infringement or unenforceability" may be raised "in any action involving the validity or infringement of a patent. " § 282(b)(2012 ed.). Based in part on § 282 and commentary thereon, legislative history, and historical practice, the Federal Circuit has held that laches can bar damages incurred prior to the commencement of suit, but not injunctive relief. *A. C. Aukerman Co. v. R. L. Chaides Constr. Co.*, 960 F. 2d 1020, 1029–1031, 1039–1041(1992)(en banc). We have not had occasion to review the Federal Circuit's position.

16. MGM pretends otherwise, but the cases on which it relies do not carry the load MGM would put on them. Morgan, described supra, at 1970, n. 7, is apparently MGM's best case, for it is cited 13 times in MGM's brief. See Brief for Respondents 8, 9, 14, 16, 18, 19, 25, 31, 34, 35, 36, 40, 47; post, at 1979, 1982, 1984–1985. Morgan, however, does not so much as hint that laches may bar claims for discrete wrongs, all of them occurring within a federal limitations period. Part II–A of that opinion, dealing with the separate–accrual rule, held that "[e]ach discrete discriminatory act starts a new clock for filing charges alleging that act," regardless of whether "past acts" are time barred. 536 U. S. , at 113, 122 S. Ct. 2061. Parts II–B and II–C of the opinion then distinguished separately accruing wrongs from hostile–work–environment claims, cumulative in effect and extending over long periods of time. Id. , at 115–117, 121, 122 S. Ct. 2061. Laches could be invoked, the Court reasoned, to limit the continuing violation doctrine's potential to rescue untimely claims, not claims accruing separately within the limitations period. Bay Area Laundry, described, along with Morgan, supra, at 1970, n. 7, is similarly featured by MGM. See also post, at 1982–1983, 1984. But that opinion considered laches only in the context of a federal statute calling for action "[a]s soon as practicable."29 U. S. C. § 1399(b)(1); see 522 U. S. , at 205, 118 S. Ct. 542. Patterson v. Hewitt, 195 U. S. 309, 25 S. Ct. 35, 49 L. Ed. 214(1904), described by MGM as a case resembling Petrella's, see Tr. of Oral Arg. 32–33, 53, barred equitable claims that were timely under state law. When state law was the reference, federal courts some-

times applied laches as a further control. See supra, at 1968–1969; *Russell v. Todd*, 309 U. S. 280,288,n. 1,60 S. Ct. 527,84 L. Ed. 754(1940) ("Laches may bar equitable remedy before the local statute has run."). No federal statute of limitations figured in Patterson.

17. E. g. ,a party's infancy or mental disability,absence of the defendant from the jurisdiction,fraudulent concealment. See S. Rep. No. 1014,85th Cong. ,1st Sess. ,2–3(1957) (hereinafter Senate Report).

18. The legislative history to which the dissent refers,post,at 1982,speaks of "equitable situations on which the statute of limitations is generally suspended,"Senate Report 3,and says nothing about laches shrinking the time Congress allowed.

19. The dissent worries that a plaintiff might sue for profits "every three years…until the copyright expires."Post,at 1981;see post,at 1979. That suggestion neglects to note that a plaintiff who proves infringement will likely gain forward-looking injunctive relief stopping the defendant's repetition of infringing acts.

20. As earlier noted,see supra,at 1972,n. 11,the Court of Appeals did not reach the question whether evidentiary prejudice existed. 695 F. 3d,at 953.

21. Although MGM,in its answer to Petrella's complaint,separately raised both laches and estoppel as affirmative defenses,see Defendants' Answer to Plaintiff's Complaint in No. CV 09–0072(CD Cal.),the courts below did not address the estoppel plea.

22. While reliance or its absence may figure importantly in this case,we do not suggest that reliance is in all cases a sine qua non for adjustment of injunctive relief or profits.

新闻界公益公司（上诉人）

华尔街在线有限责任公司等（被上诉人）

第 17-571 号
开庭时间：2019 年 1 月 8 日
判决时间：2019 年 3 月 4 日

案情摘要与裁判要旨

上诉人新闻界公益公司（以下简称"新闻界"，一家新闻机构）将作品许可给被上诉人华尔街在线有限责任公司（简称"华尔街在线"，一家新闻网站）。新闻界以许可协议终止后华尔街在线未能将以往新闻文章从网站移除为由，起诉华尔街在线及其所有者版权侵权。此前，新闻界向版权局申请登记这些新闻文章，但版权登记官尚未回应登记申请。《美国法典》第17卷第411条（a）款规定："任何美国人作品按本编规定完成版权登记前……不得就侵犯作品版权行为提起民事诉讼。"地区法院裁定驳回新闻界的诉讼请求，联邦第十一巡回上诉法院维持这一裁定，认为"只有当版权局登记了作品，作品才视为按第411条（a）款完成版权登记"。联邦最高法院裁定，只有当版权局准予登记作品，登记工作才算完成，版权人才能提起侵权之诉。但作品登记后，版权人可以就登记前和登记后实施的侵权行为主张损失赔偿。

金斯伯格大法官发表了判决意见，其他大法官一致赞同。

新闻界公益公司（上诉人）诉华尔街在线有限责任公司等（被上诉人）

*886《美国法典》第17卷第411条（a）款强制要求尽快办理版权登记，规定："任何美国人作品按本编规定完成版权登记前……不得就侵犯作品版权行为提起民事诉讼。"本案的争议在于，按第17卷要求"完成版权登记"究竟是指版权人提交符合要求的登记申请材料和作品样本并缴纳费用，还是指版权局审查后准予登记？本法院赞同联邦第十一巡回上诉法院的观点，认为版权局准予登记才能称得上完成版权登记，版权人方可启动侵权之诉。一旦作品登记后，版权人可以就*887登记前和登记后实施的侵权行为主张损失赔偿。

上诉人新闻界为一家提供在线资讯的新闻机构。新闻界将其新闻作品许可给被上诉人华尔街在线——一家新闻网站。根据许可协议，华尔街在线终止协议前需将新闻界提供的内容从其网站移除。华尔街在线终止了协议，但继续展示新闻界以往提供的内容。新闻界以版权侵权为由起诉华尔街在线及其所有者杰罗德·伯登。起诉状称，新闻界已"就许可给华尔街在线的文章向版权局提出了登记申请"（调卷令申请附录第18a[1]）。因登记官尚未回应新闻界的登记申请[2]，地区法院根据华尔街在线和杰罗德·伯登的动议，裁定驳回原告的诉讼请求，联邦第十一巡回上诉法院维持了这一裁决。之后，版权登记官拒绝为新闻界声称遭华尔街在线侵权的文章办理登记手续。[3]

为解决各巡回上诉法院关于第411条（a）款所指登记完成时间上的争议，本法院批准了调卷令状申请。参见《美国判例汇编》，第585卷，——；《最高法院判例汇编》第138卷，起始页2707；《美国判例汇编律师版·第二辑》201卷，起始页1095（2018年裁决）。对比案件如《联邦法院判例汇编·第三辑》第856卷，引证页1341页（本案下级法院的裁决）：版权登记官登记版权即为根据第411条（a）款完成版权登记；又如 Cosmetic Ideas, Inc. v. IAC/Interactivecorp 案，《联邦法院判例汇编·第三辑》第606卷，起始页612，引证页621（联邦第九巡回上诉法院2010年裁决）：版权局收到登记申请人"完整申请资料"，即为根据第411条（a）款完成版权登记。

I

根据1976年《版权法案》及相关修订内容,"作者创作的具有独创性……且固定在某种有形介质上的作品"受版权保护,代表类型有文字作品、音乐作品和戏剧作品[《美国法典》第17卷第102条(a)款]。作品一经创作完成,作者便享有复制权、发行权、展览权等垄断性权利。参见第106条及 Eldred v. Ashcroft 案,《美国判例汇编》第537卷,起始页186,引证页195;《最高法院判例汇编》第123卷,起始页769;《美国判例汇编律师版·第二辑》第154卷,起始页683(2003年裁决):"联邦版权保护始于作品创作完成之时。"根据《版权法案》第501条(b)款,版权人有权就侵犯其垄断性权利的行为提起民事诉讼。

但前往法院提起侵权诉讼之前,版权人一般须遵从第411条(a)款之规定"完成版权登记"。因此,尽管版权独立于登记手续而存在[第408条(a)款],但版权登记类似于穷尽行政救济原则要求,版权人必须满足登记要求方可起诉以执行其权利(见口头辩论笔录第35页)。

*888 在个别情况下,版权人可以在办理登记前提起侵权诉讼。对于发行前易招致侵权的作品,尤其是电影或乐曲,版权人可以在准备发行时申请预登记[《版权法案》第408条(f)款(2)项;《美国联邦法规》第37编第202.16条(b)款(1)项,2018]。此时,版权局仅对登记申请"实施有限的审查",并在"完成预登记"后通知申请人[第202.16条(c)款(7)项,(c)款(10)项]。一旦完成预登记,版权人便可以起诉侵权人[《美国法典》第17卷第411条(a)款]。然而,预登记仅仅是"正式登记手续的准备步骤"(《关于某些未公开版权主张的预登记规则》,《联邦公报》2005年第70号第42286页),版权人单凭预登记就提起侵权诉讼将面临被驳回起诉的风险,除非版权人在预登记的作品发行时或被侵权后立刻提出正式登记申请[第408条(f)款(3)至(4)项]。又如,版权人在"完成版权登记"前可以起诉侵犯其现场直播作品的权利,但如果版权人在作品首次传输后的三个月内未能"完成版权登记",则权利人将面临被驳回起诉的风险［第411条（c）款］。因此，即便是这些例外情形，版权人也必须最终通过正式登记作品以维持其诉讼权利。

II

各当事人均认同，除了上述与本案无关的例外情形，根据第411条（a）款，版权人只有"完成版权登记"才能提起侵权诉讼。新闻界与华尔街在线的争议在于，第411条（a）款之"完成版权登记"是指版权人提交登记申请书及相关材料并缴纳费用，还是指版权局准予登记。新闻界提出了第一种解读方式——"申请说"，而华尔街在线则提出了第二种解读方法——"准予登记说"。本法院认为，"准予登记说"是对第411条（a）款文本唯一正确解读。因此，本法院不赞同新闻界的"申请说"。

A

根据第411条（a）款，当版权局准予登记一件作品版权[4]，版权人才"完成版权登记"，并可以提起侵权之诉。第411条（a）款第一句规定，"在版权主张预登记或登记之前，不得就侵权行为提起民事诉讼"。该款下一句就该原则设定了一个例外："作品样本、申请书和登记费用"按要求提交后，版权局拒绝准予注册的，版权人"可以提起民事诉讼，但需要告知登记官"。第411条（a）款前两句放在一起，聚焦的是版权局的行为——同意＊889或拒绝登记一项版权主张。

如果登记申请本身足以"完成"登记，那么第411条（a）款第二句——允许登记申请人在申请遭拒后提起诉讼——便显得多余。试想，如果版权人在提出版权登记申请后便可立刻起诉版权侵权，无需等待登记官是否准予登记的决定，那么允许登记申请人在申请遭拒后提起诉讼还有何意义？"申请说"主张者坚称，第411条（a）款第二句仅仅是要求版权人将侵权诉讼告知登记官（见上诉人陈述第29-32页）。这一解读将意味着国会在同一法条多个连续且相关的语句中多次使用"登记"一词但却赋予了不同意思：第411条（a）款第一句中"登记"意指版权人提出登记申请之行为,而第二句中的"登记"则包含登记官审查申请之意。该解读方式不可信,本法院不予接受。参见 Mid-Con Freight Systems, Inc. v. Michigan Pub. Serv. Comm'n 案,《美国判例汇编》第 545 卷,起始页 440,引证页 448;《最高法院判例汇编》第 125 卷,起始页 2427;《美国判例汇编律师版·第二辑》第 162 卷,起始页 418(2005 年裁决):拒绝将相关联句子中使用的"相同词语"理解为"指代完全不同的事物"。

第 411 条(a)款第三句,也是最后一句,让本法院进一步确认该条要求登记官准予或拒绝登记之行为先于版权人提起侵权诉讼。第三句允许登记官"作为争议版权应否准予登记诉讼的当事人"。如果在登记官就登记申请作出决定前便可以起诉侵权并由法院作出裁决,那么法院将失去登记官的评判帮助,允许登记官作为诉讼当事人也就失去意义。

本法院认为,第 411 条(a)款的"登记"是指登记官的行为,《版权法案》其他条款印证了本法院的这一解读。第 410 条规定,如果登记官"经审查"认为,"所提交样本构成版权法保护的客体",且"其他法律和形式要件也……得到满足,登记官将准予登记并核发登记证给申请人"[第 410 条(a)款]。但如果登记官认为所提交样本"不构成版权法保护的客体,或登记请求因其他任何原因无效",登记官将拒绝登记[第 410 条(b)款]。可见,第 410 条确认了登记申请不同于登记,且申请是登记的前置程序。第 410 条(d)款进一步规定,如果版权局登记了一项版权,或法院后来裁定被拒绝登记的请求是应准予登记的版权客体,"版权登记生效之日"为版权人将合乎规定的申请材料提交版权局之日。如果按要求提交申请材料就视为完成登记,那么也就没有必要再明确"版权登记生效之日"。

如果提交合乎规定的申请材料即意味着完成登记,那么第 408 条(f)款的预登记选择同样失去意义。前面在 887-888 页提到,预登记程序使得那些发行前易招致侵权的作品的版权人在获准或被拒绝版权登记前得以执行其垄断性权利。而如果版权人只要完成登记申请手续便可以立刻起诉版权侵权,那么发行前易招致侵权的作品的版权人也就没有理由去申请办理预登记手续[对比 TRW Inc. v. Andrews 案,《美国判例汇编》第 534 卷,起始页 19,引证页 29;《最高法院判例汇编》第 122 卷,起始页 441;《美国判例汇编律师版·第二辑》第 151 卷,起始页 339(2001 年裁决):如果一

新闻界公益公司（上诉人）诉华尔街在线有限责任公司等（被上诉人）

种解读方式会使得某法条仅在极例外情形下有意义，*890 而在其他场合均显多余，法院将拒绝这种解读方式］。

B

新闻界不服联邦第十一巡回上诉法院的裁决，首要理由是《版权法案》使用"短语'完成登记'及其被动形式'登记被完成'"来描述版权人提交申请材料的行为，而非版权局对登记申请作出的回应（见上诉人陈述第21页）。新闻界坚称，第411条（a）款要求"按本编规定完成版权登记"最有可能指版权人遵从制定法的具体规定提出登记申请。为支持自己的主张，新闻界援引了《版权法案》中看似使用"完成登记"或其变体来指代版权人行为的条款［同上，见22-26页，引述的条款有《美国法典》第17卷第110条、第205条（c）款、第408条（c）款（3）项、第411条（c）款和第412条（2）项］。此外，新闻界还坚称其解读方式反映了绝大部分版权登记申请最终都获批这一现实（见上诉人陈述第41页）。

不过新闻界也承认，《版权法案》有时也用"登记"一词指代版权局而非版权人的行为［同上，第27-28页，引述《美国法典》第17卷第708条（a）款］。因此，新闻界也认同，在确定制定法所用"登记"一词含义时，须"考查该词使用的具体语境"（上诉人陈述第29页）。本法院在前面第888-890页解释过，第411条（a）款的具体语境只容许一种解释，那就是"完成版权登记"只能指版权局准予登记之行为，而非版权人提出注册申请之行为。

新闻界对第411条（a）款的相反理解部分误读了《版权法案》1976年的某些修订对法案的意义。1976年修订前，第411条（a）款对应的内容为："在按本编规定提交作品样本并登记作品前，不得就该作品提起版权侵权诉讼和程序。"参见《美国法典》第17卷第13条（1970年修订）。新闻界认为，恰是该内容抛出了本法院现在要解决的争议问题，即版权人的登记申请本身是否意味着完成版权登记。新闻界注意到，联邦第二巡回上诉法院在 *Vacheron & Constantin-Le Coultre Watches, Inc. v. Benrus Watch Co.* 案［《联邦上诉法院判例汇编·第二辑》第260卷，起始页637（1958年裁决）］中考虑了该问题（上诉人陈述第32-34页）。在该案中，据勒恩德·

汉德法官的意见,法院认为,提交版权登记手续的版权人在登记申请遭拒后不得立刻起诉侵权（Vacheron 案,《联邦上诉法院判例汇编·第二辑》第 260 卷,引证页 640-641 页）。相反,版权人必须首先通过提起针对登记官的职责履行的行诉讼获得登记证书。但该案的少数意见法官认为,版权人的登记申请足以准许版权人启动侵权之诉（同上,引证页 645）。

新闻界认为,国会 1976 年关于登记要求的修订支持了 Vacheron 案少数意见法官的立场（上诉人陈述第 34-36 页）。本法院对此不予认可。相反,本法院认为 1976 年的修订变化表明国会支持勒恩德·汉德法官的观点,即触发版权人诉权的是登记官的行为。在拟定第 411 条（a）款时,国会既重申了登记先于侵权诉讼这一基本原则,也在该款第二句增加了一项例外,以规范未准予版权登记的情形（见参议院 1976 年第 94-1476 号报告,第 157 页）。如果 1976 年国会修订《版权法案》真如新闻界所言是为了确认版权人提出登记申请后便可即刻提起侵权诉讼,那么这项例外也就没有什么价值。如果版权人提起版权登记申请后便可以立刻起诉侵权人,那么版权人也就没有必要等到申请遭拒后再取得制定法授权去起诉。[5]

同样值得注意的是,1976 年《版权法案》修订后的多年里,国会阻止了旨在删除第 411 条（a）款及其登记要求的尝试。1988 年,为执行《伯尔尼公约》禁止对某些作品强加形式要求之规定,国会将外国人作品移出第 411 条（a）款规制的范畴［见第 9 条（b）款（1）项,《美国制定法大全》第 102 卷,第 2859 页］。虽然有建议彻底废弃第 411 条（a）款的登记要求（见参议院 1988 年第 100-352 号报告,第 36 页）,但国会维持了对美国人作品的登记要求［见第 411 条（a）款］。国会紧接着在 1993 年曾考虑过但最终还是拒绝采纳允许版权人提交版权登记申请后立刻起诉侵权的建议（见参议院 1993 年第 103-338 号报告,第 4 页）。2005 年,针对发行前易招致侵权的作品,国会提供了预登记选择（见 2005 年《艺术家权利与防盗用法案》第 104 条,《美国制定法大全》第 119 卷,第 221 页；同上,第 887-888 页）。预登记措施是国会对众多就发行前易招致侵权的作品废除版权登记呼声的回应（《联邦公报》第 70 卷,起始页 42286）。后来,国会又数次维持了登记手续作为侵权诉讼前置程序的做法,拒绝了废除登记要求或将登记程序等同于版权人的登记申请行为而非登记官行为的建议。

新闻界公益公司（上诉人）诉华尔街在线有限责任公司等（被上诉人）

新闻界还辩称，既然登记并非获得版权保护的要件［《美国法典》第17卷第408条（a）款］，那么第411条（a）款也不应理解为妨碍版权人在按规定提交版权登记申请材料后行使其权利（上诉人陈述第37页）。但正如前面第887-888页解释的那样，作品无论登记与否，《版权法案》通过赋予创作者垄断性权利并禁止他人侵权，以保障版权人的利益。如果侵权发生在版权人申请版权登记之前，那么版权人可以最终获赔登记前因侵权遭受的损失，包括侵权人的收益（第504条），版权人只需要在起诉前申请并获准版权登记即可。一旦登记官同意或拒绝登记作品，版权人便可申请禁令阻止正在发生的侵权，并请求法院颁布命令，要求侵权人销毁侵权材料［第502条、第503条（b）款］。

然而，新闻界认为，如果侵权发生在版权局审查登记申请之时，"准予登记说"会在等待期内剥夺版权人的权利［上诉人陈述第41页；同时见P. Goldstein著《版权法》第3.15节，第3：154.2页（第三版，2018年增补）：认为申请说是"更好的规则"；M. Nimmer & D. Nimmer著《版权法》第2卷，第7.16节［B］［3］［a］、［b］［ii］（2018版）：登记申请为侵权诉讼的先决条件，而版权登记证书则是作品为版权法保护的客体的初步证明］。除了规定一般登记规则的第411条（a）款，国会对《版权法案》其他内容的精雕细琢表明其已关注这一问题。在408条（f）款规定的预登记选择里，允许发行前易招致侵权作品的版权人在登记官决定是否准予登记前起诉侵权［见第411条（a）款］。对于现场直播，国会作出了类似决定［第411条（c）款；如前所述，第888页][6]。但对于其他作品，根据第411条（a）款的一般规定，版权人在提起侵权诉讼前新闻界必须等待登记官的决定。

新闻界忧心，如果《版权法案》规定的三年诉讼时效在版权局就登记申请作出决定前届满，那么版权人将无法执行自己的权利（上诉人陈述第41页）。新闻界未免多虑了，因为现在版权登记的平均周期一般为七个月，这给版权人留有充裕的时间在登记官作出决定后再去起诉侵权，甚至起诉版权登记申请提交前发生的侵权行为（参见美国版权局"版权登记处理周期"，2018年10月2日发布，网址：https：//www.copyright.gov/registration/docs/processing-times-faqs.pdf，最后访问日期2019年3月1日）。

的确，现有制定法可能并未如国会过去预想的那样运行。版权登记花费的时间已经从1956年的一到两周增加至如今的数月之久［见审计总署1982年《提高版权登记效率报告》（编号：GAO-AFMD-83-13）第3页；"版权登记处理周期"］。迟延登记很大程度上是由于版权局人手和预算短缺，这些问题国会可以疏解，法院则鞭长莫及［W. 帕特里著，《版权》第17：83节（2019年版）］。虽然版权登记迟延是一个不幸现象，但本法院无权修改国会制定的第411条（a）款。

综上，本法院的结论是：《美国法典》第17卷第411条（a）款之"完成版权登记"并非指提交版权登记申请之时，而是指登记官收到符合规定的登记申请后决定准予登记之时。因此，本法院维持联邦第十一巡回上诉法院的裁决。

注释

［1］版权登记官是指版权局局长，由国会图书馆馆长任命［《美国法典》第17卷第701条（a）款］。《版权法案》授予登记官"履行第17卷赋予的一切行政职能和义务"（同上）。

［2］版权局当初之所以延迟审查新闻界的登记申请，是因为新闻界用以支付登记申请费的支票遭新闻界开户银行拒绝兑付（见法庭之友意见书附录1a）。

［3］版权局拒绝登记的决定是否合理不是本法院讨论的问题。

［4］第411条（a）款主要内容有："任何美国人作品按本编规定完成版权预登记或登记前，不得就侵犯作品版权行为提起民事诉讼。然而，在任何情况下，如果版权人已经按要求将作品样本、申请书和登记费用交给版权局后，版权局拒绝准予注册的，版权人可以提起民事诉讼，但需要告知登记官并向其提交起诉状的副本一份。登记官自己有权决定要不要作为争议版权应否准予登记诉讼的当事人……"

［5］新闻界声称，如果版权人在版权局遭遇了长时间的延误，他将被迫提起针对登记官职责履行的诉讼，以强迫登记官对登记申请作出决定，这恰是 *Vacheron & Constantin-Le Coultre Watches, Inc. v. Benrus Watch Co.* 案［《联邦上诉法院判例汇编·第二辑》第260卷，起始页637（1958年裁

决）]暴露出来的问题。但国会对这一问题的答案在第411条（a）款的第二句，即允许版权人在登记申请遭拒后提起侵权诉讼，而并未废除版权登记为侵权诉讼先决程序的规则。

[6]此外，除了《版权法案》中预登记诉讼相关规定，版权局还允许版权人选择申请的快速审查通道，但需额外支付800美元[参见美国版权局"特别申请程序"（2017年第10号通告第1-2页）]。在一些例外情形中，尤其是"诉讼正在进行或即将发生"，版权局允许版权人走"特别申请程序"通道，并将"尽全力……在5个工作日内完成审查工作"[《美国版权实务指南》第623.2，623.4（2017年第三版）]。

FOURTH ESTATE PUBLIC BENEFIT

CORPORATION, Petitioner v.

WALL-STREET. COM, LLC, et al.

No. 17-571

Argued January 8, 2019

Decided March 4, 2019

https://www.supremecourt.gov/opinions/18pdf/17-571_e29f.pdf

**FOURTH ESTATE PUBLIC BENEFIT CORPORATION,Petitioner v.
WALL-STREET.COM,LLC,et al.**

*886 Impelling prompt registration of copyright claims, 17 U. S. C. § 411 (a) states that "no civil action for infringement of the copyright in any United States work shall be instituted until...registration of the copyright claim has been made in accordance with this title. " The question this case presents: Has "registration... been made in accordance with [Title 17]" as soon as the claimant delivers the required application, copies of the work, and fee to the Copyright Office; or has "registration... been made" only after the Copyright Office reviews and registers the copyright? We hold, in accord with the United States Court of Appeals for the Eleventh Circuit, that registration occurs, and a copyright claimant may commence an infringement suit, when the Copyright Office registers a copyright. Upon registration of the copyright, however, a copyright owner can recover *887 for infringement that occurred both before and after registration.

Petitioner Fourth Estate Public Benefit Corporation (Fourth Estate) is a news organization producing online journalism. Fourth Estate licensed journalism works to respondent Wall-Street. com, LLC (Wall-Street), a news website. The license agreement required Wall-Street to remove from its website all content produced by Fourth Estate before canceling the agreement. Wall-Street canceled, but continued to display articles produced by Fourth Estate. Fourth Estate sued Wall-Street and its owner, Jerrold Burden, for copyright infringement. The complaint alleged that Fourth Estate had filed "applications to register [the] articles [licensed to Wall-Street] with the Register of Copyrights. " App. to Pet. for Cert. 18a. [1] Because the Register had not yet acted on Fourth Estate's applications, [2] the District Court, on Wall-Street and Burden's motion, dismissed the complaint, and the Eleventh Circuit affirmed. 856 F. 3d 1338 (2017). Thereafter, the Register of Copyrights refused registration of the articles Wall-Street had allegedly infringed. [3]

We granted Fourth Estate's petition for certiorari to resolve a division among U. S. Courts of Appeals on when registration occurs in accordance with § 411(a). 585 U. S. ——, 138 S. Ct. 2707, 201 L. Ed. 2d 1095 (2018). Compare, e. g. , 856 F. 3d at 1341 (case below) (registration has been made under § 411(a) when the Register of Copyrights registers a copyright), with, e. g. , *Cosmetic Ideas, Inc. v. IAC/Interactivecorp*, 606 F. 3d 612, 621 (C. A. 9 2010) (registration has been made under § 411(a) when the copyright claimant's "complete application" for registration is received by the Copyright Office).

I

Under the Copyright Act of 1976, as amended, copyright protection attaches to "original works of authorship"—prominent among them, literary, musical, and dramatic works— "fixed in any tangible medium of expression." 17 U. S. C. § 102 (a). An author gains "exclusive rights" in her work immediately upon the work's creation, including rights of reproduction, distribution, and display. See § 106; *Eldred v. Ashcroft*, 537 U. S. 186, 195, 123 S. Ct. 769, 154 L. Ed. 2d 683 (2003) ("[F]ederal copyright protection ... run[s] from the work's creation."). The Copyright Act entitles a copyright owner to institute a civil action for infringement of those exclusive rights. § 501(b).

Before pursuing an infringement claim in court, however, a copyright claimant generally must comply with § 411(a)'s requirement that "registration of the copyright claim has been made." § 411(a). Therefore, although an owner's rights exist apart from registration, see § 408(a), registration is akin to an administrative exhaustion requirement that the owner must satisfy before suing to enforce ownership rights, see Tr. of Oral Arg. 35.

*888 In limited circumstances, copyright owners may file an infringement suit before undertaking registration. If a copyright owner is preparing to distribute a work of a type vulnerable to predistribution infringement—notably, a movie or musical composition—the owner may apply for preregistration. § 408(f)(2); 37 CFR § 202.16(b)(1)(2018). The Copyright Office will "conduct a limited review" of the application and notify the claimant "[u]pon completion of the preregistration." § 202.16(c)(7), (c)(10). Once "preregistration ... has been made," the copyright claimant may institute a suit for infringement. 17 U. S. C. § 411(a). Preregistration, however, serves only as "a preliminary step prior to a full registration." Preregistration of Certain Unpublished Copyright Claims, 70 Fed. Reg. 42286 (2005). An infringement suit brought in reliance on preregistration risks dismissal unless the copyright owner applies for registration promptly after the preregistered work's publication or infringement. § 408(f)(3)–(4). A copyright owner may also sue for infringement of a live broadcast before "registration...has been made," but faces dismissal of her suit if she fails to "make registration for the work" within three months of its first transmission. § 411(c). Even in these exceptional scenarios, then, the copyright owner must eventually pursue registration in order to maintain a suit for infringement.

II

All parties agree that, outside of statutory exceptions not applicable here, § 411 (a) bars a copyright owner from suing for infringement until "registration...has been made." Fourth Estate and Wall-Street dispute, however, whether "registration...has been made" under § 411(a) when a copyright owner submits the application, materials, and fee required for registration, or only when the Copyright Office grants registration. Fourth Estate advances the former view—the "application approach"—while Wall-Street urges the latter reading—the "registration approach." The registration approach, we conclude, reflects the only satisfactory reading of § 411(a)'s text. We therefore reject Fourth Estate's application approach.

A

Under § 411(a), "registration...has been made," and a copyright owner may sue for infringement, when the Copyright Office registers a copyright. [4] Section 411(a)'s first sentence provides that no civil infringement action "shall be instituted until preregistration or registration of the copyright claim has been made." The section's next sentence sets out an exception to this rule: When the required "deposit, application, and fee...have been delivered to the Copyright Office in proper form and registration has been refused," the claimant "[may] institute a civil action, if notice thereof...is served on the Register." Read together, § 411 (a)'s opening sentences focus not on the claimant's act of applying for registration, but on action by the Copyright Office—namely, its registration  889 or refusal to register a copyright claim.

If application alone sufficed to "ma[ke]" registration, § 411(a)'s second sentence—allowing suit upon refusal of registration—would be superfluous. What utility would that allowance have if a copyright claimant could sue for infringement immediately after applying for registration without awaiting the Register's decision on her application? Proponents of the application approach urge that §411(a)'s second sentence serves merely to require a copyright claimant to serve "notice[of an infringement suit]…on the Register." See Brief for Petitioner 29-32. This reading, however, requires the implausible assumption that Congress gave "registration" different meanings in consecutive, related sentences within a single statutory provision. In §411(a)'s first sentence, "registration" would mean the claimant's act of filing an application, while in the section's second sentence, "registration" would entail the Register's review of an application. We resist this improbable construction. See, e.g., *Mid-Con Freight Systems, Inc. v. Michigan Pub. Serv. Comm'n*, 545 U.S. 440, 448, 125 S. Ct. 2427, 162 L. Ed. 2d 418(2005)(declining to read "the same words" in consecutive sentences as "refer[ring] to something totally different").

The third and final sentence of §411(a) further persuades us that the provision requires action by the Register before a copyright claimant may sue for infringement. The sentence allows the Register to "become a party to the action with respect to the issue of registrability of the copyright claim." This allowance would be negated, and the court conducting an infringement suit would lack the benefit of the Register's assessment, if an infringement suit could be filed and resolved before the Register acted on an application.

Other provisions of the Copyright Act support our reading of "registration," as used in §411(a), to mean action by the Register. Section 410 states that, "after examination," if the Register determines that "the material deposited constitutes copyrightable subject matter" and "other legal and formal requirements…[are] met, the Register shall register the claim and issue to the applicant a certificate of registration." §410(a). But if the Register determines that the deposited material "does not constitute copyrightable subject matter or that the claim is invalid for any other reason, the Register shall refuse registration." §410(b). Section 410 thus confirms that application is discrete from, and precedes, registration. Section 410 (d), furthermore, provides that if the Copyright Office registers a claim, or if a court later determines that a refused claim was registrable, the "effective date of [the work's] copyright registration is the day on which" the copyright owner made a proper submission to the Copyright Office. There would be no need thus to specify the "effective date of a copyright registration" if submission of the required materials qualified as "registration."

Section 408(f)'s preregistration option, too, would have little utility if a completed application constituted registration. Preregistration, as noted *supra*, at 887–888, allows the author of a work vulnerable to predistribution infringement to enforce her exclusive rights in court before obtaining registration or refusal thereof. A copyright owner who fears prepublication infringement would have no reason to apply for preregistration, however, if she could instead simply complete an application for registration and immediately commence an infringement suit. Cf. *TRW Inc. v. Andrews*, 534 U. S. 19, 29, 122 S. Ct. 441, 151 L. Ed. 2d 339 (2001) (rejecting an interpretation that "would in practical effect render ☆890[a provision] superfluous in all but the most unusual circumstances").

B

Challenging the Eleventh Circuit's judgment, Fourth Estate primarily contends that the Copyright Act uses "the phrase 'make registration' and its passive-voice counterpart 'registration has been made' " to describe submissions by the copyright owner, rather than Copyright Office responses to those submissions. Brief for Petitioner 21. Section 411(a)'s requirement that "registration...has been made in accordance with this title," Fourth Estate insists, most likely refers to a copyright owner's compliance with the statutory specifications for registration applications. In support, Fourth Estate points to Copyright Act provisions that appear to use the phrase "make registration" or one of its variants to describe what a copyright claimant does. See *id.*, at 22–26 (citing 17 U. S. C. §§ 110, 205(c), 408(c)(3), 411(c), 412(2)). Furthermore, Fourth Estate urges that its reading reflects the reality that, eventually, the vast majority of applications are granted. See Brief for Petitioner 41.

Fourth Estate acknowledges, however, that the Copyright Act sometimes uses "registration" to refer to activity by the Copyright Office, not activity undertaken by a copyright claimant. See *id.*, at 27–28 (citing 17 U. S. C. § 708(a)). Fourth Estate thus agrees that, to determine how the statute uses the word "registration" in a particular prescription, one must "look to the specific context" in which the term is used. Brief for Petitioner 29. As explained *supra*, at 888–890, the "specific context" of § 411(a) permits only one sensible reading: The phrase "registration… has been made" refers to the Copyright Office's act granting registration, not to the copyright claimant's request for registration.

Fourth Estate's contrary reading of § 411(a) stems in part from its misapprehension of the significance of certain 1976 revisions to the Copyright Act. Before that year, § 411(a)'s precursor provided that "[n]o action or proceeding shall be maintained for infringement of copyright in any work until the provisions of this title with respect to the deposit of copies and registration of such work shall have been complied with." 17 U. S. C. § 13(1970 ed.). Fourth Estate urges that this provision posed the very question we resolve today—namely, whether a claimant's application alone effects registration. The Second Circuit addressed that question, Fourth Estate observes, in *Vacheron & Constantin-Le Coultre Watches, Inc. v. Benrus Watch Co.*, 260 F. 2d 637(1958). Brief for Petitioner 32–34. In that case, in an opinion by Judge Learned Hand, the court held that a copyright owner who completed an application could not sue for infringement immediately upon the Copyright Office's refusal to register. *Vacheron*, 260 F. 2d at 640–641. Instead, the owner first had to obtain a registration certificate by bringing a mandamus action against the Register. The Second Circuit dissenter would have treated the owner's application as sufficient to permit commencement of an action for infringement. *Id.* , at 645.

Fourth Estate sees Congress' 1976 revision of the registration requirement as an endorsement of the *Vacheron* dissenter's position. Brief for Petitioner 34–36. We disagree. The changes made in 1976 instead indicate Congress' agreement with Judge Hand that it is the Register's action that triggers a copyright owner's entitlement to sue. In enacting 17 U. S. C. § 411(a), Congress both reaffirmed the general rule that registration must precede an infringement suit, and added an * 891 exception in that provision's second sentence to cover instances in which registration is refused. See H. R. Rep. No. 94–1476, p. 157(1976). That exception would have no work to do if, as Fourth Estate urges, Congress intended the 1976 revisions to clarify that a copyright claimant may sue immediately upon applying for registration. A copyright claimant would need no statutory authorization to sue after refusal of her application if she could institute suit as soon as she has filed the application.

Noteworthy, too, in years following the 1976 revisions, Congress resisted efforts to eliminate § 411(a) and the registration requirement embedded in it. In 1988, Congress removed foreign works from § 411(a)'s dominion in order to comply with the Berne Convention for the Protection of Literary and Artistic Works' bar on copyright formalities for such works. See § 9(b)(1), 102 Stat. 2859. Despite proposals to repeal § 411(a)'s registration requirement entirely, however, see S. Rep. No. 100-352, p. 36(1988), Congress maintained the requirement for domestic works, see § 411(a). Subsequently, in 1993, Congress considered, but declined to adopt, a proposal to allow suit immediately upon submission of a registration application. See H. R. Rep. No. 103-338, p. 4(1993). And in 2005, Congress made a preregistration option available for works vulnerable to predistribution infringement. See Artists' Rights and Theft Prevention Act of 2005, § 104, 119 Stat. 221. See also *supra*, at 887-888. Congress chose that course in face of calls to eliminate registration in cases of predistribution infringement. 70 Fed. Reg. 42286. Time and again, then, Congress has maintained registration as prerequisite to suit, and rejected proposals that would have eliminated registration or tied it to the copyright claimant's application instead of the Register's action. [5]

Fourth Estate additionally argues that, as "registration is not a condition of copyright protection," 17 U. S. C. § 408(a), § 411(a) should not be read to bar a copyright claimant from enforcing that protection in court once she has submitted a proper application for registration. Brief for Petitioner 37. But as explained *supra*, at 887-888, the Copyright Act safeguards copyright owners, irrespective of registration, by vesting them with exclusive rights upon creation of their works and prohibiting infringement from that point forward. If infringement occurs before a copyright owner applies for registration, that owner may eventually recover damages for the past infringement, as well as the infringer's profits. § 504. She must simply apply for registration and receive the Copyright Office's decision on her application before instituting suit. Once the Register grants or refuses registration, the copyright owner may also seek an injunction barring the infringer from continued violation of her exclusive rights and an order requiring the infringer to destroy infringing materials.

§§ 502,503(b).

Fourth Estate maintains, however, that if infringement occurs while the Copyright Office is reviewing a registration application, the registration approach will deprive the owner of her rights during the waiting period. Brief for Petitioner 41. *892 See also 1 P. Goldstein, Copyright §3.15, p. 3:154.2(3d ed. 2018 Supp.) (finding application approach "the better rule"); 2 M. Nimmer & D. Nimmer, Copyright §7.16[B][3][a],[b][ii](2018)(infringement suit is conditioned on application, while prima facie presumption of validity depends on certificate of registration). The Copyright Act's explicit carveouts from §411(a)'s general registration rule, however, show that Congress adverted to this concern. In the preregistration option, §408(f), Congress provided that owners of works especially susceptible to prepublication infringement should be allowed to institute suit before the Register has granted or refused registration. See §411(a). Congress made the same determination as to live broadcasts. §411(c); see *supra*, at 888.[6] As to all other works, however, §411(a)'s general rule requires owners to await action by the Register before filing suit for infringement.

Fourth Estate raises the specter that a copyright owner may lose the ability to enforce her rights if the Copyright Act's three-year statute of limitations runs out before the Copyright Office acts on her application for registration. Brief for Petitioner 41. Fourth Estate's fear is overstated, as the average processing time for registration applications is currently seven months, leaving ample time to sue after the Register's decision, even for infringement that began before submission of an application. See U. S. Copyright Office, Registration Processing Times (Oct. 2, 2018) (Registration Processing Times), https://www.copyright.gov/registration/docs/processing-times-faqs.pdf (as last visited Mar. 1, 2019).

True, the statutory scheme has not worked as Congress likely envisioned. Registration processing times have increased from one or two weeks in 1956 to many months today. See GAO, Improving Productivity in Copyright Registration 3 (GAO-AFMD-83-13 1982); Registration Processing Times. Delays in Copyright Office processing of applications, it appears, are attributable, in large measure, to staffing and budgetary shortages that Congress can alleviate, but courts cannot cure. See 5 W. Patry, Copyright §17:83(2019). Unfortunate as the current administrative lag may be, that factor does not allow us to revise § 411(a)'s congressionally composed text.

For the reasons stated, we conclude that "registration...has been made" within the meaning of 17 U. S. C. § 411(a) not when an application for registration is filed, but when the Register has registered a copyright after examining a properly filed application. The judgment of the Court of Appeals for the Eleventh Circuit is accordingly

Affirmed.

Footnotes

1. The Register of Copyrights is the "director of the Copyright Office of the Library of Congress" and is appointed by the Librarian of Congress. 17 U. S. C. § 701(a). The Copyright Act delegates to the Register "[a]ll administrative functions and duties under[Title 17]." *Ibid.*

2. Consideration of Fourth Estate's filings was initially delayed because the check Fourth Estate sent in payment of the filing fee was rejected by Fourth Estate's bank as uncollectible. App. to Brief for United States as *Amicus Curiae* 1a.

3. The merits of the Copyright Office's decision refusing registration are not at issue in this Court.

4. Section 411(a) provides, in principal part: "[N]o civil action for infringement of the copyright in any United States work shall be instituted until preregistration or registration of the copyright claim has been made in accordance with this title. In any case, however, where the deposit, application, and fee required for registration have been delivered to the Copyright Office in proper form and registration has been refused, the applicant is entitled to institute a civil action for infringement if notice thereof, with a copy of the complaint, is served on the Register of Copyrights. The Register may, at his or her option, become a party to the action with respect to the issue of registrability of the copyright claim..."

5. Fourth Estate asserts that, if a copyright owner encounters a lengthy delay in the Copyright Office, she may be forced to file a mandamus action to compel the Register to rule on her application, the very problem exposed in *Vacheron & Constantin-Le Coultre Watches, Inc. v. Benrus Watch Co.*, 260 F. 2d 637(C. A. 2 1958), see *supra*, at 890. But Congress' answer to *Vacheron*, codified in § 411(a)'s second sentence, was to permit an infringement suit upon refusal of registration, not to eliminate Copyright Office action as the trigger for an infringement suit.

6. Further, in addition to the Act's provisions for preregistration suit, the Copyright Office al-

lows copyright claimants to seek expedited processing of a claim for an additional $800 fee. See U. S. Copyright Office, Special Handling: Circular No. 10, pp. 1-2(2017). The Copyright Office grants requests for special handling in situations involving, *inter alia*, "[p]ending or prospective litigation," and "make[s] every attempt to examine the application…within five working days." Compendium of U. S. Copyright Practices § 623. 2, 623. 4(3d ed. 2017).

里米尼街公司等（上诉人）

甲骨文美国公司等

第 17-1625 号
开庭日期：2019 年 1 月 14 日
裁决日期：2019 年 3 月 4 日

案情摘要与裁判要旨

陪审团在认定里米尼街公司（Rimini Street）侵犯甲骨文公司（Oracle）多项版权后，判决被告支付赔偿金。紧接着，地区法院也判决被告负担费用，包括1280万美元的诉讼费用（含专家证人费、电子取证费、陪审团咨询费）。第九巡回上诉法院维持了1280万美元诉讼费用的判决，认为该费用包含了联邦法律涉及费用的一般性条款（《美国法典》第28卷第1821条和第1920条）所准予地区法院支持的六类费用之外的费用。尽管如此，联邦第九巡回上诉法院认为上述赔偿金额是恰当的，理由是《版权法案》赋予了地区法院判决赔偿版权纠纷胜诉方"全部费用"的自由裁量权。里米尼街公司上诉至联邦最高法院。联邦最高法院批准了调卷令状申请，以消除各上诉法院关于《版权法案》第505条所用"全部费用"一词解释的分歧。

甲骨文公司基于三种理由，认为其包含专家证人费、电子取证费、陪审团咨询费的1280万美元诉讼费用主张是合理的：首先，甲骨文公司称，"全部"一词授权法院要求败诉方负担第1821条和第1920条所列项目之外的费用；其次，甲骨文公司主张《版权法案》中"全部费用"一词为历史术语，意思多于第1821条和第1920条所列内容；最后，甲骨文公司抛出了种种冗余说辞。

甲骨文公司抛出的上述理由，联邦最高法院均不予认同，认为《版权法案》第505条之"全部费用"一词应限于规制费用的一般性条款（《美国法典》第28卷1821条和第1920

条）所规定的六项费用。联邦第九巡回上诉法院的判决被部分推翻,并发回重审。

卡瓦纳大法官发表了判决意见,其他大法官一致赞同。

*875《版权法案》赋予地区法院在版权纠纷中支持胜诉方"全部费用"的自由裁量权*876（《美国法典》第 17 卷第 505 条）。在规范"费用"的一般制定法中，国会明确了六项诉讼费用属于应赔偿的费用（《美国法典》第 28 卷第 1821 条、第 1920 条）。本案的争议在于，《版权法案》所指"全部费用"能否包含国会在一般法中明确的六项诉讼费用之外的费用。根据相关制定法和本法院判例，答案是否定的。"全部"一词是表达数量用词，并不能将"费用"的外延拓展至一般法所列费用类型之外。在版权案件中，法院根据第 505 条判决支持的"全部费用"也因此仅限于一般法所列的六种费用类型，具体见第 1821 条和第 1920 条。本法院推翻了联邦第九巡回上诉法院判决中与此相关的内容，并将案件发回，要求联邦第九巡回上诉法院按本观点进一步审理。甲骨文公司开发并许可他人使用面向企业和非营利组织的数据及运行管理软件。同时，甲骨文公司还向客户提供软件支持服务。

里米尼街公司向甲骨文公司的客户提供第三方软件支持服务，该业务导致里米尼街公司与甲骨文公司形成竞争关系。

甲骨文公司在内华达州的联邦地区法院起诉里米尼街公司及其首席执行官，并根据《版权法案》及多个其他联邦及州法律提出索赔要求。甲骨文公司诉称，里米尼街公司在向甲骨文公司客户提供软件支持服务的过程中，未经许可复制了甲骨文公司的软件。

一陪审团认定里米尼街公司侵犯了甲骨文公司多项版权，并且里米尼街公司及其首席执行官都违反了加利福尼亚州和内华达州计算机访问法案。陪审团要求里米尼街公司就版权侵权及违反州计算机访问法案分别赔偿甲骨文公司 3560 万美元和 1440 万美元。紧接着，地区法院命令被告向甲骨文公司额外支付 2850 万美元的律师费和 495 万美元的费用，后上诉法院将后者缩减至 340 万美元。地区法院还要求被告支付 1280 万美元的诉讼费用，涵盖专家证人费、电子取证费和陪审团咨询费。

本案争议的问题是这笔 1280 万美元的诉讼费用。就此问题，联邦第九巡回上诉法院维持了这笔费用的裁决。该院注意到，授权地区法院判决败诉方赔偿胜诉方费用的《美国法典》第 28 卷第 1821 条和第 1920 条只列出了六类费用，并且也承认这笔 1280 万美元的诉讼费用并不在所述六类费用之列。但遵从上诉法院之前的判例，联邦第九巡回上诉法院认为这笔额外费用仍旧是合理的，原因是《版权法案》第505条允许法院判决赔偿"全部费用"。在联邦第九巡回上诉法院看来，"全部费用"并不局限于第1821条和第1920条确定的六类费用［《联邦上诉法院判例汇编·第三辑》第879卷，第965-966页（2018判决）］。

本法院批准了调卷令状申请，以消除各上诉法院关于《版权法案》第505条"全部费用"一词是否意味着法院有权判决支持第1821条和第1920条确定的六类费用之外的费用的分歧。参见《美国判例汇编》第585卷——；《最高法院判例汇编》第139卷，起始页52；《美国判例汇编律师版·第二辑》第201卷，起始页1130（2018年判决）。对比《联邦上诉法院判例汇编·第三辑》第879卷，引证页965-966；*Twentieth Century Fox Film Corp. v. Entertainment Distributing* 案，《联邦上诉法院判例汇编·第三辑》第429卷，起始页869（联邦第九巡回上诉法院，2005年判决）；和 *877 Artisan Contractors Assn. of Am. ,Inc. v. Frontier Ins. Co.* 案，《联邦上诉法院判例汇编·第三辑》第275卷，起始页1038（联邦第十一巡回上诉法院，2001年判决）；*Pinkham v. Camex ,Inc.* 案，《联邦上诉法院判例汇编·第三辑》第84卷，起始页292（联邦第八巡回上诉法院1996年判决）。

II

A

国会在先后制定的两百多部不同主题的联邦法案中，明确授权法院判决案件败诉方负担胜诉方诉讼费用，《版权法案》是其中之一。该法案规定，地区法院审理版权案件时，"可视案情允许一方或向一方（不包括美国政府或其官员）主张全部费用"（《美国法典》第17卷第505条）。

作为规范"费用"的一般法，《美国法典》第28卷1821条和第1920条确定了六类联邦法院可以判决支持的费用，并且国会还详细规定了特定费用的具体计算方法。第1821条和第1920条从根本上划定了在具体主题的联邦法案中"费用"的边界。

第 1821 条和第 1920 条确立了一项默认规则，也设定了国会立法的基准。遵从这一基本规则，一些联邦法案中仅使用"费用"一词。在此类案件中，联邦法院只能在第 1821 条和第 1920 条规定的六类费用范围内要求败诉方负担费用。国会也有权准予法院在某类案件中判决败诉方承担一般法中六类之外的费用。例如，某些联邦法案就超越了第 1821 条和第 1920 条的限制，明确规定了专家证人费或律师费。参见 West Virginia Univ. Hospitals, Inc. v. Casey 案，《美国判例汇编》第 499 卷，起始页 83，引证页 89 及脚注 4；《最高法院判例汇编》第 111 卷，起始页 1138；《美国判例汇编律师版·第二辑》第 113 卷，起始页 68（1991 年判决）。事实上，《版权法案》明确规定了律师费和费用（《美国法典》第 17 卷第 505 条）。修订 1976 年《版权法案》的同届国会还在制定的其他几部法案中明确支持律师费（见 Casey 案，《美国判例汇编》第 499 卷，引证页 88；《最高法院判例汇编》第 111 卷，起始页 1138）。但没有明确授权，法院不得判决支持第 1821 条和第 1920 条未列之费用。

本法院判例一直秉承这一态度，三个案件可以佐证。

在 Crawford Fitting Co. v. J. T. Gibbons, Inc. 案中，争议问题是法院能否依据《联邦民事程序规则》第 54 条（d）款支持专家证人费的主张。第 54 条（d）款授权法院判决支持"费用"，但未明确提及专家证人费。参见《美国判例汇编》第 482 卷，起始页 437，引证页 441；《最高法院判例汇编》第 107 卷，起始页 2494；《美国判例汇编律师版·第二辑》第 96 卷，起始页 385（1987 年判决）。在定义哪些花费称得上"费用"时，《美国法典》第 28 卷第 1821 条和第 1920 条同样也未包括专家证人费。本法院因此决定不支持胜诉方专家证人费的主张——当胜诉方寻求法院支持其专家证人费的主张时，联邦法院应遵守《美国法典》第 28 卷第 1821 条（b）款，除非合同或制定法另有明确相反的约定或规定。

《美国法典》第 42 编第 1988 条授权法院在民事诉讼中判决支持"费用"主张，本法院在 Casey 案中对该条进行了解释。在 Casey 案中，本法院认为，Crawford Fitting 案"阐明《美国法典》第 28 卷第 1821 条和第 1920 条已划定联邦法院可以判决败诉方负担的诉讼费用的全部，除非另有明确的制定法授权"（《美国判例汇编》第 499 卷，引证页 86，《最高法院判例汇编》第 111 卷，起始页 1138）。遵从 Crawford Fitting 案，本法院在 Casey 案的结论是第 1988 条并未授权法院判决败诉方负担专家证人费，因为第 1988 条并未就专家证人费给出"明确的制定法授权"。

在 Arlington Central School Dist. Bd. of Ed. v. Murphy 案，本法院考虑了允许法院判决支持费用的《残障人士教育法案》。该案争议的问题在于，《残障人士教育法案》所指"费用"是否包含专家证人费。本法院再次解释，"费用"一词"一般并不包含专家证人费"。参见《美国判例汇编》第 548 卷，起始页 291，引证页 297；《最高法院判例汇编》第 126 卷，起始页 2455；《美国判例汇编律师版·第二辑》第 165 卷，起始页 526（2006 年判决）。同样见 Taniguchi v. Kan Pacific Saipan, Ltd. 案［《美国判例汇编》第 566 卷，起始页 560，引证页 573；《最高法院判例汇编》第 132 卷，起始页 1997；《美国判例汇编律师版·第二辑》第 182 卷，起始页 903（2012 年判决）］，本法院明确："除非一部制定法明确提及证人费，否则不得视为该制定法同意要求败诉方负担证人费。"（Murphy 案，《美国判例汇编》第 548 卷，引证页 301；《最高法院判例汇编》第 126 卷，起始页 2455，引用自 Crawford Fitting 案，《美国判例汇编》第 482 卷，引证页 445；《最高法院判例汇编》第 107 卷，起始页 2494）。

总结来看，本法院的判例确立了一个清晰的原则：制定法允许判决支持"费用"并不能理解为授权法院要求败诉方负担第 1821 条和第 1920 条规定的六类之外的费用，除非有明确相反的制定法规定，见 Murphy 案（《美国判例汇编》第 548 卷，引证页 301；《最高法院判例汇编》第 126 卷，起始页 2455：要求"明确"授权）、Casey 案（《美国判例汇编》第 499 卷，引证页 86；《最高法院判例汇编》第 111 卷，起始页 1138：要求"明确"授权）和 Crawford Fitting 案（《美国判例汇编》第 482 卷，引证页 439；《最高法院判例汇编》第 107 卷，起始页 2494：要求"明确制定法授权"）。

本案中，《版权法案》并未明确授权法院判决支持第 1821 条和第 1920 条所列六类之外的诉讼费用，第 1821 条和第 1920 条也并未明确授权法院支持专家证人费、电子取证费和陪审团咨询费。这些费用被包括在地区法院要求败诉方向甲骨文公司负担的 1280 万美元的诉讼费用中，里米尼街公司因此认为这笔诉讼费用不合理。

B

甲骨文公司为支持其 1280 万美元费用的主张，提出三个主要论点，但本法院最终认为这些论点均缺乏说服力。

第一，尽管甲骨文公司承认，如果《版权法案》仅使用"费用"一词，自己便会输掉诉讼，但强调《版权法案》在"费用"前面加了"全部"一词。甲骨文公司辩称，"全部"一词授权法院判决败诉方负担第 1821 条和第 1920 条六项之外的费用。对此，本法院不予赞同。"全部"一词为形容数量的用词，描述的是所修饰名词的全部量度。参见《美国传统词典》第 709 页（2011 年第五版）、《牛津英语词典》第 247 页（1989 年第二版）。本法院在之前的判决中解释过，该词"作为形容词、修饰名词，是要从一个大类里挑选出具有一定特征的子类"。参见 *Weyerhaeuser Co. v. United States Fish and Wildlife Serv.* 案，《美国判例汇编》第 586 卷，——，——；《最高法院判例汇编》第 139 卷，起始页 361，引证页 368；《美国判例汇编律师版·第二辑》第 202 卷，起始页 269（2018 年判决）。

因此《版权法案》第 505 条中的形容词"全部"并未改变 *879 "费用"一词的本义。相反，"全部费用"指的是相关制定法支持的所有"费用"。"全部费用"中的"全部"（full）与该词在其他常见短语中的用法无异："满月"（full moon）指的是月亮，而不是火星；"全套早餐"（full breakfast）指的是早餐而非午餐；"全季票套餐"（full season ticket plan）指的是门票而非热狗。同理，"全部费用"指的是"费用"，而非其他花费。

因此，这里的争议取决于"费用"的含义。之前解释过，"费用"一词指费用相关联邦制定法（具体指第 1821 条和第 1920 条）所涉及的费用，"全部费用"也应指联邦制定法所规定的全部费用。

第二，甲骨文公司主张《版权法案》中的"全部费用"一词是历史概念，包含的意思多于第 1821 条和第 1920 条列举的内容。对此，本法院同样不赞成。

一些背景知识：从 1789 年到 1853 年，联邦法院判决支持费用的依据是诉讼地相关的州法律。参见 *Crawford Fitting* 案，《美国判例汇编》第 482

卷，引证页 439-440；《最高法院判例汇编》第 107 卷，起始页 2494。*Alyeska Pipeline Service Co. v. Wilderness Society* 案，《美国判例汇编》第 421 卷，起始页 240，引证页 247-250；《最高法院判例汇编》第 95 卷，起始页 1612；《美国判例汇编律师版·第二辑》第 44 卷，起始页 141（1975 年判决）。1853 年，国会改变了遵从州法律的做法。同年，国会通过并经总统菲尔莫尔签署生效了内容广泛的联邦法案，确定了联邦法院可以判决支持的费用项目（*Crawford Fitting* 案，《美国判例汇编》第 482 卷，引证页 440；《最高法院判例汇编》第 107 卷，起始页 2494；《美国制定法大全》第 10 卷，第 161 页）。该法案即 1853 年《费用法案》，其内容"延续至今"，成为第 1821 条和第 1920 条，"核心规则未显现出任何明显变化"（*Crawford Fitting* 案，《美国判例汇编》第 482 卷，引证页 440；《最高法院判例汇编》第 107 卷，起始页 2494）。本法院已经说过，第 1821 条和第 1920 条为联邦法院确立了内容全面的费用支持清单。

现在再补充一些版权法背景知识。"全部费用"一词出现在英国第一部版权方面的制定法中，即 1710 年《安妮法案》（安娜女王即位第八年通过的第 19 部法案，第 8 条）。在美国，1831 年《版权法案》借用了英国版权法中的表述，并同样使用了"全部费用"这一术语（1831 年 2 月 3 日法案第 12 条，《美国制定法大全》第 4 卷，第 438-439 页）。该术语出现在版权法案之后的每一次修订中，包括 1976 年最新一次实质性修订版本中（见 1870 年 7 月 8 日法案第 108 条，《美国制定法大全》第 16 卷，第 215 页；1909 年《版权法案》40 条，《美国制定法大全》第 35 卷，第 1084 页；1976 年《版权法案》第 505 条，《美国制定法大全》第 90 卷，第 2586 页）。

甲骨文公司辩称，英国版权制定法之"全部费用"允许法官判决败诉方负担全部诉讼费用，内容多于任何制定法中关于费用的项目。在甲骨文公司看来，国会在 1831 年《版权法案》中从英国法借用"全部费用"一词时一定是承袭了这一意思，并且 1831 年《版权法案》中"全部费用"的含义统领国会 1853 年及之后的所有规范费用的相关法案。

首先，本法院在 *Crawford Fitting* 案中解释过，在解读费用相关制定法含义时，法院不应开展详尽的历史调查，并且无论涉及费用的特定主题法案是何时制定的，均应执行第 1821 条和第 1920 条（《美国判例汇编》第 482

卷，引证页 445；《最高法院判例汇编》第 107 卷，起始页 2494）。*Crawford Fitting* 案确立的规则意味着无需进行此类历史调查，并确认《版权法案》所指"全部费用"必须参照第 1821 条和第 1920 条解读。

无论如何，甲骨文公司的历史概念主张本身就难以自圆其说。甲骨文公司未能说服本法院，让本法院认为自 1831 年以来，"全部费用"在英国法或美国 *880 法中的确切含义广于费用相关制定法中列举的全部项目。相反，自 1831 年起，联邦法院是根据相关州法律规定的费用项目来判决费用承担的（同上，引证页 439-440，《最高法院判例汇编》第 107 卷，起始页 2494；*Alyeska Pipeline* 案，《美国判例汇编》第 421 卷，引证页 250；《最高法院判例汇编》第 95 卷，起始页 1612）。彼时的州法律倾向于使用"全部费用"一词，以区别于当时州法律中普遍存在的一半费用、两倍费用或三倍费用等。这一用法与该短语的日常意思并无二致。当时的"全部"一词与今日意思相同，即"完全，全部，非残缺的或部分的"。参见诺亚·韦伯斯特《美国英语词典》第一版第 89 页（1828 年）；同时见塞缪尔·约翰逊《英语词典》第一版第 817 页（1773 年）："完全的，以至于不再想要或缺乏任何；完全，没有减损；在最高程度"。在当时，全部费用不包括州法律规定项目以外的费用。

不仅如此，1831 年以来的判例法也同样反驳了甲骨文公司的历史解读。如果甲骨文公司的历史描绘是正确的，那么联邦法院自 1831 年以来就应该会要求败诉方负担多于当时相关制定法规定的费用类型。但里米尼街公司指出，1831 年（即"全部费用"一词首次出现在《版权法案》之年）至 1976 年（即《版权法案》最后一次实质性修订之年）的 800 多个版权裁决中，无一例要求败诉方负担相关州或联邦法律所列费用项目之外的费用类型（口头辩论笔录第 7 页）。对此主张，甲骨文公司并未予以反驳。与《版权法案》第 505 条相关的诸多判例中，除了 2005 年联邦第九巡回上诉法院的 *Twentieth Century Fox* 案（《联邦上诉法院判例汇编·第三辑》第 429 卷，起始页 869），甲骨文公司也未能引述其他任何判决支持专家证人费或本案其他争议费用的案例。联邦第九巡回上诉法院在本纠纷中的判决遵循的就是上述案例。

鉴于自 1831 年以来"全部费用"术语的一般含义以及 1831 年以来的

判例,甲骨文公司的历史解读难以令人信服。"全部费用"的含义最科学的解读方式是自 1831 年至今未有变化,即指相关费用制定法中列明的全部费用。

第三,甲骨文公司抛出了种种冗余说法。该公司辩称,如果里米尼街公司的说法成立,那么"全部"在短语中就纯粹成了冗余词。本法院不予赞同。自 1831 年至 1976 年,败诉方负担费用是强制的(见第 40 条,《美国制定法大全》第 35 卷,第 1084 页;第 12 条,《美国制定法大全》第 4 卷,第 438-439 页)。在此期间,"全部"一词同时确定了法院判决败诉方负担费用的下限和上限。换言之,"全部费用"规则要求法院判定败诉方负担相关法律支持的全部费用。

甲骨文公司声称,对"全部费用"的这一解读即便在 1976 年以前说得通,在 1976 年以后其含义也发生了变化。在这一年,国会修订了《版权法案》,使得费用救济从"强制"变为法院可自由裁量的内容(第 505 条,《美国制定法大全》第 90 卷,第 2586 页)。甲骨文公司认为,在国会允许法院自由裁量费用之后,地区法院有权要求败诉方负担最高 *881 100% 的费用,因此里米尼街公司对"全部"一词的解读意味着"费用"一词即便前面增加"全部"一词也未发生变化。甲骨文公司据此认为,如果假定 1976 年国会所用"全部"一词并非冗余词,那么国会一定是借此表达第 1821 条和第 1920 条所列费用项目之外的费用之意。

因为诸多原因,本法院并不认可这一主张。

首先,即便 1976 年后"全部"一词的含义缺乏延续性,"费用"的含义也从未发生变化。"费用"依然是指第 1821 条和第 1920 条所列诸项费用。很难想象国会 1976 年修订法律将费用的裁决由强制变为法院自由裁量时,会悄无声息地增加法院判决版权诉讼败诉方负担费用的种类。

其次,甲骨文公司的解读本身也会使《版权法案》第 505 条第二句(涵盖律师费)变得明显冗余。该条第二句为:"除非本编另有规定,法院可以再要求败诉方向胜诉方支付合理的律师费,作为费用的一部分。"参见《美国法典》第 17 卷第 505 条。如果甲骨文公司关于"全部费用"涵盖所有诉讼花费的主张是正确的,那么第 505 条第一句就应视为已涵盖律师费,进而第二句就变得明显冗余。为了避免冗余,甲骨文公司的解读产生了新

英美最高法院版权裁判文书选译（2010—2020）

的冗余。

最后，即便甲骨文公司关于"全部"一词因1976年版权法修订而变得无关紧要或冗余的主张是正确的，甲骨文公司也过分强调了法条冗余的影响。冗余并非庭辨高招。本法院已指出，在规范费用的制定法中，"冗余并不鲜见"。参见 Marx v. General Revenue Corp. 案，《美国判例汇编》第568卷，起始页371，引证页385；《最高法院判例汇编》第133卷，起始页1166；《美国判例汇编律师版·第二辑》第185卷，起始页242（2013年判决）。如果对制定法的某种解释会产生冗余，而另一种解释会避免冗余，那么两种解释之间的差异反倒可以给更好地解释制定法提供线索，但也仅仅是线索而已。有时候对制定法更好、更全面的阐释是需要承认冗余存在的。

……

《版权法案》授权联邦法院判决支持版权诉讼一方的"全部费用"。该短语意指规范费用的一般法——第1821条和第1920条——所列费用诸项目。本法院推翻联邦第九巡回上诉法院判决中与此相关的内容，并将此案发回，要求联邦第九巡回上诉法院按本观点继续审理。

兹判决如上。

RIMINI STREET, INC., et al., Petitioners v.

ORACLE USA, INC., et al.

No. 17-1625

Argued January 14, 2019

Decided March 4, 2019

https://www.supremecourt.gov/opinions/18pdf/17-1625_lkhn.pdf

*875 The Copyright Act gives federal district courts discretion to award "full costs" to a party in copyright litigation. *876 17 U.S.C. § 505. In the general statute governing awards of costs, Congress has specified six categories of litigation expenses that qualify as "costs." See 28 U.S.C. §§ 1821,1920. The question presented in this case is whether the Copyright Act's reference to "full costs" authorizes a court to award litigation expenses beyond the six categories of "costs" specified by Congress in the general costs statute. The statutory text and our precedents establish that the answer is no. The term "full" is a term of quantity or amount; it does not expand the categories or kinds of expenses that may be awarded as "costs" under the general costs statute. In copyright cases, § 505's authorization for the award of "full costs" therefore covers only the six categories specified in the general costs statute, codified at §§ 1821 and 1920. We reverse in relevant part the judgment of the U.S. Court of Appeals for the Ninth Circuit, and we remand the case for further proceedings consistent with this opinion. Oracle develops and licenses software programs that manage data and operations for businesses and non-profit organizations. Oracle also offers its customers software maintenance services.

Rimini Street sells third-party software maintenance services to Oracle customers. In doing so, Rimini competes with Oracle's software maintenance services.

Oracle sued Rimini and its CEO in Federal District Court in Nevada, asserting claims under the Copyright Act and various other federal and state laws. Oracle alleged that Rimini, in the course of providing software support services to Oracle customers, copied Oracle's software without licensing it.

A jury found that Rimini had infringed various Oracle copyrights and that both Rimini and its CEO had violated California and Nevada computer access statutes. The jury awarded Oracle $35.6 million in damages for copyright infringement and $14.4 million in damages for violations of the state computer access statutes. After judgment, the District Court ordered the defendants to pay Oracle an additional $28.5 million in attorney's fees and $4.95 million in costs; the Court of Appeals reduced the latter award to $3.4 million. The District Court also ordered the defendants to pay Oracle $12.8 million for litigation expenses such as expert witnesses, e-discovery, and jury consulting.

That $12.8 million award is the subject of the dispute in this case. As relevant here, the U. S. Court of Appeals for the Ninth Circuit affirmed the District Court's $12. 8 million award. The Court of Appeals recognized that the general federal statute authorizing district courts to award costs, 28 U. S. C. §§ 1821 and 1920, lists only six categories of costs that may be awarded against the losing party. And the Court of Appeals acknowledged that the $12. 8 million award covered expenses not included within those six categories. But the Court of Appeals, relying on Circuit precedent, held that the District Court's $12. 8 million award for additional expenses was still appropriate because § 505 permits the award of "full costs," a term that the Ninth Circuit said was not confined to the six categories identified in §§ 1821 and 1920. 879 F. 3d 948,965-966(2018).

We granted certiorari to resolve disagreement in the Courts of Appeals over whether the term "full costs" in § 505 authorizes awards of expenses other than those costs identified in §§ 1821 and 1920. 585 U. S. ----, 139 S. Ct. 52, 201 L. Ed. 2d 1130(2018). Compare 879 F. 3d at 965-966; *Twentieth Century Fox Film Corp. v. Entertainment Distributing*, 429 F. 3d 869(C. A. 9 2005), with ★877 *Artisan Contractors Assn. of Am. , Inc. v. Frontier Ins. Co.* , 275 F. 3d 1038(C. A. 11 2001); *Pinkham v. Camex, Inc.* , 84 F. 3d 292(C. A. 8 1996).

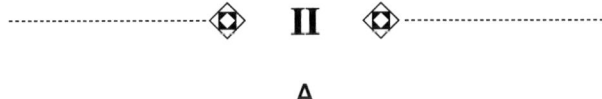

II

A

Congress has enacted more than 200 subject-specific federal statutes that explicitly authorize the award of costs to prevailing parties in litigation. The Copyright Act is one of those statutes. That Act provides that a district court in a copyright case "in its discretion may allow the recovery of full costs by or against any party other than the United States or an officer thereof. " 17 U. S. C. § 505.

In the general "costs" statute, codified at §§ 1821 and 1920 of Title 28, Congress has specified six categories of litigation expenses that a federal court may award as "costs," [1] and Congress has detailed how to calculate the amount of certain costs. Sections 1821 and 1920 in essence define what the term "costs" encompasses in the subject-specific federal statutes that provide for an award of costs.

Sections 1821 and 1920 create a default rule and establish a clear baseline against which Congress may legislate. Consistent with that default rule, some federal statutes simply refer to "costs." In those cases, federal courts are limited to awarding the costs specified in §§ 1821 and 1920. If, for particular kinds of cases, Congress wants to authorize awards of expenses beyond the six categories specified in the general costs statute, Congress may do so. For example, some federal statutes go beyond §§ 1821 and 1920 to expressly provide for the award of expert witness fees or attorney's fees. See *West Virginia Univ. Hospitals, Inc. v. Casey*, 499 U. S. 83, 89, n. 4, 111 S. Ct. 1138, 113 L. Ed. 2d 68 (1991). Indeed, the Copyright Act expressly provides for awards of attorney's fees as well as costs. 17 U. S. C. § 505. And the same Congress that enacted amendments to the Copyright Act in 1976 enacted several other statutes that expressly authorized awards of expert witness fees. See *Casey*, 499 U. S. at 88, 111 S. Ct. 1138. But absent such express authority, courts may not award litigation expenses that are not specified in §§ 1821 and 1920.

Our precedents have consistently adhered to that approach. Three cases illustrate the point.

In *Crawford Fitting Co. v. J. T. Gibbons, Inc.*, the question was whether courts could award expert witness fees under Rule 54(d) of the Federal Rules of Civil Procedure. Rule 54(d) authorizes an award of "costs" but does not expressly refer to expert witness fees. 482 U. S. 437, 441, 107 S. Ct. 2494, 96 L. Ed. 2d 385 (1987). In defining what expenses qualify as "costs," §§ 1821 and 1920 likewise do not include expert witness fees. We therefore held that the prevailing party could not obtain *878 expert witness fees: When "a prevailing party seeks reimbursement for fees paid to its own expert witnesses, a federal court is bound by the limit of §1821(b), absent contract or explicit statutory authority to the contrary." *Id.*, at 439, 107 S. Ct. 2494.

In *Casey*, we interpreted 42 U. S. C. § 1988, the federal statute authorizing an award of "costs" in civil rights litigation. We described *Crawford Fitting* as holding that §§ 1821 and 1920 "define the full extent of a federal court's power to shift litigation costs absent express statutory authority to go further." 499 U. S. at 86, 111 S. Ct. 1138. In accord with *Crawford Fitting*, we concluded that §1988 does not authorize awards of expert witness fees because §1988 supplies no "'explicit statutory authority' " to award expert witness fees. 499 U. S. at 87, 111 S. Ct. 1138 (quoting *Crawford Fitting*, 482 U. S. at 439, 107 S. Ct. 2494).

In *Arlington Central School Dist. Bd. of Ed.* v. *Murphy*, we considered the Individuals with Disabilities Education Act, which authorized an award of costs. The question was whether that Act's reference to "costs" encompassed expert witness fees. We again explained that "costs" is " 'a term of art that generally does not include expert fees. ' "548 U. S. 291, 297, 126 S. Ct. 2455, 165 L. Ed. 2d 526 (2006); see also *Taniguchi v. Kan Pacific Saipan, Ltd.* , 566 U. S. 560, 573, 132 S. Ct. 1997, 182 L. Ed. 2d 903 (2012). We stated: "[N]o statute will be construed as authorizing the taxation of witness fees as costs unless the statute 'refer[s] explicitly to witness fees. ' "*Murphy*, 548 U. S. at 301, 126 S. Ct. 2455 (quoting *Crawford Fitting*, 482 U. S. at 445, 107 S. Ct. 2494).

Our cases, in sum, establish a clear rule: A statute awarding "costs" will not be construed as authorizing an award of litigation expenses beyond the six categories listed in § § 1821 and 1920, absent an explicit statutory instruction to that effect. See *Murphy*, 548 U. S. at 301, 126 S. Ct. 2455 (requiring " 'explici[t]' " authority); *Casey*, 499 U. S. at 86, 111 S. Ct. 1138 (requiring " 'explicit' " authority); *Crawford Fitting*, 482 U. S. at 439, 107 S. Ct. 2494 (requiring "explicit statutory authority").

Here, the Copyright Act does not explicitly authorize the award of litigation expenses beyond the six categories specified in § § 1821 and 1920. And § § 1821 and 1920 in turn do not authorize an award for expenses such as expert witness fees, e-discovery expenses, and jury consultant fees, which were expenses encompassed by the District Court's $12. 8 million award to Oracle here. Rimini argues that the $12. 8 million award therefore cannot stand.

B

To sustain its $12. 8 million award, Oracle advances three substantial arguments. But we ultimately do not find those arguments persuasive.

First, although Oracle concedes that it would lose this case if the Copyright Act referred only to "costs," Oracle stresses that the Copyright Act uses the word "full" before "costs." Oracle argues that the word "full" authorizes courts to award expenses beyond the costs specified in §§ 1821 and 1920. We disagree. "Full" is a term of quantity or amount. It is an adjective that means the complete measure of the noun it modifies. See American Heritage Dictionary 709(5th ed. 2011); Oxford English Dictionary 247(2d ed. 1989). As we said earlier this Term: "Adjectives modify nouns—they pick out a subset of a category that possesses a certain quality." *Weyerhaeuser Co.* v. *United States Fish and Wildlife Serv.*, 586 U. S. --,--, 139 S. Ct. 361, 368, 202 L. Ed. 2d 269(2018).

The adjective "full" in § 505 therefore does not alter the meaning of the word *879 "costs." Rather, "full costs" are all the "costs" otherwise available under law. The word "full" operates in the phrase "full costs" just as it operates in other common phrases: A "full moon" means the moon, not Mars. A "full breakfast" means breakfast, not lunch. A "full season ticket plan" means tickets, not hot dogs. So too, the term "full costs" means *costs*, not other expenses.

The dispute here, therefore, turns on the meaning of the word "costs." And as we have explained, the term "costs" refers to the costs generally available under the federal costs statute—§§ 1821 and 1920. "Full costs" are all the costs generally available under that statute.

Second, Oracle maintains that the term "full costs" in the Copyright Act is a historical term of art that encompasses more than the "costs" listed in the relevant costs statute—here, §§ 1821 and 1920. We again disagree.

Some general background: From 1789 to 1853, federal courts awarded costs and fees according to the relevant state law of the forum State. See *Crawford Fitting*, 482 U. S. at 439–440, 107 S. Ct. 2494; *Alyeska Pipeline Service Co.* v. *Wilderness Society*, 421 U. S. 240, 247–250, 95 S. Ct. 1612, 44 L. Ed. 2d 141(1975). In 1853, Congress departed from that state-focused approach. That year, Congress passed and President Fillmore signed a comprehensive federal statute establishing a federal schedule for the award of costs in federal court. *Crawford Fitting*, 482 U. S. at 440, 107 S. Ct. 2494; 10 Stat. 161. Known as the Fee Act of 1853, that 1853 statute has "carried forward to today" in §§ 1821 and 1920 " 'without any apparent intent to change the controlling rules.' " *Crawford Fitting*, 482 U. S. at 440, 107 S. Ct. 2494. As we have said, §§ 1821 and 1920 provide a comprehensive schedule of costs for proceedings in federal court.

Now some copyright law background: The term "full[c]osts" appeared in the first copyright statute in England, the Statute of Anne. 8 Anne c. 19, § 8(1710). In the United States, the Federal Copyright Act of 1831 borrowed the phrasing of English copyright law and used the same term, "full costs. " Act of Feb. 3, 1831, § 12, 4 Stat. 438–439. That term has appeared in subsequent revisions of the Copyright Act, through the Act's most recent substantive alterations in 1976. See Act of July 8, 1870, § 108, 16 Stat. 215; Copyright Act of 1909, § 40, 35 Stat. 1084; Copyright Act of 1976, § 505, 90 Stat. 2586.

Oracle argues that English copyright statutes awarding "full costs" allowed the transfer of all expenses of litigation, beyond what was specified in any costs schedule. According to Oracle, Congress necessarily imported that meaning of the term "full costs" into the Copyright Act in 1831. And according to Oracle, that 1831 meaning overrides anything that Congress enacted in any costs statute in 1853 or later.

To begin with, our decision in *Crawford Fitting* explained that courts should not undertake extensive historical excavation to determine the meaning of costs statutes. We said that §§ 1821 and 1920 apply regardless of when individual subject-specific costs statutes were enacted. 482 U. S. at 445, 107 S. Ct. 2494. The *Crawford Fitting* principle eliminates the need for that kind of historical analysis and confirms that the Copyright Act's reference to "full costs" must be interpreted by reference to §§ 1821 and 1920.

In any event, Oracle's historical argument fails even on its own terms. Oracle has not persuasively demonstrated that as of 1831, the phrase "full costs" had an established meaning in English or American ✶880 law that covered more than the full amount of the costs listed in the applicable costs schedule. On the contrary, the federal courts as of 1831 awarded costs in accord with the costs schedule of the relevant state law. See *id.* , at 439–440, 107 S. Ct. 2494; *Alyeska Pipeline*, 421 U. S. at 250, 95 S. Ct. 1612. And state laws at the time tended to use the term "full costs" to refer to, among other things, full cost awards as distinguished from the half, double, or treble cost awards that were also commonly available under state law at the time. [2] That usage accorded with the ordinary meaning of the term. At the time, the word "full" conveyed the same meaning that it does today: "Complete;

entire; not defective or partial."1 N. Webster, An American Dictionary of the English Language 89 (1828); see also 1 S. Johnson, A Dictionary of the English Language 817 (1773) ("Complete, such as that nothing further is desired or wanted; Complete without abatement; at the utmost degree"). Full costs did not encompass expenses beyond those costs that otherwise could be awarded under the applicable state law.

The case law since 1831 also refutes Oracle's historical argument. If Oracle's account of the history were correct, federal courts starting in 1831 presumably would have interpreted the term "full costs" in the Copyright Act to allow awards of litigation expenses that were not ordinarily available as costs under the applicable costs schedule. But Rimini points out that none of the more than 800 available copyright decisions awarding costs from 1831 to 1976—that is, from the year the term "full costs" first appeared in the Copyright Act until the year that the Act was last significantly amended—awarded expenses other than those specified by the applicable state or federal law. Tr. of Oral Arg. 7. Oracle has not refuted Rimini's argument on that point. Oracle cites no § 505 cases where federal courts awarded expert witness fees or other litigation expenses of the kind at issue here until the Ninth Circuit's 2005 decision adopting the interpretation of § 505 that the Ninth Circuit followed in this case. See *Twentieth Century Fox*, 429 F. 3d 869.

In light of the commonly understood meaning of the term "full costs" as of 1831 and the case law since 1831, Oracle's historical argument falls short. The best interpretation is that the term "full costs" meant in 1831 what it means now: the full amount of the costs specified by the applicable costs schedule.

Third, Oracle advances a variety of surplusage arguments. Oracle contends, for example, that the word "full" would be unnecessary surplusage if Rimini's argument were correct. We disagree. The award of costs in copyright cases was *mandatory* from 1831 to 1976. See § 40, 35 Stat. 1084; § 12, 4 Stat. 438–439. During that period, the term "full" fixed both a floor and a ceiling for the amount of "costs" that could be awarded. In other words, the term "full costs" required an award of 100 percent of the costs available under the applicable costs schedule.

Oracle says that even if that interpretation of "full costs" made sense before 1976, the meaning of the term "full costs" changed in 1976. That year, Congress amended the Copyright Act to make the award of costs discretionary rather than mandatory. See § 505, 90 Stat. 2586. According to Oracle, after Congress made the costs award discretionary, district courts could award any amount of costs up *881 to 100 percent and so Rimini's reading of the word "full" now adds nothing to "costs." If we assume that Congress in 1976 did not intend "full" to be surplusage, Oracle argues that Congress must have employed the term "full" to mean expenses beyond the costs specified in § § 1821 and 1920.

For several reasons, that argument does not persuade us.

To begin with, even if the term "full" lacked any continuing significance after 1976, the meaning of "costs" did not change. The term "costs" still means those costs specified in § § 1821 and 1920. It makes little sense to think that Congress in 1976, when it made the award of full costs discretionary rather than mandatory, silently expanded the kinds of expenses that a court may otherwise award as costs in copyright suits. [3]

Moreover, Oracle's interpretation would create its own redundancy problem by rendering the second sentence of § 505 largely redundant. That second sentence provides: "Except as otherwise provided by this title, the court may also award a reasonable attorney's fee to the prevailing party as part of the costs." 17 U. S. C. § 505. If Oracle were right that "full costs" covers all of a party's litigation expenditures, then the first sentence of § 505 would presumably already cover attorney's fees and the second sentence would be largely unnecessary. In order to avoid some redundancy, Oracle's interpretation would create other redundancy.

Finally, even if Oracle is correct that the term "full" has become unnecessary or redundant as a result of the 1976 amendment, Oracle overstates the significance of statutory surplusage or redundancy. Redundancy is not a silver bullet. We have recognized that some "redundancy is 'hardly unusual' in statutes addressing costs." *Marx v. General Revenue Corp.*, 568 U. S. 371, 385, 133 S. Ct. 1166, 185 L. Ed. 2d 242(2013). If one possible interpretation of a statute would cause some redundancy and another interpretation would avoid redundancy, that difference in the two interpretations can supply a clue as to the better interpretation of a statute. But only a clue. Sometimes the better overall reading of the statute contains some redundancy.

* * *

The Copyright Act authorizes federal district courts to award "full costs" to a party in copyright litigation. That term means the costs specified in the general costs statute, §§ 1821 and 1920. We reverse in relevant part the judgment of the Court of Appeals, and we remand the case for further proceedings consistent with this opinion.

It is so ordered.

英国最高法院篇

联合王国最高法院 2011 第 39 号案件
对英格兰和威尔士上诉法院 2009 第 1328 号民事案件的上诉

卢卡斯影业有限公司等（上诉人）

安斯沃斯及另一人（被上诉人）

审理人：菲利普斯勋爵 院长
　　　　沃克勋爵
　　　　黑尔女勋爵
　　　　曼斯勋爵
　　　　柯林斯勋爵

裁决日期：2011 年 7 月 27 日
开庭日期：2011 年 3 月 7 日、8 日、9 日

案情摘要与裁判要旨[*]

1997年,首部《星球大战》电影在美国上映。这部电影取得了巨大的商业成功。本上诉涉及电影中所用诸多道具的知识产权,特别是帝国冲锋队的头盔。卢卡斯影业有限公司(以下简称"卢卡斯影业")拥有为《星球大战》系列电影创作的艺术作品的版权。此前,乔治·卢卡斯先生(以下简称"卢卡斯先生")构思了影片的故事情节和人物角色。1974年至1976年,卢卡斯先生构思了身着"法西斯式白色盔甲套装"的帝国冲锋队这一恐怖角色,后由艺术家拉尔夫·麦考瑞先生(以下简称"麦考瑞先生")通过绘画形式从视觉上呈现出来,并由尼克·彭博顿(以下简称"彭博顿先生")和安德鲁·安斯沃斯先生(以下简称"安斯沃斯先生")制作模型。安斯沃斯先生制作了多个真空吸塑头盔原型,待卢卡斯先生认可了头盔的最终版本后,安斯沃斯先生为电影拍摄制作了50个头盔。在2004年,本案第一被上诉人安斯沃斯先生用他最初使用的工具制作了多个帝国冲锋队头盔和盔甲以及其他道具,并向公众出售。

2005年,卢卡斯影业在美国加利福尼亚州中区联邦地方法院起诉安斯沃斯先生。2006年,卢卡斯影业获得了赔偿金额为2000万美元的缺席判决,但判决未得到执行。卢卡斯影业在英国高等法院也提起了诉讼,提出了多项主张,包括版

---

[*] 受篇幅所限,本译文与判决书只提供了第一部分内容。——译者注

权侵权主张、执行美国判决赔偿 1000 万美元的主张,以及根据美国版权法提出的多项主张。2008 年 4 月至 5 月,高等法院开庭审理了此案,驳回了卢卡斯影业所有基于英国版权法的权利主张,并认为,因美国法院不具有对安斯沃斯先生和其公司的属人管辖权,故其判决在英国不予执行。

上诉法院认同高等法院关于美国法院判决在英国不可执行的意见,并认为,头盔中的任何知识产权都应归属于卢卡斯影业。在最高法院,争议的问题为头盔是否为雕塑,以及根据 1988 年《版权、外观设计与专利法案》(以下简称"1988 年法案")第 51 条和第 52 条提出的抗辩是否应予以支持。基于下级法院所给出的理由,最高法院维持他们所作判决的主体部分。

沃克勋爵和柯林斯勋爵撰写判决书,菲利普斯勋爵和黑尔女勋爵持赞同意见。

案件简介

1.1997 年，首部《星球大战》电影（为承接前传和后传，后更名为《星球大战 4：新希望》）在美国上映。这部电影取得了巨大的商业成功，并斩获了奥斯卡最佳服装设计奖。本上诉涉及电影中所用诸多道具的知识产权，其中最重要的是帝国冲锋队的头盔。初审法官（曼恩法官）在判决书｛案号：[2008] EWHC 1878 (Ch)，2009 年《弗利特街判例汇编》，起始页 103，第 2 段和第 121 段｝中提到：

"帝国冲锋队的头盔时常出现在影片镜头中。帝国冲锋队的士兵们身穿白色盔甲，头戴能够遮盖住整个面部的白色头盔……在影片中，头盔是服装整体的一部分，用于区分人物角色并展现该角色的某些特征，如忠诚、力量、威慑力及意志力，在某种程度上也可以避免暴露身份。头盔既是服装，也是道具。"

就本终审上诉而言，当事人均认同，可将头盔视作决定胜诉结果的范式案例。

2. 初审法官的判决书清晰完整地阐明了案件事实，就本上诉而言，只需要简要概括案件事实就足够了。卢卡斯先生构思了影片的故事情节和人物角色。1974 年至 1976 年，卢卡斯先生构思了身着"法西斯式白色盔甲套装"的帝国冲锋队这一恐怖角色，后由艺术家麦考瑞先生通过绘画形式呈现出来，并由（自由美工师兼道具制作人）彭博顿先生和（精于真空吸塑成型技艺的）安斯沃斯先生制作模型。彭博顿先生先用黏土制作了头盔模型，经数次调整后，最终获得卢卡斯先生的认可。安斯沃斯先生则制作了多个真空吸塑头盔原型，待卢卡斯先生认可了头盔的最终版本后，安斯沃斯先生为电影拍摄制作了 50 个头盔。上述事实均发生在英国。尽管卢卡斯先生身在加利福尼亚州，他的公司也位于此，但是电影在埃尔斯特里拍摄时（电影也曾在突尼斯取景），他居住在英国。

3. 第一上诉人系卢卡斯先生名下的一家加利福尼亚公司；第二上诉人系卢卡斯先生名下的一家英国公司；第三上诉人系负责集团许可授权业务的一家加利福尼亚公司，系第一上诉人的全资子公司。这三家公司统称为"卢卡斯影业"，都拥有为《星球大战》系列电影创作的艺术作品的版权。除了《星球大战》系列电影获得巨大商业成功外，卢卡斯影业还成功地操办了许可业务,包括许可帝国冲锋队的道具模型及装备。发生诉讼的原因是,在2004年,本上诉的第一被上诉人安斯沃斯先生用他最初使用的工具制作了多个帝国冲锋队头盔和盔甲以及其他道具(此处无需详述),并向公众出售。第二被上诉人系安斯沃斯先生名下的一家私人公司。为方便起见,可以将安斯沃斯先生视为唯一被上诉人。

4. 安斯沃斯先生在美国出售了他制作的部分成品(总价值介于8000美元至30 000美元)。2005年,卢卡斯影业在美国加利福尼亚州中区联邦地方法院起诉安斯沃斯先生。2006年,卢卡斯影业获得了赔偿金额为2000万美元的缺席判决,其中1000万美元是根据《兰哈姆法案》获得的三倍赔偿。但整个判决未得到执行。卢卡斯影业在英国高等法院大法官庭也提起了诉讼。再次修改后的起诉状根据英国法提出了多项主张,包括:版权侵权主张(救济请求第1段至第10段),执行美国判决赔偿1000万美元的主张(第11段),以及根据美国版权法提出的多项主张(第12段至第17段)。

5. 2008年4月至5月,高等法院开庭审理了此案,审理持续了17天,并于2008年7月31日宣读判决。曼恩法官驳回了卢卡斯影业所有基于英国版权法的权利主张(以及其他一些本次终审上诉不再提出的权利主张)。曼恩法官认为,安斯沃斯先生制作的头盔是对麦考瑞先生及其他卢卡斯影业工作人员原创作品的实质性复制。但因为头盔并非雕塑,并且安斯沃斯先生根据1988年法案第51条和第52条(针对安斯沃斯先生复制了麦考瑞先生作品的主张)进行抗辩,所以卢卡斯影业基于英国版权法的权利主张未获支持。曼恩法官也未支持安斯沃斯先生在反诉中提出的自己对头盔享有版权的主张。

6. 曼恩法官认为,因美国法院不具有对安斯沃斯先生和其公司的属人管辖权,故其判决在英国不予执行。但他认为,卢卡斯影业的美国版权主张可以在英国法院提起诉讼,并且认为安斯沃斯先生和其公司的确侵犯了卢卡斯影业的权利。

7. 上诉法院{案号:[2009] EWCA Civ 1328,《判例汇编之衡平法庭系列》2010年卷,起始页503}认同曼恩法官关于美国法院判决在英国不可执行的意见,当事人也未就这一点继续上诉。上诉法院也认为,头盔中的任何知识产权都应归属于卢卡斯影业,并且本法院也未允许安斯沃斯先生就这一点进行反上诉。在本法院，争议的问题为头盔是否为雕塑，以及根据1988年法案第51条和第52条提出的抗辩是否应予以支持（关于这些，上诉法院都认同曼恩法官的意见）和在美国的版权主张是否可以在英国起诉（在这一点上，上诉法院并不认同曼恩法官的意见）。根据1988年法案，只有在本案的头盔属于雕塑（进而构成艺术作品）的情况下，才会产生第51条和第52条的问题。在上诉法院，卢卡斯影业放弃了头盔作为工艺美术作品应被视为艺术作品的观点。

第一部分：英国版权法问题

现行制定法规定

8. 本法院在全面了解立法历史的基础上，决定从现行立法，即1988年法案开始讨论。根据1988年法案第1条第（1）款（a）项，版权是一种存在于独创的文学、戏剧、音乐或艺术作品中的财产权。包括电影在内的其他作品，均属于第1条（1）款（b）项和（c）项的范畴。根据第4条（1）款，版权法所称的"艺术作品"是指：

"（a）图形作品、照片、雕塑或拼贴，不论艺术品质如何，

（b）建筑作品，包括建筑物或建筑物模型，或者

（c）工艺美术作品。"

根据第4条（2）款，"雕塑"包括为制作雕塑而做的铸型或模型。

9. 第51条和第52条在1988年法案的第一编第三章（"与版权作品有关的允许行为"）中。第三章包含了基于一般理由的各种免责规定，包括合理使用（第29条至第31条）、教育、存档和其他公共目的（第32条至第50条）。第62条包含对永久公开展示的建筑、雕塑及工艺美术作品的一般性豁免。

10. 修订后的第51条（"外观设计文件和模型"）规定：

"（1）根据外观设计制作物品或者复制根据外观设计所制作的物品的行为，不侵犯外观设计文件或记录、呈现该外观设计之模型的版权，但艺术作品或创作字体之外观设计除外。

（2）将依第（1）款制作的不侵犯版权的任何物品向公众发行、在电影中使用或向公众传播的，也不侵犯版权。

(3) 本条中：

'外观设计'是指对一物品全部或部分形状或构造（不论内部或外部）的任何方面的设计，但不包括表面装饰；

'外观设计文件'是指对外观设计以绘图、文字描述、照片、存贮于电脑的数据或其他方式的任何记录。"

11. 第 52 条（"使用源于艺术作品的外观设计的后果"）规定如下：

"（1）本条适用于版权人或被许可人以下述方式利用艺术作品：

（a）以工业过程制作被本编视为该作品复制件的物品的行为，

（b）在联合王国或其他地方出售上述物品。

（2）自这些物品首次销售的日历年年底起算至 25 年结束后，以制造任何类型物品的方式复制此作品、为制作任何类型物品而实施的任何行为，以及实施与所制作物品相关的任何行为，都不侵犯该作品的版权。

（3）依第（1）款所述方式仅利用部分艺术作品的，第（2）款只适用于该相关部分。

（4）国务大臣可以颁布命令规定：

（a）明确在何种情况下制作一件物品或任何种类物品应视为本条所称的以工业过程制作；

（b）将在他看来主要属于具有文学或艺术特征的物品排除在本条效力范围之外。

（5）国务大臣的此类命令应以行政立法性文件颁布，上议院或下议院可以通过决议废止。

（6）本条：

（a）所称的物品不包括电影；

（b）所称的物品销售包括售卖、租售，或为上述目的做售卖、租售准备。"

12. 保护文学或艺术作品的版权会影响他人自由制造和销售立体物品，这两个条款旨在（以不同方式）对这一影响加以限制。在 *British Leyland Motor Corporation Ltd v. Armstrong Patents Co Ltd* 案（《判例汇编之上诉法院系列》1986 年卷，起始页 577）中，上议院提出了一个激进且富有争议的解决方案，尽管议会当时正在审议后来成为 1988 年法案的议案。相比之下，

第51条提供了更加条理化的解决方案，它适用于外观设计文件或模型的最终产品不属于艺术作品的情形。第52条（除了国务大臣确定的例外情况）适用于艺术作品（在得到版权人许可后）被以工业过程生产复制件并销售的形式利用的情形。

13. 根据1988年法案第52条（4）款制定的1989年《版权（工业过程和除外物品）（第2号）令》（1989年行政立法性文件第1070号，以下称"1989年令"）第2条规定，如果将一件特定艺术作品制作出50个以上的复制件（且它们不属于同一套复制件），那么该复制件应视为是通过工业过程制造。1989年令［在第3条（1）款（a）项］也规定了第52条的例外："雕塑作品，但不包括通过工业过程大量制作，用作或意图用作模型或样式的铸型或模型。"

立法历史：1911年法案之前

14. 只有回顾立法历史，才好理解这些条款，特别是第51条和第52条。但不巧的是，这段立法历史本身就极为复杂。正如布里奇勋爵在 British Leyland 案（《判例汇编之上诉法院系列》1986年卷，起始页577，引证页619）中所描述的那样，1911年《版权法案》（以下简称"1911年法案"）是"制订版权保护综合性法典的第一次尝试"。1911年法案第1条（1）款与1988年法案第1条（1）款（a）项极为相似（除了"不论艺术品质如何"等表述未出现在1911年法案中外），并且它给人的印象是体现了恰如其分的对称原则，为人类各种形式的创作提供平等保护。但任何此类印象都具有误导性。至1911年法案通过之时，始于1709年《版权法案》（以下简称"1709年法案"）的英国版权立法已有两个世纪的历史。大部分时间里，1709年法案主要关注的是保护印刷文字，即出版的文学作品。此外，最初有关文学版权立法的目的是保护印刷书商（早期出版商）和书店的商业利益，并管控未经许可的出版物（且可能是反动出版物），而非维护作者的法律和精神权利。《科平杰和斯科恩·詹姆斯论版权》（2010年第十六版）第2章第8段至第42段，以及康沃尔、卢埃林和阿普林的《知识产权：专利权、版权、商标权及邻接权》（2010年第七版）第10章第1段到第41段，对英国版权立法历史的概括非常有用。

15. 1709年法案保护文学作品、书籍及其他著述。在18世纪，版权保护范围（因制定法）扩大到版画，后又（基于对1709年法案的自由阐释）扩大至音乐和戏剧作品。根据1798年乔治三世颁布的立法（乔治三世即位第38年通过的第71部法案），立体艺术作品被纳入版权保护范围，但由于1798年的法案文本很糟糕，几乎没有提供实际保护［艾伦伯格勋爵在 *Gahagan v. Cooper* 案中的主张，《坎贝尔巡回案例汇编》第3卷，起始页111，引证页113（1811年裁决）："该法案似乎是为了击垮自己设定的目标而制定"］。该法案后被1814年《雕塑版权法案》（以下简称"1814年法案"）所取代。1814年法案在开头用散乱无章的话语来描述受保护作品的类别：

"任何新的、独创的雕塑，或模型，或复制件，或单人像或群像的铸型，或任一半身人像或半身群像的铸型，或人像任一部位或多个部位的铸型，不论是否身着衣物。"

然后法案用更笼统的表达，指出受保护的作品类别为"雕塑创作主题中的任何事物"。雕塑需要留有创作者的姓名和完成日期。直到1862年《美术作品版权保护法案》（以下简称"1862年法案"）的颁布，绘画、图画和照片才得到保护。1862年法案将作品的注册作为版权保护的要件。建筑作品直到1911年法案颁布后才受保护（1911年法案也将"工艺美术作品"引入到第35条"艺术作品"的定义中）。

16. 1814年法案的效力一直持续到1911年法案生效——在此之前，1814年法案依然是唯一给予所有立体作品长时间版权保护的法案。在19世纪，随着机械化大生产的飞速发展，在工业设计师和生产者群体中产生了防止他人抄袭外观设计、实施不正当竞争的明显需求。议会决定设计一项新的权利以进行保护，这项权利被称作"版权"（正如上诉法院在其判决书第24段中所述，以"版权"命名这项新的权利令人感到非常困惑），但它与文学和艺术作品的版权有两点不同：一是，它要求所有者对外观设计进行注册；二是，它的保护期限要比对文学和艺术作品短得多。以上两点也是1839年《外观设计版权法案》所采用方案的本质特征，该法案后来为1842年《外观设计法案》所废止并取代。曾向一些纺织品印花设计授予版权的早期立法，后来因新的注册制度而废止。不过，1814年法案对雕塑的版权保护却得以保留下来。

17. 1850 年《外观设计版权法案》修订了有关已注册外观设计的规则，之后 1883 年《专利、外观设计与商标法案》（以下简称"1883 年法案"）第三编进行了进一步修订和统一，（就 1911 年以前的立法而言）最后经 1907 年《专利和外观设计法案》（以下简称"1907 年法案"）再次修订。这段立法历史的大部分细节与本案无益，但值得注意的是，尽管注册外观设计的保护期限在逐渐延长，但总是要比文学或艺术作品版权的保护期限短得多。此外，由于早期立法对外观设计的保护具有不确定性，雕塑作品的外观设计被排除在立法中"外观设计"一词的范畴之外（见 1883 年法案第 60 条和 1907 年法案第 93 条）。

18. 关于 1814 年法案，仅需提及一项司法裁决，即 Britain v. Hanks Bros & Co 案 [《判例时代汇编》，第 86 卷，起始页 765（1902 年裁决）]。审理本案的赖特法官认为，判例汇编所称的"马背上士兵或骑马随从的金属玩具模型"应作为雕塑受版权保护。该模型由原告企业合伙人威廉·布列登设计制作。判例报道没有提及模型的大小，但很明显，它们的尺寸要大到足以刻上制作者姓名和完成日期。法官采纳的专家证据称，这些玩具模型是"结构比例恰当且展现技术知识与技能的艺术产品"。法官似乎认为，此案中的模型介于可保护与无需保护之间，但法官更倾向于认为模型应受保护。

19. 上诉法院认为，"……很难从此案中得到太多借鉴"（第 59 段）。上诉人案中的一个次要点是，头盔与本法院在 Britain 案中描述的模型一样，都是"制作技艺精湛的模型，设计的目的是吸引收藏家，但也可能会成为收藏家孩子们的玩物"（第 82 段）。

立法历史：自 1911 年法案起

20. 在 George Hensher Ltd v. Restawile Upholstery（Lancs）Ltd 案（《判例汇编之上诉法院系列》1976 年卷，起始页 64，引证页 89-91）中，西蒙勋爵认为，1911 年法案之所以赋予"工艺美术作品"完全的版权保护，还应归功于威廉·莫里斯和约翰·鲁斯金发起的工艺美术运动所带来的影响。西蒙勋爵认为，"工艺美术作品"这一表达系复合短语，必须从整体上理解

（见第 91 页）。此观点最近得到了澳大利亚高等法院判例［*Swarbrick v. Burge* 案，《英联邦判例汇编》第 232 卷，起始页 336（2007 年裁决）］的支持。

21. 1911 年法案第 22 条规定：

"（1）本法案不适用于可以根据 1907 年法案进行注册的外观设计，虽可以根据 1907 年法案注册、但未用作或未打算用作模型或样式供工业过程批量生产的外观设计除外。

（2）1907 年法案第 86 条确立的一般规则，可用来决定在何种条件下一项外观设计应被视为用于前述目的。"

判断是否为工业过程生产的方法（根据到目前仍旧适用的 1920 年《外观设计细则》第 89 条）和 1989 年令中的判断方法（前述第 13 段提到的）相同。

22. 正如怀康特·毛姆在 *King Features Syndicate Inc v. O & M Kleeman Ltd* 案（《判例汇编之上诉法院系列》1941 年卷，起始页 417，引证页 427）中所观察到的，如果第 22 条（1）款重新表述如下，那么该条中双重否定的效果就更容易理解了：

"本法案适用于可以根据 1907 年法案进行注册的外观设计，但该外观设计需未用作或未打算用作通过任何工业过程批量生产的模型或样式。除此例外情形，本法案不适用于可以根据 1907 年法案进行注册的其他外观设计。"

King Features Syndicate Inc v. O & M Kleeman Ltd 案与已出版并享有艺术版权的连环画《大力水手》衍生出来的玩偶有关。该案的主要问题在于，使用工业生产这一意图于何时形成？法官们判定，该意图自始存在。

23. 1919 年《专利与外观设计法案》对 1907 年法案进行了修订，用新定义替换了 1907 年法案第 93 条"外观设计"的定义。新定义提到了"通过任何工业过程"应用的特征，且没有明确将雕塑外观设计规定为例外。1911 年法案第 22 条的表述方式，等于是收回了雕塑作品可以大量生产复制的特权地位，这一影响在 *Pytram Ltd v. Models（Leicester）Ltd* 案（《判例汇编之衡平法庭系列》1930 年第 1 卷，起始页 639）中得以体现。在该案中，童子军协会委托制作一个狼崽头部模型，该模型将被用作模具来批量生产固定在木杆顶部的混凝纸质地模型。克劳森法官驳回了原告认为其拥有原创模型版权的主张。克劳森法官认同该模型是一件雕塑作品,但根据修订后的1907年法案,它不属于不可以注册的外观设计,也不属于第22条(1)款的例外,因为"制作该模型的目的在于使原告能够提供大量的图腾杆"(第647页)。

24. "二战"后,立法又走了回头路。1947年,天鹅委员会建议将雕塑作品再次排除在可注册外观设计之外。1949年《注册外观设计法案》第1条(3)款和(4)款明确将主要性质为文学或艺术的物品排除在可注册外观设计之外。1949年《外观设计细则》(以下简称"1949年法案")(行政立法性文件1949年第2368号)第26条第(1)款排除了"雕塑作品,但不包括通过任何工业过程批量生产的、用作或打算用作模型或样式的铸型或模型"。这种措辞(重现于1989年令中)紧随1911年法案第22条第(1)款的规定,必须要遵从上议院在 *King Features* 案关于该条款的裁决来解读。

25. 1956年《版权法案》(以下简称"1956年法案")废止了1911年法案。1956年法案第10条("关于工业外观设计的特殊例外情况")重申了版权和外观设计权之间的界限,后经1968年《外观设计版权法案》修订,第10条(3)款对包含可以根据1949年法案进行注册的外观设计的任何作品设置了15年版权保护期。但针对根据1949年法案所制定细则排除在外的外观设计,第10条(4)款规定了一项例外,并且现行1989年《注册外观设计细则》第26条照搬了1949年法案第26条。

26. 1956年法案将"不论艺术品质如何"表述引入了第3条(1)款(a)项"艺术作品"的定义中。这看似是1956年法案将地图、图表、平面图从文学作品重新归类为艺术作品的结果,但是这种新的措辞与上述(c)项中"工艺美术作品"的定义相矛盾。在 *Hensher* 案(《判例汇编之上诉法院系列》1976年卷,起始页64,引证页94)中,西蒙勋爵提出的解释可能并不能使人完全信服,但共识是,在法院版权案件中并不会评价文学作品或艺术作品的优劣。

27. 上诉法院从其对立法历史的调查(判决书第21段至第39段)中得出两个一般性结论:第一,从版权和注册外观设计权之间的关系来推断

1988年法案中"雕塑"的含义几乎没有或完全没有帮助（第40段和第41段）；第二，"外观设计"和"艺术作品"是两个不同的概念（第42段和第43段）。除了（1988年法案第三编引入的）未注册外观设计权，外观设计权相关立法关注的是具有视觉吸引力的特征。版权保护则在意一件作品是否落入1988年法案规定的特定作品类型中，"并不取决于对其外观设计特征的进一步分析或识别"。

"雕塑"的含义

28. 曼恩法官和上诉法院都全面回顾了英国及英联邦权威文献中"雕塑"的含义。他们准确地总结道，一些一审决定未能给予他们真正的帮助，因此没有必要再研究这些一审决定。需要讨论的判决（按时间顺序）分别为：新西兰上诉法院 *Wham-O Manufacturing Co v. Lincoln Industries Ltd* 案（1985年《专利、外观设计与商标判例汇编》，起始页127；1984年《新西兰判例汇编》第1卷，起始页641）的判决；福尔克纳法官对 *Breville Europe Plc v. Thorn EMI Domestic Appliances Ltd* 案（1995年《弗利特街判例汇编》，起始页77）的判决；莱迪法官对 *Metix(UK)Ltd v. G H Maughan(Plastics)Ltd* 案（1997年《弗利特街判例汇编》，起始页718）的判决；以及安杰尔法官（在澳北区开庭）对 *Wildash v. Klein* 案（2004年《知识产权判例汇编》第61卷，起始页324）的判决。

29. 在讨论上述四个案件之前，有必要进一步介绍一下上议院 *Hensher* 案（《判例汇编之上诉法院系列》1976年卷，起始页64）的裁决。由于卢卡斯影业不再主张头盔是工艺美术作品，也就没必要过多介绍 *Hensher* 案。曼恩法官相当详细地讨论了该案，提请人们留意识别该裁决背后真正原则的难度。据称，卢卡斯影业放弃上述主张的原因在于，1988年法案第4条（1）款（c）项旨在包含主要目的为功能性的物品，这些物品因此不能被视为雕塑［上诉人书面事实陈述第22条（2）款］。功能性和艺术性的相对意义对本上诉极为重要。尽管 *Hensher* 案的裁决用词很艰涩，但总体倾向于从法律用语的一般含义去理解（见里德勋爵第78页、莫里斯勋爵第81页、迪尔霍恩子爵第86至87页、西蒙勋爵第91页以及吉尔布兰登勋爵第97页），尽管他们在这一原则的具体应用上差异巨大。关于"雕塑"的含义，也需要采用相同的方法去解读。

30. 新西兰上诉法院的 Wham-O 案涉及飞盘（一种因其空气动力特性而用于户外游戏的轻质塑料盘）。林肯在新西兰制作并售卖飞盘，该行为被指控侵犯了威猛奥的外观设计图纸、木质模型、模具及最终模压塑料产品的版权。1962年《新西兰版权法案》的相关条款与1988年法案的相关条款相似但不相同。初审时，穆勒法官认为，木质模型应作为雕塑受版权保护，并且模具和最终产品都是雕刻品。上诉法院维持原判，尽管他们不认为最终产品是雕塑（法官未作阐释）。判决书的大部分内容是分析推理过程，并最终得出了相当令人惊讶的结论：模具和最终产品都是雕刻品。飞盘的木质模型是雕塑且只有木质模型是雕塑这一结论似乎主要是基于这一事实：只有木质模型是手工制作的，而模具和最终产品都是工业生产的。首席大法官戴维森认为（1985年《专利、外观设计与商标判例汇编》，起始页127）：

"在我们看来，将使用模压塑料工艺制造的诸如塑料飞盘玩具等实用物品视为版权法案意义上的雕塑是不恰当的。"

31. Breville 案涉及的是烤三明治机。有人对用于生产加热盘压铸模型的石膏形状（加热盘须具有与压制在烤三明治上的相同的扇形）主张版权。福尔克纳法官认为，本案不存在侵权，但又认为石膏形状应受版权保护。他（第94页）说道：

"我无法理解1956年法案第3条中'雕塑'一词为什么不是指该词的一般字典含义，而是指第48条（1）款的拓展含义，该条款规定，'雕塑'包括为制作雕塑目的所用的任何铸型或模型。"

他援引 Wham-O 案裁决的部分内容得出了这个结论，Wham-O 案裁决认可飞盘木质模型的版权。他还援引了《简明牛津词典》对"雕塑"的下述定义：

"通过钻凿石头、雕刻木头、模塑黏土、铸造金属或相似工艺，以圆雕或浮雕形式来展示物品或抽象外观设计的艺术；一件雕塑品。"

32. 福尔克纳法官是经验丰富的知识产权法官，但在 Breville 案中，他似乎忽略了法条中"为制作雕塑目的"等词语的重要意义，也忽略了词典定义中"艺术"一词的重要性。以下是上诉法院的观点（第66段）：

"福尔克纳法官在 Breville 案（1995年《弗利特街判例汇编》，起始页

77）中考虑的石膏形状❶也出现了同样的'不属于创作表达形式'的情况。一般而言，没有市民——自然也没有律师——会认为烤三明治机或其任何部分是一件雕塑作品，即使它的确做出了'扇形'三明治。那么，为什么版权律师会持不同观点呢？在像 *Breville* 案和 *Wham-O* 案（1985年《专利、外观设计与商标判例汇编》，起始页127）中，完全强调或几乎完全强调创造方式所产生的结果是违背常识的，而且在我们看来，这样做也是错误的。正如曼恩法官所说，无论多么失败的作品，都必然有一些艺术表达元素。"

33. 上诉法院在判决书靠前的位置（第49段和第50段，还有第70段）对"雕塑"一词应用于工艺流程和产品（知识产权律师熟知上述术语）场景的含义时，都强调了"为制作雕塑目的"这一点。几个世纪以来，制作金属雕像和其他铸造艺术品基本上都要通过三个阶段的工艺流程：首先是制作黏土或其他延展性材料模型；其次是根据模型制作模具；最后是浇铸，即将金属熔液倒进模具中以生产艺术品（毫无疑问还要再经过适当修整处理）。版权保护也因此［根据1988年法案第4条（2）款］扩大到为制作雕塑目的而制造的铸型或模型。但并非每一件工业铸型产品或浇铸产品都是雕塑。正如上诉法院所观察到的（第50段）：

"铸型或浇铸一般是用于以塑料或某种金属为原料制成最终产品的工业过程。它被用于生产数百万件的普通家用物品，通常没有一件物品会被描述成雕塑。汽车就是一个明显示例。一些物品有资格作为注册外观设计受到保护，进而被1911年法案第22条（1）款排除在外，但它们有资格成为'雕塑'吗？"

34. 再来简单看一下 *Metix* 案。该案中，莱迪法官准确地驳回了认为用于制作与流体混合器搭配使用的暗盒（法官称其看起来像双筒皮下注射器）的模具具有艺术版权的主张。莱迪法官也是经验丰富的知识产权法官，他做了些一般性分析（第721页和第722页）：

"法律被一些试图拓宽版权法案保护范围的尝试困扰着。虽然无法精准判断什么是雕塑、什么不是雕塑，但我认为米德先生已接近问题的核心。他认为，雕塑是经艺术家之手制作的立体作品。在我看来，没有理由将

---

❶ 原文中"plastic shapes"拼写错误，应为"plaster shapes"。——译者注

1988年法案中'雕塑'一词的外延拓展到超出普通民众所理解的范畴。"

由莱迪法官记录的米德先生对"雕塑"的表述似乎是唯一一个没有引发任何方面负面评论的定义或近似定义。

35. *Wildash v. Klein* 案（2004年《知识产权判例汇编》第61卷，起始页324）和 *Metix* 案一样，对本案的意义不在于它裁定了什么，而在于它对一般性问题的讨论（包括对部分复制的见解，不过这与本案无关）。本案是有关两位女性之间的不幸纠纷。两人分别制作了描绘当地野生动物的工艺品，并在市场上售卖。起初两人合作，但之后相互控告对方侵犯自己的版权。该工艺品由丝线制成，原材料还有（在此处判决书摘要中提及的内容较少）玻璃棒、玻璃块、铜箔等。法官认为，这些工艺品是雕塑，又或者是工艺美术作品。他引用了新西兰上诉法院在 *Wham-O* 案中的观点（雕塑应当在某种意义上以立体形式表达雕刻者的理念），也引用了莱迪法官在 *Metix* 案中的观点。关于复制，该法官也引用了霍夫曼勋爵在 *Designers Guild Ltd v. Russell Williams (Textiles) Ltd* 案（2000年《判例汇编周报》合订本第1卷，起始页2416，引证页2423）中对狐狸和刺猬的神秘描述，认为这一神秘描述暗指以赛亚·伯林爵士1953年所著论文中的典故。事实上，正如罗纳德·德沃金教授在其新作《刺猬的正义》一书中所说，以赛亚爵士暗指的是公元前7世纪古希腊抒情诗人阿尔奇洛克斯的一句格言：

"狐狸知道很多事情，但刺猬知道一件大事"（原文为 πολλ'οιδ'αλωπηξ, αλλ'εχινο ς έν μεγα）。

曼恩法官和上诉法院的判决

36. 曼恩法官主要从上述判决中推断出了确立1988年法案中"雕塑"一词含义的"指导原则，而非僵硬死板的要求"。这些指导原则记录在其判决书第118段下9个不同编号的分段中。上诉法院在（《判例汇编之衡平法庭系列》2010年卷，起始页503）第54段引用了曼恩法官判决书第118段的全部内容，并整体上予以赞同。这些指导原则易于理解，我们就不再重复引用。

37. 与上议院在 *Henscher* 案（《判例汇编之上诉法院系列》1976年卷，起始页64）中的裁决一样，前三个分段注意到，一般英语用法即便不是决

卢卡斯影业有限公司等（上诉人）诉安斯沃斯及另一人（被上诉人）

定性的，也依然很重要。第四项指导原则（判决不对艺术价值作出判断）成文于1988年法案第4条（1）款（a）项，这是共识。法院不应将自己界定为艺术价值的裁判者，而是应关注艺术目的（"艺术家之手"）。第五项指导原则（并非每一个理念的立体表达都可以视为雕塑）也无可争议，但前提是"理念"被理解为覆盖任何创意，包括功能性的和艺术性的（皇家大律师布洛赫先生在上诉法院对此质疑，但上诉人在本法院的书面事实陈述并未对此提出异议，特别是在第7段和第14段）。

38. 在高等法院和上诉法院，以及在双方向本法院提交或发表的书面或口头意见中，争论焦点都是如何正确看待兼具（某种）艺术性和（某种）实用功能的立体物品。这些问题在曼恩法官剩余的指导原则里得到了回应。上诉人的书面事实陈述给出了一些世界闻名的例子：构成雅典伊瑞克提翁神殿一部分的女像柱，佛罗伦萨圣洛伦佐圣器收藏室中的美第奇墓，以及罗马的特莱维喷泉。这些例子似乎比较特殊，倒不是因为它们具有突出的价值，而是因为它们都具有强大的建筑元素，并且建筑作品具有功能性这一事实并不会影响其受版权保护的资格。本案提及的其他人工制品，如大英博物馆中的里布切斯特头盔，或一套盛装的中世纪盔甲，还有精美家具、乐器、银器和陶器，都会自然而然地归入工艺美术作品中。但上诉人已明确表示，不再主张本案的帝国冲锋队头盔是工艺美术作品。

39. 相反，上诉人称，上述头盔完全不具有实用功能。他们的主张是，鉴于头盔完全是艺术性的，因而是雕塑。他们的书面事实陈述第7段内容如下：

"本案不涉及功能性问题，因为本案所涉物品完全没有功能性目的。帝国冲锋队的头盔和盔甲不是为了保持佩戴者温暖或体面，也不是为了保护佩戴者在星际战争中不受伤害。它们唯一的目的是给观影者留下视觉印象，因此它们是艺术作品。"

40. 曼恩法官对此持不同看法。他说道（第121段，此处我们引用曼恩法官判决书的第1段）：

"头盔是服装和道具的结合体，但其主要功能是实用性。即便说它有意表达某种东西，也是出于实用性目的。虽然它作为一件物品有意义，并意图传达某种思想，但在构思和制作头盔时并没有这些意图，头盔的构思和制作不过是为了塑造电影中的人物形象。在我看来，这并未赋予头盔莱迪法官测试中所谓的固有、必要的艺术创作。"

41. 上诉法院持相同看法（第 79 段和第 80 段）：

"布洛赫先生通过强调冲锋队的虚构和想象本质，力图回避我们列举的真实士兵头盔用作电影道具的例子……

但是该论点混淆了冲锋队队员的虚构本质和电影中对他的真实描绘。尽管头盔和盔甲是虚构的，但它们依然可以被辨识出来是头盔和盔甲，并在电影场景内具有作为冲锋队装备的功能。"

分析

42. 在本法院，上诉人对曼恩法官和上诉法院的推论提出了质疑。皇家大律师桑普顿先生说，法官将头盔描述为具有实用性这一点很奇怪，并认为，只有认定头盔在"电影场景内"具有与真实头盔相同的功能性目的，上诉法院才应认为头盔具有功能性目的。

43. 这一点令人感到十分困惑。《星球大战》系列电影设定的背景是虚构的未来科幻世界。背景设定在过去的战争电影（如《光荣之路》描绘了第一次世界大战期间的法国军队，《赎罪》描绘了在敦刻尔克的英国远征军）至少是基于历史事实的。战壕中或海滩上的演员和群众演员可能戴着真的钢盔，或者（由于无法找到数量足够、式样正确的真钢盔）他们也可能戴着涂成卡其色的塑料头盔。不论是何种情况，（用曼恩法官的话说）头盔是"服装和道具的结合体"，目的是提高电影的艺术效果。它们是生产过程的一部分，正如莱迪法官在 *Metix* 案判决书第 721 页所言。这里莱迪法官引用了惠特福德法官在 *Davis（J & S）（Holdings）Ltd v. Wright Health Group Ltd* 案（1988 年《专利、外观设计与商标判例汇编》，起始页 403，引证页 410-412）中的意见。在本案中，生产过程是制作长篇故事电影。

44. 将"雕塑"一词用于指称电影制作过程中所使用的 20 世纪军用头盔，无论它是真实头盔还是由其他材料制成的复制件，也无论它对电影成片的艺术效果贡献有多大，都不符合该词语的日常用法。将该词语用于指称帝国冲锋队的头盔所引发的争论就更加激烈了，因为人们联想到了身穿统一白色盔甲的邪恶克隆士兵形象。但是称得上是艺术作品的，是卢卡斯先生和其公司创作的电影《星球大战》。头盔是电影制作过程中的一个元素，从这个意义上来说，头盔具有实用性。

45. 以上是曼恩法官和上诉法院的共同认识，分别在各自判决书的第121段和第80段。在知识产权案件中，经常需要就诸如显而易见性、创造性和复制等问题作出裁判结论，上诉级别法院在介入初审法院判决时，一般都非常谨慎。在 *Designers Guild* 案（2000年《判例汇编周报》合订本第1卷，起始页2416，引证页2423-2424）中，霍夫曼勋爵指出，出现这种情况有两个原因。第一是初审法院的法官看到并听审了证人，而上诉级别法院没有。霍夫曼勋爵继续说道：

"第二，因为上诉裁决涉及将并不精准明了的法律标准应用于重要性各不相同的特征组合上，所以我认为这属于上诉级别法院不应轻易推翻初审法官裁决的案件类型，除非初审法官犯了原则性错误（见 *Pro Sieben Media AG v. Carlton UK Television Ltd* 案，1991年《判例汇编周报》合订本第1卷，起始页605，引证页612-613）。我赞同巴克斯顿法官在 *Norowzian v. Arks Ltd (No 2)* 案（2000年《弗利特街判例汇编》，起始页363，引证页370）中的观点：'在没有迹象表明初审法官犯了原则性错误的情况下，当事人来到上诉法院，不要指望上诉法院的法官或这些法官中的至少两名法官的印象会与初审法官不同。'"

二次上诉案件尤其如此。同样地，霍夫曼法官在 *Biogen Inc v. Medeva plc* 案（1997年《专利、外观设计与商标判例汇编》，起始页1，引证页45）中也是如此评述，这一点众所周知，无需重复。

46. 上诉法院遵从了霍夫曼勋爵在 *Designers Guild* 案中的论述（第78段），在我们看来，这是正确做法。在为期17天的庭审中，曼恩法官听取了多位证人提供的关于头盔和其他人工制品的证据。尽管他的判决书篇幅很长、内容全面，但他也不可能记录每一个有助于得出其结论的细节。他的初审判决没有法律错误，也未得出明显站不住脚的结论。在这一点上，上诉法院维持其裁决是正确的。

47. 我们基于下级法院所给出的理由维持他们所作判决的主体部分。但是（冒着显得无趣的风险），我们对上诉法院判决书第77段中的"大象测试"（"难以名状却一看便知"）没有多大兴趣。动物学家都能轻易辨认出大象，并且他们中的大多数人也一定能够清晰准确地描述出其关键识别特征。但相比之下，法官，即使是经验丰富的知识产权法官，也做不到未卜先知并立刻得出准确结论，也没有法官会宣称自己有这样的能力。法官阅读、听取证据（经常包括专家证据），阅读、听取辩护意见，并采取上诉法院所称的多因子分析方法。此外，法官必须论证得出判决的理由。

48. 还有一个方面上诉法院未予重视，但在我们看来它是支持初审法官结论的，那就是议会制订法律以保护立体人工制品的外观设计人和制作者免于面对不正当竞争的一般性政策考虑。在回顾立法历史后，上诉法院认为（第 40 段），无法从版权和注册外观设计权之间的关系中获取任何帮助。我们对此不予认同，尤其是考虑到相对较新的未注册外观设计权。从二者的关系，我们可以认识到确立立体物品保护背后逐步显现出来的立法目的（尽管这一过程缓慢而艰难），立体物品保护完全不同于对文学版权的无差别保护，作品类别不同，保护期限也不同。艺术作品（雕塑和工艺美术作品）享有最全面的保护；接下来是"吸引眼球的"作品（*AMP Inc v. Utilux Pty Ltd* 案，1971 年《弗利特街判例汇编》，起始页 572）；然后根据 1988 年法案第三编，扩展到对纯功能性物品（典型例子是汽车排气系统）提供适度水平的保护。尽管不受待见客体的保护期限正逐渐延长，但版权保护的期限要长得多。保护期限差异的背后是良好的政策考虑，并且在我们看来，法院也不应鼓励完全版权保护的范围向外扩张。

第 51 条和第 52 条

49. 上诉人认同，如果头盔没有资格成为 1988 年法案所定义的雕塑，那么针对侵犯麦夸里先生绘画版权的主张，安斯沃斯先生就可以根据第 51 条进行抗辩，并且本案也就不再涉及第 52 条的问题。出于完整性考虑，上诉法院在判决书第 83 段至第 98 段讨论了这两个条款，此处无需赘述。我们驳回基于英国版权法的上诉。

[2011] UKSC 39
On appeal from: [2009] EWCA Civ 1328

Lucasfilm Limited and others (Appellants) v.

Ainsworth and another (Respondents)

before

Lord Phillips, President
Lord Walker
Lady Hale
Lord Mance
Lord Collins

JUDGMENT GIVEN ON

27 July 2011

Heard on 7, 8 and 9 March 2011

https://www.supremecourt.uk/cases/docs/uksc-2010-0015-judgment.pdf

Introduction

1. The first Star Wars film (later renamed "Star Wars Episode IV - A New Hope" in order to provide for "prequels" as well as sequels) was released in the United States in 1977. It was an enormous commercial success. It won an Oscar for best costume design. This appeal is concerned with intellectual property rights in various artefacts made for use in the film. The most important of these was the Imperial Stormtrooper helmet to which the trial judge (Mann J) referred in his judgment([2008]EWHC 1878(Ch), [2009]FSR 103, paras[2] and [121]):

"One of the most abiding images in the film was that of the Imperial Stormtroopers. These were soldiers clad in white armour, including a white helmet which left no part of the face uncovered…The purpose of the helmet was that it was to be worn as an item of costume in a film, to identify a character, but in addition to portray something about that character-its allegiance, force, menace, purpose and, to some extent, probably its anonymity. It was a mixture of costume and prop."

The parties are agreed that for the purposes of this final appeal the helmet can be taken as the paradigm case that will be decisive of the outcome.

2. The facts are set out in the judge's clear and thorough judgment. For present purposes a brief summary will suffice. The film's story-line and characters were conceived by Mr George Lucas. Between 1974 and 1976 Mr Lucas's concept of the Imperial Stormtroopers as threatening characters in "fascist white-armoured suits" was given visual expression in drawings and paintings by an artist, Mr Ralph McQuarrie, and three-dimensional form by Mr Nick Pemberton (a freelance scenic artist and prop-maker) and Mr Andrew Ainsworth (who is skilled in vacuum-moulding in plastic). Mr Pemberton made a clay model of the helmet, which was adapted several times until Mr Lucas was happy with it. Mr Ainsworth produced several prototype vacuum-moulded helmets. Once Mr Lucas had approved the final version Mr Ainsworth made 50 helmets for use in the film. These events all took place in England. Although Mr Lucas and his companies are based in California he had come to live in England while the film was made at Elstree (there was also filming on location in Tunisia).

3. The first appellant is a Californian corporation owned by Mr Lucas. The second appellant is an English company owned by Mr Lucas. The third appellant is a

Californian corporation responsible for the group's licensing activities; it is wholly owned by the first appellant. Between them these three companies own copyrights in the artistic works created for the Star Wars films, and they can be referred to generally as "Lucasfilm". Apart from the huge commercial success of the Star Wars films, Lucasfilm has built up a successful licensing business which includes licensing models of Imperial Stormtroopers and their equipment. This litigation has come about because in 2004 Mr Ainsworth, the principal respondent in this appeal, used his original tools to make versions of the Imperial Stormtrooper helmet and armour, and other artefacts that it is not necessary to detail, for sale to the public. The second respondent is a private company owned by Mr Ainsworth but for practical purposes Mr Ainsworth can be treated as the only respondent.

4. Mr Ainsworth sold some of the goods that he produced (to the value of at least $8,000 but not more than $30,000) in the United States. In 2005 Lucasfilm sued Mr Ainsworth in the United States District Court, Central District of California, and in 2006 it obtained a default judgment for $20m, $10m of which represented triple damages under the Lanham Act. The whole judgment remains unsatisfied. Lucasfilm also commenced proceedings in the Chancery Division of the English High Court. The re-amended particulars of claim put forward a variety of claims under English law, including infringement of copyright (paras (1) to (10) of the prayer for relief); a claim for enforcement of the United States judgment to the extent of $10m (para (11)); and claims under United States copyright law (paras (12) to (17)).

5. The trial occupied 17 days during April and May 2008. In his judgment delivered on 31 July 2008 Mann J dismissed all Lucasfilm's claims based on English copyright law (together with some other claims that are no longer pursued). He held that the helmet made by Mr Ainsworth was a substantial reproduction of original work carried out by Mr McQuarrie and other persons working for Lucasfilm. But the English copyright claims failed because the helmet was not a work of sculpture and Mr Ainsworth had defences (to a claim that he was reproducing Mr McQuarrie's work) under sections 51 and 52 of the Copyright Designs and Patents Act 1988 ("the 1988 Act"). The judge also dismissed Mr Ainsworth's counterclaim based on his own claim to copyright in the helmet.

6. The judge held that the United States judgment was unenforceable for want of personal jurisdiction over Mr Ainsworth and his company. But he held that Lucasfilm's United States copyright claims were justiciable in England and that Mr Ainsworth and his company had infringed those rights.

7. The Court of Appeal([2009]EWCA Civ 1328,[2010]Ch 503)agreed with the judge that the United States judgment is unenforceable, and there is no further appeal on that point. The Court of Appeal also agreed with the judge that any intellectual property rights in the helmet belong to Lucasfilm, and this Court has refused Mr Ainsworth permission to cross-appeal on that point. The issues that are open in this Court are whether the helmet was a sculpture and the defences under sections 51 and 52 of the 1988 Act(on all of which the Court of Appeal agreed with the judge)and justiciability in England of the United States copyright claims(on which the Court of Appeal disagreed with the judge). The issues on sections 51 and 52 arise only if the helmet was a sculpture(and so an artistic work)within the meaning of the 1988 Act. In the Court of Appeal Lucasfilm abandoned its alternative contention that the helmet qualified as an artistic work because it was a work of artistic craftsmanship.

Part I: English copyright law issues

Current statutory provisions

8. The Court has been taken to the full legislative history but it is better to start with the current legislation, that is the 1988 Act. Under section 1(1)(a) copyright is a property right which subsists in original literary, dramatic, musical or artistic works. Other works, including films, come in under section 1(1)(b) and (c). By section 4(1) "artistic work" means, for copyright purposes,

"(a) a graphic work, photograph, sculpture or collage, irrespective of artistic quality,

(b) a work of architecture being a building or a model for a building, or

(c) a work of artistic craftsmanship."

By section 4(2) "sculpture" includes a cast or model made for purposes of sculpture.

9. Sections 51 and 52 are in Part I, Chapter III of the 1988 Act (acts permitted in relation to copyright works). Chapter III contains a variety of exemptions from liability on general grounds, including fair dealing (sections 29–31) and educational, archival and other public purposes (sections 32–50). Section 62 contains a general exemption for buildings, sculpture and works of artistic craftsmanship on permanent public display.

10. Section 51 (design documents and models) as amended provides as follows:

"(1) It is not an infringement of any copyright in a design document or model recording or embodying a design for anything other than an artistic work or a typeface to make an article to the design or to copy an article made to the design.

(2) Nor is it an infringement of the copyright to issue to the public, or include in a film or communicate to the public, anything the making of which was, by virtue of subsection (1), not an infringement of that copyright.

(3) In this section—

'design' means the design of any aspect of the shape or configuration (whether internal or external) of the whole or part of an article, other than surface decoration; and

'design document' means any record of a design, whether in the form of a drawing, a written description, a photograph, data stored in a computer or otherwise."

11. Section 52 (effect of exploitation of design derived from artistic work) provides as follows:

"(1) This section applies where an artistic work has been exploited, by or with the licence of the copyright owner, by—

(a) making by an industrial process articles falling to be treated for the purposes of this Part as copies of the work, and

(b) marketing such articles, in the United Kingdom or elsewhere.

(2) After the end of the period of 25 years from the end of the calendar year in which such articles are first marketed, the work may be copied by making articles of any description, or doing anything for the purpose of making articles of any

description, and anything may be done in relation to articles so made, without infringing copyright in the work.

(3) Where only part of an artistic work is exploited as mentioned in subsection (1), subsection(2) applies only in relation to that part.

(4) The Secretary of State may by order make provision-

(a) as to the circumstances in which an article, or any description of article, is to be regarded for the purposes of this section as made by an industrial process;

(b) excluding from the operation of this section such articles of a primarily literary or artistic character as he thinks fit.

(5) An order shall be made by statutory instrument which shall be subject to annulment in pursuance of a resolution of either House of Parliament.

(6) In this section-

(a) references to articles do not include films; and

(b) references to the marketing of an article are to its being sold or let for hire or offered or exposed for sale or hire."

12. These two sections operate so as to limit(in different ways) the influence of literary or artistic copyright on other persons' freedom to make and market three-dimensional objects. Section 51 applies where the end-product of a design document or model is not an artistic work. It provides a more principled answer to the problem to which the House of Lords gave a radical and controversial solution in *British Leyland Motor Corporation Ltd v. Armstrong Patents Co Ltd*[1986] AC 577 while the Bill which became the 1988 Act was before Parliament. Section 52 applies(subject to exceptions specified by the Secretary of State) where there is an artistic work, but that work has been exploited(with the consent of the copyright owner) by industrial production of copies to be marketed.

13. The Copyright(Industrial Process and Excluded Articles)(No 2) Order 1989(SI 1989/1070)("the 1989 Order"), made under section 52(4) of the 1988 Act, provides(para 2) for an article to be regarded as made by an industrial process if it is one of more than 50 articles which are to be treated as copies of a particular artistic work(and are not together a set). The Order also provides(para 3(1)(a))

for the exclusion from section 52 of "works of sculpture, other than casts or models used or intended to be used as models or patterns to be multiplied by any industrial process."

Legislative history: before the 1911 Act

14. These provisions (and especially sections 51 and 52) are difficult to understand without reference to their legislative history. Unfortunately the history is itself quite complicated. The Copyright Act 1911 ("the 1911 Act") was (as Lord Bridge observed in *British Leyland* [1986] AC 577, 619) "the first attempt to provide a comprehensive code of copyright protection". Section 1(1) of the 1911 Act was in terms similar to those of section 1(1)(a) of the 1988 Act, (except that the words "irrespective of artistic quality" did not appear in the 1911 Act), and it may give the impression of embodying a well-proportioned symmetrical principle providing equal protection to every form of human creativity. Any such impression would be misleading. When the 1911 Act was passed there had already been two centuries of legislative history, starting with the Copyright Act 1709 ("the 1709 Act"), and for most of that time it was the protection of printed words —published literary works—that was the law's principal concern. Moreover the original legislative purpose of laws on literary copyright was the protection of the commercial interests of stationers (the early publishers) and booksellers, and the control of unlicensed (and possibly subversive) publications, rather than the vindication of the legal and moral rights of authors. There are useful summaries of the history of English copyright law in *Copinger and Skone James on Copyright*, 16th ed (2010), paras 2-08 to 2-42, and *Cornish, Llewelyn and Aplin, Intellectual Property: Patents, Copyright, Trade Marks and Allied Rights*, 7th ed (2010), paras 10-01 to 10-41.

15. The 1709 Act protected literary works, books and other writings. During the 18th century protection was extended (by statute) to engravings and (by a liberal interpretation of the 1709 Act) to musical and dramatic compositions. Three-dimensional works of art were brought within the scope of copyright by a statute enacted in 1798, 38 Geo III c 71, but it was very badly drafted and offered little practi-

cal protection (Lord Ellenborough said in *Gahagan v. Cooper* (1811) 3 Camp 111, 113 that "The statute seems to have been framed with a view to defeat its own object"). This Act was replaced by the Sculpture Copyright Act 1814 ("the 1814 Act"). The class of protected works was described in discursive terms, starting with

"any new and original sculpture, or model, or copy, or cast of the human figure or human figures, or of any bust or busts, or of any part or parts of the human figure, clothed in drapery or otherwise,"

and continuing in broader terms, referring to "any matter being subject of invention in sculpture." The sculpture was required to bear the maker's name and the date when it was made. Paintings, drawings and photographs were not protected until the Fine Arts Copyright Act 1862 ("the 1862 Act"). The 1862 Act required registration as a condition of protection. Architectural works were not protected until the 1911 Act (which also introduced works of "artistic craftsmanship" into the definition of "artistic work" in section 35 of that Act).

16. The 1814 Act remained in force until the coming into force of the 1911 Act, and was until then the only statute that gave long-term copyright protection to any three-dimensional works. During the 19th century the rapid expansion of mechanical mass-production produced an obvious need for industrial designers and manufacturers to be protected against unfair competition by copying of their designs. Parliament decided that protection should be provided by a new right which was (rather confusingly, as the Court of Appeal said in para[24] of its judgment) called copyright, but which differed in two respects from literary and artistic copyright. First, the proprietor was required to register his design. Second, the period of protection was much shorter. Those were the essential features of the scheme introduced by the Copyright of Designs Act 1839, repealed and replaced by the Designs Act 1842. Earlier legislation granting copyright to the design of a range of printed textiles was repealed and replaced by the new system of registration, but copyright in sculpture under the 1814 Act was preserved.

17. The law as to registered designs was amended by the Copyright of Designs Act 1850, was further amended and consolidated by Part III of the Patents, Designs

and Trade Marks Act 1883("the 1883 Act") and finally(as regards legislation before the 1911 Act) was further amended by the Patents and Designs Act 1907("the 1907 Act"). Most of the detail of this history is irrelevant for present purposes. But it is to be noted that although the periods of protection for registered designs were progressively extended, they were always much shorter than the period for literary or artistic copyright. It is also to be noted that after an uncertain start in the early statutes, a design for a work of sculpture was excluded from the statutory definition of "design" (section 60 of the 1883 Act and section 93 of the 1907 Act).

18. Only one judicial decision on the 1814 Act calls for mention, that is *Britain v. Hanks Bros & Co*(1902) 86 LT 765. Wright J held that copyright protection as sculpture was available to what the report refers to as "toy metal models of soldiers on horseback, or mounted yeomen." The models were designed and made by William Britain, a partner in the plaintiff firm. The report does not say how large the models were, but they were evidently large enough for each to have stamped on it the maker's name and the date of its manufacture. There was expert evidence, which the judge accepted, that the models were "artistic productions, in that the anatomy is good, and that the modelling shows both technical knowledge and skill." The judge seems to have regarded the case as near the borderline, but was prepared to hold that the models were entitled to protection.

19. The Court of Appeal observed(para[59]) that it is "difficult...to take too much from this case." A minor point in the appellants' case is that that is just what the Court did(para[82]) in describing the *Britain* models as "highly crafted models designed to appeal to the collector but which might be played with by his children."

Legislative history : the 1911 Act and afterwards

20. The introduction by the 1911 Act of full copyright protection for "a work of artistic craftsmanship" was ascribed by Lord Simon, in *George Hensher Ltd v. Restawile Upholstery(Lancs) Ltd*[1976] AC 64, 89-91, to the influence of the Arts and Crafts movement inspired by William Morris and John Ruskin. Lord Simon's view(at p 91) was that the expression is a composite phrase which must be construed

as a whole, and that view has had recent support from the High Court of Australia (*Swarbrick v. Burge*(2007)232 CLR 336).

21. Section 22 of the 1911 Act provided as follows:

"(1)This Act shall not apply to designs capable of being registered under the Patents and Designs Act 1907, except designs which, though capable of being so registered, are not used or intended to be used as models or patterns to be multiplied by any industrial process.

(2)General rules under section 86 of the Patents and Designs Act 1907 may be made for determining the conditions under which a design shall be deemed to be used for such purposes as aforesaid."

The test for production by an industrial process was(by rule 89 of the Designs Rules 1920, and so far as now material) the same as that in the 1989 Order(mentioned in para[13]above).'

22. The effect of the double negative in section 22(1)can be more easily understood, as Viscount Maugham observed in *King Features Syndicate Inc v. O & M Kleeman Ltd*[1941]AC 417,427,if it is rewritten:

"This Act shall apply to designs capable of being registered under[the 1907 Act], which are not used or intended to be used as models or patterns to be multiplied by any industrial process. With that exception this Act shall not apply to designs capable of being registe red under[the 1907 Act]."

The main issue in that case(which was concerned with "Popeye" dolls derived from published comic strips enjoying artistic copyright)was the time at which the intention of use for industrial production had to be formed. The Lords decided that the intention must have been there from the start.

23. The Patents and Designs Act 1919 amended the 1907 Act by substituting for the definition in section 93 of the 1907 Act a new definition of "design" which referred to features applied "by any industrial process" and did not make an express exception for a design for a sculpture. Because of the way that section 22 of the 1911 Act was framed, this had the effect of withdrawing from works of sculpture their specially privileged position in relation to mass-production of copies. Its effect

was illustrated by *Pytram Ltd v. Models (Leicester) Ltd* [1930] 1 Ch 639. The Boy Scouts Association commissioned a model of a wolf-cub's head which was to be used to produce a permanent mould for the production of large numbers of papier-maché models to be attached to the top of wooden poles. Clauson J dismissed the plaintiff's claim to copyright in the original model. He accepted that the model was a work of sculpture, but it was not automatically exempt from registration under the 1907 Act as amended, and it did not come within the exception in section 22(1) because (p 647) "The whole point in the preparation of this model was to enable the plaintiffs to supply totem poles in large quantities."

24. After the second world war there was a legislative shift back again. In 1947 the Swan Committee recommended that works of sculpture should again be excluded from registrable designs. The Registered Designs Act 1949 provided (section 1(3) and (4)) for exclusions from registration of articles which were primarily literary or artistic in character. Rule 26(1) of the Designs Rules 1949 (SI 1949/2368) excluded "works of sculpture other than casts or models used or intended to be used as models or patterns to be multiplied by any industrial process." This wording (now reproduced in the 1989 Order) followed section 22(1) of the 1911 Act and must be construed in line with the House of Lords' decision on that section in *King Features*.

25. The 1911 Act was repealed by the Copyright Act 1956 ("the 1956 Act"). Section 10 of the 1956 Act (special exception in respect of industrial designs) restated the boundaries between copyright and design right. As amended by the Design Copyright Act 1968, section 10(3) set a 15-year limit on copyright protection for any work in respect of which a corresponding design could have been registered under the 1949 Act. But section 10(4) made an exception for designs excluded from registration by rules made under the 1949 Act; and rule 26 of the Designs Rules 1949 has now been replicated by rule 26 of the Registered Designs Rules 1989.

26. The 1956 Act introduced the words "irrespective of artistic quality" into para(a) of its definition of "artistic work" in section 3(1). This was, it seems, as a result of maps, charts and plans being reclassified by the 1956 Act as artistic rather

than literary works. The new wording sits rather uneasily with "works of artistic craftsmanship" in para(c) of the same definition. In *Hensher*[1976] AC 64,94, Lord Simon suggested an explanation which some may not find wholly convincing. But it is common ground that in copyright cases the court is not concerned with passing judgment on the merits of either literary or artistic works.

27. The Court of Appeal drew two general conclusions from its own survey of the legislative history(which occupies paras[21] to[39] of the judgment). The first ([40] and [41]) was that there is little or no assistance as to the meaning of "sculpture" in the 1988 Act to be derived from the relationship between copyright and registered design rights. The second([42] and [43]) is that "design" and "artistic work" are different concepts. Apart from unregistered design right(introduced by Part III of the 1988 Act), design right statutes are concerned with features that have visual appeal. Copyright protection depends on a work falling within a particular category specified in the 1988 Act: "It does not depend upon a further analysis or identification of its design features."

The meaning of "sculpture"

28. Both the judge and the Court of Appeal undertook a full review of English and Commonwealth authority as to the meaning of "sculpture". They rightly concluded that some first-instance decisions gave them no real assistance, and it is unnecessary to go into them again. The judgments that call for discussion are(in chronological order) those of the Court of Appeal of New Zealand in *Wham-O Manufacturing Co v. LincolnIndustries Ltd*[1985] RPC 127,[1984] 1 NZLR 641; of Falconer J in *Breville Europe Plc v. Thorn EMI Domestic Appliances Ltd*[1995] FSR 77;of Laddie J in *Metix(UK) Ltd v. G H Maughan(Plastics) Ltd*[1997] FSR 718;and of Angel J(sitting in the Supreme Court of the Northern Territory) in *Wildash v. Klein* (2004) 61 IPR 324.

29. Before discussing these four cases it is appropriate to make a further brief reference to the decision of the House of Lords in *Hensher*[1976] AC 64. Since Lucasfilm is no longer contending that the helmet is a work of artistic craftsmanship it

is unnecessary to make much further reference to *Hensher*, which Mann J discussed at some length, drawing attention to the difficulty of identifying the true principle of the decision. The reason why that contention has been abandoned is stated (para 22 (2) of the appellants' printed case) to be that section 4(1)(c) of the 1988 Act is intended to comprise articles whose purpose is primarily functional, and which cannot therefore qualify as sculpture. The relative significance of the functional and the artistic is central to this appeal. The speeches in *Hensher*, difficult though they are, show a general inclination to start with the ordinary meaning of the words of the statute (see Lord Reid at p 78, Lord Morris at p 81, Viscount Dilhorne at pp 86-87, Lord Simon at p 91 and Lord Kilbrandon at p 97), however much they differed as to the application of that principle. The same approach is called for in relation to the meaning of "sculpture".

30. In *Wham-O* the Court of Appeal of New Zealand was concerned with frisbees (light plastic discs used in outdoor games because of their aerodynamic qualities). Lincoln made and marketed in New Zealand frisbees which were alleged to infringe Wham-O's copyright in design drawings, wooden models, moulds and the final plastic moulded products. The relevant parts of the Copyright Act 1962 of New Zealand were similar but not identical to those of the 1988 Act. At first instance Moller J held that the wooden models were copyright as sculptures and that the moulds and final products were engravings. The Court of Appeal upheld this result, while holding that the final products were not sculptures (a point left open by the judge). Much of the judgment is taken up with reasoning leading to the rather surprising conclusion that the moulds and final products were engravings. The finding that the wooden model of a frisbee-and that alone was a sculpture seems to have been based mainly on the fact that only the model had been made by hand, and the moulds and final products had been made industrially. Davison CJ stated ([1985] RPC 127, 157):

"It seems to us inappropriate to regard utilitarian objects such as plastic flying discs, manufactured as toys, by an injection moulding process, as items of sculpture for the purposes of the Copyright Act."

31. The *Breville* case was concerned with sandwich toasters. Copyright was claimed for plaster shapes made for the production of die-cast moulds of the heating plates(which were required to have the same scalloped shape as was to be impressed on the toasted sandwiches). Falconer J held that there had been no infringement, but went on to express the view that the plaster shapes were protected by copyright. He stated(at p 94):

"I do not see why the word 'sculpture' in section 3 of the Copyright Act 1956 should not receive its ordinary dictionary meaning except in so far as the scope of the word is extended by section 48(1) which provides that 'sculpture'includes any cast or model made for purposes of sculpture."

In reaching this conclusion he relied on the part of the *Wham-O* decision which recognised copyright in the wooden model of a frisbee. He also relied on the Concise Oxford Dictionary's definition of "sculpture":

"Art of forming representations of objects etc or abstract designs in the round or in relief by chiselling stone, carving wood, modelling clay, casting metal, or similar processes; a work of sculpture."

32. Falconer J was a very experienced intellectual property judge but in *Breville* he seems to have overlooked the significance of the words "for purposes of sculpture" in the statute and the significance of the first word, "Art", in the dictionary definition. That was the view of the Court of Appeal(para[66]):

"The same['far removed from the creation of expressive form'] goes for the plastic shapes considered by Falconer J in the *Breville* case[1995]FSR 77. No ordinary citizen- indeed no ordinary lawyer would regard a sandwich toaster or any part of it as a work of sculpture even if it did produce 'scalloped' sandwiches. So why should a copyright lawyer take a different view? A total or almost total emphasis on the manner of creation, as in the *Breville* case and *Wham-O* case[1985] RPC 127 produces a result which offends common sense and in our view is wrong. There must, as Mann J said, be some element of artistic expression however unsuccessful."

33. The point about "for purposes of sculpture" is underlined by some obser-

vations earlier in the judgment of the Court of Appeal (paras [49] and [50], and again at para [70]) as to the word "sculpture" being applicable both to a process and to a product (terms familiar to intellectual property lawyers). Over the centuries statues and other works of art cast in metal have been produced by what is basically a three-stage process: first by making a model in clay or some other malleable material; then by taking a mould from the model; and then by casting, that is, pouring molten metal into the mould to produce the work of art (followed no doubt by appropriate finishing). Copyright protection is therefore extended (currently by section 4(2) of the 1988 Act) to a cast or model made for purposes of sculpture. But not every product of industrial casting or moulding is sculpture. As the Court of Appeal observed (para [50]):

"Casting or moulding is an industrial process commonly used where the end product is made of plastic or metal of some kind. It is used in the production of millions of ordinary household objects, none of which would usually be described as sculptures. A motor car is but one obvious example. Some would have qualified for protection as registered designs so as to be excluded under section 22(1) of the 1911 Act. But would they have qualified as 'sculpture'?"

34. *Metix* can be taken more shortly. It was a case in which Laddie J rightly rejected a claim to artistic copyright in moulds used for making cartridges used in conjunction with flow mixers (the judge described them as looking like double-barrelled hyperdermic syringes). Laddie J, another very experienced intellectual property judge made some general observations (at pp 721-722):

"The law has been bedevilled by attempts to widen out the field covered by the Copyright Acts. It is not possible to say with precision what is and what is not sculpture, but I think Mr Meade was close to the heart of the issue. He suggested that a sculpture is a three-dimensional work made by an artist's hand. It appears to me that there is no reason why the word 'sculpture' in the 1988 Act, should be extended far beyond the meaning which that word has to ordinary members of the public."

Mr Meade's formulation as recorded by Laddie J seems to be the only suggested definition or near-definition that has not attracted adverse comment from any quarter.

35. *Wildash v. Klein* (2004) 61 IPR 324, like *Metix*, is of interest not so much for what it decides as for its discussion of general issues (including the notion of copying of part, which is not an issue here). The case was an unfortunate dispute between two women, each of whom made craftwork depicting local wildlife for sale at markets. Initially they cooperated but later each accused the other of copyright infringement. The craftworks were made of wire but also (and here the summaries in the judgments below are rather sparse) glass rods, glass nuggets, copper foil and other materials. The judge held that they were sculptures or, alternatively, works of artistic craftsmanship. The judge cited the Court of Appeal of New Zealand in *Wham-O* ("sculpture should in some way express in three-dimensional form an idea of the sculptor") and also Laddie J in *Metix*. In connection with copying the judge also cited Lord Hoffmann's cryptic observation about foxes and hedgehogs in *Designers Guild Ltd v. Russell Williams (Textiles) Ltd* [2000] 1 WLR 2416, 2423, describing it as an allusion to an essay written in 1953 by Sir Isaiah Berlin; in fact Sir Isaiah was alluding, as has Professor Ronald Dworkin in his latest book, *Justice for Hedgehogs* (2011), to a saying attributed to Archilochus in the 7th century BC

"πολλ' οιδ'αλωπηξ, αλλ'εχινο ς έ ν μεγα (the fox knows many things, but the hedgehog one big thing.)"

The judgments of Mann J and the Court of Appeal

36. It was primarily from these authorities that Mann J derived what he called "guidelines, not rigid requirements" as to the meaning of sculpture in the 1988 Act. These are set out in nine numbered sub-paragraphs in para 118 of his judgment. The Court of Appeal quoted this paragraph in full, [2010] Ch 503, para [54], and was generally in agreement with it. As the guidelines are readily accessible we will not quote them again.

37. The first three note (as did the House of Lords in *Henscher* [1976] AC 64) that normal English usage is important, though not determinative. The fourth guide-

line ("no judgment is to be made about artistic worth") is in the text of section 4 (1)(a) of the 1988 Act, and is common ground. The Court is not to set itself up as an arbiter of artistic merit. But it is concerned with artistic purpose ("the artist's hand"). The fifth guideline ("not every three-dimensional representation of a concept can be regarded as a sculpture") is also uncontroversial, at any rate if "concept" is understood as covering any idea, functional as well as artistic (Mr Bloch QC challenged it in the Court of Appeal, but it is consistent with the appellants' printed case in this Court, especially paras 7 and 14).

38. In the courts below as in the parties' written and oral submissions in this Court, the argument has centred on the right approach to three-dimensional objects that have both an artistic purpose (of some sort) and a utilitarian function (of some sort). These issues are addressed in the rest of the judge's guidelines. The appellants' printed case gives some world-famous examples: the caryatids which form part of the Erectheion at Athens; the Medici tombs in the sacristy of San Lorenzo in Florence; the Trevi fountain in Rome. These seem to be rather special cases, not because of their outstanding merit but because they all have a strong architectural element, and the fact that a work of architecture is functional does not disqualify it from copyright protection. Other artefacts mentioned in the case, such as the Ribchester helmet in the British Museum or a decorated medieval suit of armour, would come more naturally under the head of works of artistic craftsmanship, together with fine furniture, musical instruments, silverware and ceramics. But the appellants have made clear that it is no longer part of their case that the Imperial Stormtrooper helmet was a work of artistic craftsmanship.

39. Instead, the appellants contend that the helmet had no practical function at all. Their case is that it is sculpture because its purpose is wholly artistic. Para 7 of their printed case puts it in these terms:

"In the present case, the question of functionality does not arise, because the articles in question have no functional purpose whatever. The Stormtroopers' helmets and armour did not exist in order to keep their wearers warm or decent or to protect them from injury in an inter-planetary war. Their sole purpose was to make a visual impression on the filmgoer. They are therefore artistic works."

40. Mann J saw it differently. He stated(para[121], and here we are picking up the quotation in the first paragraph in this judgment):

"It was a mixture of costume and prop. But its primary function is utilitarian. While it was intended to express something, that was for utilitarian purposes. While it has an interest as an object, and while it was intended to express an idea, it was not conceived, or created, with the intention that it should do so other than as part of character portrayal in the film. That, in my view, does not give it the necessary quality of artistic creation inherent in the test suggested by Laddie J."

41. The Court of Appeal took the same view(paras[79] and [80]):

"Mr Bloch seeks to avoid our example of a real soldier's helmet being used as a prop in a film by stressing the fictional and imaginary nature of the stormtroopers and what they were…

But that argument confuses the fictional nature of the stormtrooper with his physical depiction in the film. Although invented, the helmet and armour are still recognisable as such and have a function within the confines of the film as the equipment of the stormtrooper."

Discussion

42. In this Court the appellants have challenged the reasoning of the judge and the Court of Appeal. Mr Sumption QC said that it was eccentric of the judge to describe the helmet's purpose as utilitarian, and that the Court of Appeal could find it to have a functional purpose only by treating it as having the same functional purpose as a real helmet "within the confines of a film".

43. This is quite a puzzling point. The Star Wars films are set in an imaginary, science-fiction world of the future. War films set in the past(Paths of Glory, for instance, depicting the French army in the first world war, or Atonement depicting the British Expeditionary Force at Dunkirk) are at least based on historical realities. The actors and extras in the trenches or on the beaches may be wearing real steel helmets, or(because real steel helmets of the correct style are unobtainable in suffi-

cient numbers) they may be wearing plastic helmets painted khaki. In either case the helmets are there as (in the judge's words) "a mixture of costume and prop" in order to contribute to the artistic effect of the film as a film. They are part of a production process, as Laddie J said in *Metix* at p 721, citing Whitford J in *Davis (J & S)(Holdings) Ltd v. Wright Health Group Ltd* [1988] RPC 403, 410–412. In this case the production process was the making of a full-length feature film.

44. It would not accord with the normal use of language to apply the term "sculpture" to a 20th century military helmet used in the making of a film, whether it was the real thing or a replica made in different material, however great its contribution to the artistic effect of the finished film. The argument for applying the term to an Imperial Stormtrooper helmet is stronger, because of the imagination that went into the concept of the sinister cloned soldiers dressed in uniform white armour. But it was the Star Wars film that was the work of art that Mr Lucas and his companies created. The helmet was utilitarian in the sense that it was an element in the process of production of the film.

45. Those were the concurrent findings of both the judge and the Court of Appeal, in paras [121] and [80] of their respective judgments. The type of judgmental conclusion that often has to be reached in intellectual property cases—on issues such as obviousness, inventiveness, and copying—are matters on which appellate courts should be slow to interfere with the judgment of the trial judge. In *Designers Guild* [2000] 1 WLR 2416, 2423–2424, Lord Hoffmann observed that there were two reasons for this. The first is that the judge has, and the appellate court has not, seen and heard the witnesses. Lord Hoffmann continued,

"Secondly, because the decision involves the application of a not altogether precise legal standard to a combination of features of varying importance, I think that this falls within the class of case in which an appellate court should not reverse a judge's decision unless he has erred in principle: see *Pro Sieben Media AG v. Carlton UK Television Ltd* [1991] 1 WLR 605, 612–613. I agree with Buxton LJ in *Norowzian v. Arks Ltd (No 2)* [2000] FSR 363, 370 when he said: 'where it is not suggested that the judge has made any error of principle a party should not come to the Court of Appeal simply in the hope that the impression formed by the judges in this court, or at least two of them, will be different from that of the trial judge.'"

That applies with extra force in the case of a second appeal. To the same effect are Lord Hoffmann's observations in *Biogen Inc v. Medeva plc* [1997] RPC 1, 45, which are too well known to need repetition.

46. The Court of Appeal(para[78]) relied on Lord Hoffmann's observations in *Designers Guild*, and in our view it was right to do so. During the 17 days of the trial Mann J heard evidence about the helmet and the other artefacts from numerous different witnesses. Long and thorough as his judgment is, he may not have recorded every nuance that contributed to his conclusion. He did not err in law or reach an obviously untenable conclusion, and the Court of Appeal was right to uphold his decision on this point.

47. We would uphold the judgments below very largely for the reasons that they give. But(at the risk of appearing humourless) we are not enthusiastic about the "elephant test" in para[77] of the Court of Appeal's judgment("knowing one when you see it"). Any zoologist has no difficulty in recognising an elephant on sight, and most could no doubt also give a clear and accurate description of its essential identifying features. By contrast a judge, even one very experienced in intellectual property matters, does not have some special power of divination which leads instantly to an infallible conclusion, and no judge would claim to have such a power. The judge reads and hears the evidence(often including expert evidence), reads and listens to the advocates' submissions, and takes what the Court of Appeal rightly called a multi-factorial approach. Moreover the judge has to give reasons to explain his or her conclusions.

48. There is one other matter to which the Court of Appeal attached no weight, but which seems to us to support the judge's conclusion. It is a general point as to the policy considerations underlying Parliament's development of the law in order to protect the designers and makers of three-dimensional artefacts from unfair competition. After reviewing the legislative history the Court of Appeal took the view(para [40]) that there was no assistance to be obtained from the relationship between

copyright and registered design right. We respectfully disagree, especially if the relatively new unregistered design right is also taken into account. It is possible to recognise an emerging legislative purpose (though the process has been slow and laborious) of protecting three-dimensional objects in a graduated way, quite unlike the protection afforded by the indiscriminate protection of literary copyright. Different periods of protection are accorded to different classes of work. Artistic works of art (sculpture and works of artistic craftsmanship) have the fullest protection; then come works with "eye appeal" (*AMP Inc v. Utilux Pty Ltd* [1971] FSR 572); and under Part III of the 1988 Act a modest level of protection has been extended to purely functional objects (the exhaust system of a motor car being the familiar example). Although the periods of protection accorded to the less privileged types have been progressively extended, copyright protection has always been much more generous. There are good policy reasons for the differences in the periods of protection, and the Court should not, in our view, encourage the boundaries of full copyright protection to creep outwards.

Sections 51 and 52

49. The appellants accept that if the helmet did not qualify as a sculpture within the meaning of the 1988 Act, then Mr Ainsworth had a defence under section 51 to any infringement claim based on Mr McQuarrie's graphics, and section 52 does not arise. The Court of Appeal dealt with these sections, for completeness, in paras 83 to 98 of its judgment. It is unnecessary to cover the same ground again. We would dismiss the appeal so far as it is based on the English law of copyright.

联合王国最高法院 2013 第 18 号案件
对英格兰和威尔士上诉法院 2011 第 890 号民事案件的上诉

公共关系顾问协会（上诉人）

报纸许可协会等（被上诉人）

审理人：纽伯格勋爵 院长
　　　　克尔勋爵
　　　　克拉克勋爵
　　　　桑普顿勋爵
　　　　卡恩沃斯勋爵

裁决日期：2013 年 4 月 17 日
开庭日期：2013 年 2 月 11、12 日

案情摘要与裁判要旨

上诉人是由公共关系从业人员组成的行业协会,这些人员负责代表客户处理监测新闻报道等事务,方法之一是使用在线监测或搜索服务。融文集团(Meltwater group of companies)使用自动化软件程序,创建出现在报纸网站上的单词索引。客户向融文集团提供自己感兴趣的检索关键词,融文集团就此生成一份监测报告,列出以这些关键词为索引的检索结果。对于每次检索,监测报告将显示文章的开篇词句、关键词及其左右若干个词,以及超链接,使用户可以通过超链接从源网站获取文章。客户通过电子邮件接收融文集团提供的监测报告,或从后者网站上获取该报告。

1988年《版权、外观设计与专利法案》第16条至第26条授予版权人多项垄断性权利。一般来说,制作、分发受保护作品复制件或改编件是侵权行为。本上诉所涉及的问题是,未经版权人许可、暂时留存在屏幕上或网络缓存中的临时复制件是否属于侵权复制件。

一审法院判决认定,融文集团的客户无论是通过电子邮件接收监测报告,还是浏览网站以获取报告,都需要征得版权人的许可。上诉法院的裁决在效果上维持了一审法院的判决。最高法院则发表了完全不同的看法。

桑普顿勋爵起草判决意见（纽伯格勋爵、克尔勋爵、克拉克勋爵和卡恩沃斯勋爵均赞同）

争议问题

1. 本上诉涉及的重要问题是在互联网上浏览受版权保护资料所涉技术过程中版权法的适用问题。版权人拥有自己实施、授权他人实施1988年《版权、外观设计与专利法案》第16条至第26条所述多项行为的垄断性权利。一般来说，制作、分发受保护作品复制件或改编件是侵权行为。仅观看或阅读受保护作品并不构成侵权。阅读受保护书籍的盗版件，或观赏受保护绘画作品的赝品不构成侵权，但销售盗版件或制作绘画赝品则可能构成侵权。

2. 应用互联网时，一般会在几个阶段创建临时复制件。在路由器和代理服务器的传输过程中，会创建复制件。如果终端用户在其计算机上浏览网页但并未下载，所涉技术过程需要在屏幕上以及硬盘上的网络"缓存"中创建临时复制件。屏幕上显示复制件无疑是相关技术过程的重要组成部分，缺乏这一组成部分，用户将无法浏览网页。复制件将一直停留在屏幕上，直至用户离开相关网页。网络缓存的功能稍微复杂一些。这是当前互联网浏览技术的普遍特征。设计出没有网络缓存的浏览器软件是可能的，但就目前技术水平来看，其结果将是互联网无法承载当前的流量，以致无法正常运行。终端用户可以自行清理缓存，但一般情况下，如果用户不主动清理，一段时间后缓存空间就会被其他内容覆盖，具体多久之后被覆盖取决于缓存空间大小以及终端用户互联网浏览量和时间。以上是对技术过程的粗略描述，但足以满足当前需要。这些技术过程如同数字世界中的大多数事物一样，可以修改操作。网络缓存空间可通过更改用户计算机上的浏览器设置，在一定范围内进行修改。删除的资料有时可以通过专门软件或由熟练的技术人员恢复。但互联网的一般应用不具备这一高端特征，目前可以不予考虑。重点是，在这些情况下，终端用户并未主动复制网页，除非他选择将网页下载或打印出来——他的目的是查看资料。暂时留存在屏幕或网络缓存中的复制件仅仅是他使用计算机查看资料的附随结果。本上诉所涉及的问题是，未经版权人许可，暂时留存在屏幕上或网络缓存中的临时复制件是否属于侵权复制件。

3. 上诉人是由公共关系从业人员组成的行业协会,这些人员负责代表客户处理监测新闻报道等事务。监测新闻报道的方法之一是使用在线监测或搜索服务。本上诉有关融文集团向协会成员提供的服务。融文集团使用自动化软件程序,创建出现在报纸网站上的单词索引。客户向融文集团提供自己感兴趣的检索关键词,融文集团就此生成一份监测报告,列出以这些关键词为索引的检索结果。对于每次检索,监测报告将显示文章的开篇词句、关键词及其左右若干个词,以及超链接(超链接显示的文字是文章标题),使用户可以通过超链接从源网站获取文章。但值得注意的是,如果源网站设有付费墙,超链接并不能使客户绕过付费环节。客户必须按其他访客同等条件付费后,方能获取付费墙后的资料。客户通过电子邮件接收融文集团提供的监测报告,或从其网站上获取该报告。

4. 争论双方的共同基础有:第一,融文集团同意从报纸发行商处获得许可,并根据版权裁判所确定的条款提供服务;第二,融文集团的客户也需要获得报纸发行商的许可方能接受目前的服务,这一点在诉讼的早期阶段就已明确。这是因为,目前的服务会自动通过电子邮件传输监测报告,而电子邮件复制件不是临时的,它会一直存储在收件人的硬盘驱动器上,直至终端用户将其删除。本上诉争议的真正问题在于,如果融文集团的客户只从网站上获取监测报告,是否仍需要征得报纸发行商的许可?显然,如果客户从网站上下载了报告,除非经过报纸发行商的许可,否则客户制作的复制件将侵犯版权。但如果客户只是浏览网站上的资料呢?普劳德曼法官认为,仅浏览网站上的资料也需要许可,上诉法院采纳了她的意见。因为该问题影响现如今一种商业服务的运作,本法院遂同意受理本案。但同一问题可能会影响到数百万非商业性互联网用户,他们很可能未经版权人授权,在不经意间上网浏览了版权保护资料(如第三方非法上传的资料),并因此招致民事责任。观众在数字电视上收看电视节目或通过机顶盒观看付费电视节目时,也会碰到类似问题。

第 2001/29/EC 号指令

5. 2003 年根据《版权和相关条例》对 1988 年《版权、外观设计与专利法案》进行修订,增加第 28A 条,对使用计算机浏览受版权保护资料时所涉及技术过程中创建的临时复制件作出了规定,以执行欧洲议会与欧盟理事会"关于协调信息社会中版权和相关权若干方面"的 2001 年 5 月 22 日第 2001/29/EC 号指令。毫无疑问,该指令和英国制定法条款具有同等效力,为方便起见,以下参照指令条款。

6. 第 2001/29/EC 号指令可追溯至 1995 年 7 月出版的《欧盟委员会信息社会版权与相关权绿皮书》,该绿皮书指出了使用数据处理系统以"人类感官无法直接感知的形式"复制版权资料(即"数字编码")这一问题。这就需要确定一个问题,即版权人所控制的复制作品的权利"应否介入作为信息社会标志性特征的计算机和其他设备的正常应用中(数字化、中间复制、下载到主存储器)"。经过一段时间的磋商,欧盟委员会于 1997 年 12 月发布提案终稿,明确指出了本上诉涉及的问题。该提案讨论了通过互联网或其他高速网络对数字化音乐、电影或其他版权资料库中的内容以数字信号进行商业性传输以满足展示或下载目的的前景,如此一来,将取代人们对诸如书籍、磁盘、磁带等物理传输和存储媒介的需求。一方面,欧盟在政策上一直维持高水平的知识产权保护,这些技术的广泛应用可能会助长盗版;另一方面,显然有人担心,一味照搬实施为物理传输或存储媒介制定的版权法,会阻碍互联网和其他电子媒体技术的商业发展。特别需要指出的是,"电子环境中临时或附随复制"的地位存在不确定性。

7.《伯尔尼公约》第 9 条 2 款允许签署国在本国立法中确定有限的复制作品这一垄断性权利的例外情形:

"本联盟成员国有权制定法律,允许在某些特殊情况下复制作品,但这种复制不得妨害作者对作品的正常使用,也不得不合理地影响作者的合法利益。"

正如欧盟委员会 1997 年看到的那样,欧盟成员国在立法中各自执行《伯尔尼公约》第 9 条 2 款,处理以数字形式提供的版权作品时存在差异,这些差异会阻碍欧盟内部市场的发展。第 2001/29/EC 号指令(欧盟委员会 1997 年提案后附了指令的草案)的目的在于统一整个欧盟内部的规则。

8. 作为一项内部市场措施,第 2001/29/EC 号指令旨在"调整和补充"现有版权法,以"充分应对诸如新型作品利用方式的经济现实"(序文第 5 段),其目标是确保"高水平的版权保护",同时修改版权权利以许可互联

网的正常应用。序文第 31 段称:

"必须维护不同类型权利人之间以及不同类别权利人和受保护客体使用者之间权利和利益的公正平衡。各成员国必须根据新的电子环境,重新评估国内法中关于权利例外和限制的条款。"

序文第 33 段直击临时复制件问题,其内容是:

"复制权这一垄断性权利应允许某些临时复制行为作为例外。'临时复制'是指对作品短暂或附随的复制,这一复制行为构成技术过程内在且必要的组成部分,实施该复制行为的唯一目的是促成作品或其他受保护客体在互联网上通过中间媒介在第三方之间传输,或是为了便于他人能够合法地使用作品或其他受保护客体。此类复制行为不得具有独立的经济价值。符合上述条件的浏览时和缓存中产生的复制,包括那些确保传输系统高效工作的复制,都应作为复制权的此等例外,前提条件是中间媒介不会修改信息,且未干扰使用行业内广泛认可应用的技术去获取有关信息被使用的数据。经权利人授权或不为法律所禁止的使用,都应当被认为是合法的使用。"

9. 第 2001/29/EC 号指令第二章为"权利和例外"。版权人的权利分别在第 2 条"复制权"、第 3 条"传播权"和第 4 条"发行权"三个标题下阐述。第 5 条则对上述权利进行限定,第 1 款为临时复制例外,该例外仅针对第 2 条规定的复制权,具体内容为:

"第 1 段 第 2 条所谓的临时复制行为,是短暂的或附随的行为,并且是技术过程内在且必要的组成部分,其唯一目的是确保:

'(a) 在互联网上通过中间媒介在第三方之间传输,或

'(b) 合法使用作品或其他受保护客体,且此类复制行为不具有独立经济价值,此等复制行为应排除在第 2 条所规定的复制权范围之外。'

……

第 5 段 1 款至 4 款规定的例外与限制仅适用于某些特定情形,且不与对作品或其他受保护客体的正常利用相冲突,也不得无故侵害权利人的合法利益。"

第三章和第四章对数字环境中版权人权利的执行做了细致规定。

欧洲法院的判例

10. 欧洲法院在最近的三起案件中讨论了第 5 条 1 款，为欧盟成员国国内法院适用该条确立了宽泛的指导原则。这些案件分别是（按判决作出的先后顺序）：*Infopaq International A/S v. Danske Dagblades Forening* 案（案号：C-5/08，简称 "*Infopaq I*"，2010 年《弗利特街判例汇编》，起始页 495），*Football Association Premier League Ltd v. QC Leisure and Others* 案（案号：C-403/08），*Karen Murphy v. Media Protection Services Ltd*（"*Premier League*"）案（案号：C-429/08，《欧洲共同市场判例汇编》2012 年第 1 卷，起始页 769）以及 *Infopaq International A/S v. Danske Dagblades Forening* 案（案号：C-302/10，简称 "*Infopaq II*"，2012 年 1 月 17 日判决）。需要指出的是，这三起案件中，只有第一个被普劳德曼法官或上诉法院引用。他们作出判决时，*Premier League* 案和 *Infopaq II* 案都还没有定论。

Infopaq I 案

11. 在 *Infopaq I* 案（2010 年《弗利特街判例汇编》，起始页 495，第 54 段），欧洲法院将第 5 条 1 款解读为"复制行为"的豁免需满足五个条件：

"——该行为是临时的；

——该行为是短暂或附随的；

——该行为构成技术过程内在且必要的组成部分；

——该技术过程的唯一目的是使合法使用的作品或其他受保护客体在互联网上通过中间媒介在第三方之间传输；并且

——该行为没有独立的经济价值。"

这一提法在随后的判例中被以同种形式反复提及，这样一来无疑方便很多。然而，要记住：这只是一种解读。尽管这五个条件分五段分别列出，但它们并非彼此独立的条件，而是相互重叠、彼此渲染。这五个条件必须同时考查，方能达到其共同目的。判例表明，欧洲法院一贯持此种操作。

12. 尤其是在 *Infopaq I* 案中，欧洲法院采取的就是这一操作。该案源自丹麦法院的先决裁判请示，涉及商业媒体监测服务 Infopaq，该服务与融文集团的服务并无不同。争论的问题是 Infopaq 的"数据抓取方法"，即识别相关报纸摘要所用到的电子搜索方法。与本案的不同在于，*Infopaq* 案并非关于将搜索结果传递给客户的方法。然而，*Infopaq* 案的电子搜索方法确实意味着有必要从总体上考虑第 5 条 1 款如何适用于数字资料的存储和浏览。*Infopaq* 案的方法涉及在四个连续阶段创建复制件：（1）创建原始文章的扫描图像；（2）将该图像转换成可检索的文本文件；（3）从该文本文件中提取关键词及其左右各五个词，并将词语存储为文本文件；（4）打印并保存阶段（3）的文本文件。争议在于此过程中所创建复制件的短暂性与附随性问题。欧洲法院认为，如果欧盟成员国国内法院确信在相关技术需求终结时这些复制件会自动删除，即无需任何人择机干预，那么第 5 条 1 款可以适用于（1）、（2）和（3）阶段。但阶段（4）不是"短暂的"，因为只有人为决定销毁打印件时，打印件才会被销毁。

13. 虽然欧洲法院在本案中仅直接关注了前两个条件，但它是在第三个条件下解读前两个条件的。实质上，欧洲法院认为，第三个条件，即复制应当"构成技术过程内在且必要的组成部分"，意味着在技术过程完成时，只有当复制件一定会自动删除时，该复制才能视为是"临时的"或"附随的"。欧洲法院的分析首先关注的是第 5 条 1 款中的例外情形是对版权人被赋予权利的限制。

"第 56 段 在依次解释这些条件时，应当记住，根据已有判例，若一项指令的特定条款违背该指令确立的基本原则，就必须对条款进行严格解释（*Criminal Proceedings against Kapper* 案，案号 C-476/01，2004 年《欧洲法院判例汇编》第 1 卷，起始页 5205，欧洲法院，第 72 段；*Commission of the European Communities v. Spain* 案，案号 C36/05，2006 年《欧洲法院判例汇编》第 1 卷，起始页 10313，欧洲法院，第 31 段）。

第 57 段 这一传统适用于第 2001/29/EC 号指令第 5 条 1 款规定的豁免，该豁免违背了该指令确立的对受保护作品的任何复制都需要版权人授权这一基本原则。

第 58 段 鉴于豁免必须根据第 2001/29/EC 号指令第 5 条 5 款（即豁免仅限于某些特殊情形，这些特殊情形不与对作品或其他受保护客体的正常利用相冲突，也不得无故侵害权利人的合法利益）进行阐释，因此更是需要对豁免进行严格解释。"

在判决书第 61 段至第 64 段，欧洲法院总结立场如下：

"第 61 段 法院认为，据本判决第 54 段提到的第三个条件，短暂和附随的复制行为应是为了完成一个技术过程，该复制行为又构成该过程内在及必要的组成部分。在这种情况下，鉴于本判决第 57、58 段确立的原则，复制行为不得超过为完成相关技术过程所需要的限度。

第 62 段 权利人的法律确定性进一步要求，复制件的存储和删除应独立于人的择机介入，特别是受保护作品使用者的介入。这是因为，在人工介入情况下，无法确保有关人员会删除创建的复制件，或者一旦复制件的存在不再具有完成一项技术过程的功能时将其删除。

第 63 段 这一认识得到了第 2001/29/EC 号指令序言中第 33 段序文的支持，该段列举了实现浏览和缓存而产生的复制，包括那些使传输系统高效工作的复制，以作为符合该指令第 5 条 1 款所指复制行为应具备特征的示例。根据定义，这些行为是自动创建和删除的，并无人工干预。

第 64 段 鉴于上述情况，法院认为，只有当复制行为持续时间不超过完成所涉技术过程需要的时间，且该行为是自动化行为（即一旦该行为不再具有完成这一过程的功能时将被自动删除，无需人工介入）时，该行为才能被认定为第 2001/29/EC 号指令第 5 条 1 款第二个条件中所称的'短暂'行为。"

关于阶段（3）中的复制问题（包含关键词摘录的文本文件），欧洲法院补充道：

"第 66 段……应由成员国国内法院确定，一旦复制行为不再具备完成这一技术过程的功能，复制件的删除是否取决于复制件用户的意愿，以及是否存在复制件被留存的风险。"

***Premier League* 案**

14. 在 *Football Association Premier League Ltd v. QC Leisure* 案以及 *Karen Murphy v. Media Protection Services Ltd* 案（《欧洲共同市场判例汇编》2012 年第 1 卷，起始页 769）这两个重要案件中，对第 5 条 1 款边界的讨论聚焦在第四和第五个条件上，这两个条件在 *Infopaq I* 案中没有被考虑。然而，如果不将第 5 条 1 款作为一个整体来阐释，并逐个审查这五个条件的功能，就不可能认清这些条件的影响。这恰是欧洲法院在 *Premier League* 案中所做的事情。

15. 案件事实是，墨菲夫人在希腊订阅了付费电视服务，并得到一个希腊卫星解码器。但她未经版权人授权，在联合王国的酒吧里使用该解码器接收足球比赛的广播，供酒吧顾客观看。被控侵权的复制件是资料传输过程中在解码器存储单元中和电视屏幕上创建的临时复制件。这些复制件的功能类似于在网络缓存中和个人计算机屏幕上创建的复制件。从任何角度来看，被控的侵权行为都是针对墨菲夫人及其酒吧顾客作为终端用户对版权资料的"消费"。在判决书第162段至第164段，欧洲法院提醒自己，虽然必须严格解释对版权人控制复制这一当然权利的任何例外，但该权利也必须与设定例外情形的目的——鼓励新技术的开发和应用，并保障想要使用这些技术的用户的权利相平衡。欧洲法院认为，墨菲夫人受第5条1款保护。

16. 第一个问题是，墨菲夫人解码器存储单元中所谓的侵权复制件是否为第5条1款（a）和（b）项规定的两个目的之一而创建。由于它们并非为通过网络传送资料而创建，墨菲夫人只能以（b）项作为申辩理由。这就要求她论证说明这些复制件是为了其他合法用途而创建。欧洲法院认为确是如此，并如是说道：

"第168段 很明显，根据版权指令序文第33段，对作品的使用如果得到了版权人的授权，或不被相关法律所限制，应视为合法。

第169段 由于在主要诉讼程序中，争议的作品使用行为并未经版权人授权，因此，必须考虑确定争议的使用行为是否是不为法律所限制的行为。

第170段 就这一点而言，毫无疑问，这些短暂的复制行为是为了确保卫星解码器和电视屏幕能正常工作。站在电视观众的角度，这些复制行为能使他们观看受保护作品的广播。

第171段 仅在私人圈内接收这些广播——也就是说，接收广播信号并进行可视化展示——并不违背欧盟或联合王国立法，这是可以从C-403/08案中问题5的措辞得出的结论，因此该行为合法。此外，根据本案判决书第77段至第132段，如果是使用外国解码装置接收来自联合王国以外的欧盟成员国广播的信号，这种接收必须视为合法。

第 172 段 因此，本案中复制行为的唯一目的是实现版权指令第 5 条 1 款（b）项之对作品的'合法使用'。

第 173 段 因此，主要诉讼程序中争议的复制行为符合第 5 条规定的第四个条件。"

17. 判决书的这一部分对于理解当前的问题以及欧洲法院关于这一问题的整个审判规程至关重要。欧盟法律本可以径直规定，包括通过网络传播在内，任何未经授权使用版权资料的行为一律视为非法行为。事实上，欧盟经济社会委员会曾建议将委员会的原始提案修正（扩展和澄清）为未经版权人授权，"任何实质上消费受保护作品的复制"都属于非法行为（见1998 年 12 月 28 日《欧盟官方公报》407/32，第 3. 7. 1. 2 段）。但这一建议并未被采纳。在 *Premier League* 案中，欧盟法院断然拒绝了旨在将第 5 条 1 款按照与其发布时相同方法解读的尝试。由于墨菲夫人对资料的使用并不违反"相关法律"，根据第 5 条 1 款（b）项，即使未经权利人授权，该行为也是合法的。在判决书的后面部分，欧洲法院认为，墨菲夫人对资料的使用侵犯了指令第 3 条所单独规定的传播权，就这一点而言，该行为是非法的。然而，这并不影响欧洲法院的结论，即根据第 5 条 1 款（b）项，她对资料的使用是合法的。这是因为第 5 条 1 款只涉及第 2 条所定义的复制权的边界。因此，唯一要求是，相关使用符合欧盟关于复制权的立法，包括第 5 条 1 款本身。

18. 随后，欧洲法院转向第五个条件，即使用该资料所产生的"经济价值"。欧洲法院将这一条件解释为，被控侵权人对资料的使用不得具有除接收和浏览资料固有价值以外的其他价值：

"第 174 段 最后，就该条规定的第五个条件而言，技术过程中的复制行为使人能够获取受保护作品。由于受保护作品具有经济价值，获取行为必然具有经济意义。

第 175 段 然而，只要第 2001/29/EC 号指令第 5 条 1 款中规定的例外不是冗余内容，那么这种经济意义也必须具有独立性，也即超越仅接收包含受保护作品的广播所带来的经济利益，换句话说，超过了仅接收广播并进行视觉展示所产生的利益。

第 176 段 主要诉讼程序中，在卫星解码器存储内和电视屏幕上进行的

临时复制行为，构成了接收所传送有关作品广播信号过程中不可分割且非自主控制的部分。此外，这些行为的实施未受那些因此能获取到受保护作品者的影响，他们甚至没有意识到这些行为的实施。

第177段 因此，那些临时复制行为并不足以产生额外的超过仅接收该广播本身所带来的经济利益。

第178段 故而，主要诉讼程序中争议的复制行为不能视为具有独立的经济意义。这些行为满足第2001/29/EC号指令第5条1款规定的第五个条件。

第179段 此外，这一结论，以及本判决书第172段的结论（复制行为以实现合法使用为目的），还得到了该条款目的的印证，即确保新技术的开发与应用。若认为争议的复制行为不符合第2001/29/EC号指令第5条1款规定的诸条件，那么所有使用（需要进行这些复制行为以正常工作的）现代设备的观众，未经版权人授权，都不得接收包含作品的广播。这一认识无视第2001/29/EC号指令序文第31段所描绘的欧盟立法机构的愿景，将阻碍新技术的实际传播和贡献，甚至使其瘫痪。"

19. 最后，欧洲法院简单分析了指令第5条5款的要求，即该例外只有在"不与对作品或其他受保护客体的正常利用相冲突，也不得无故侵害权利人的合法利益的特定情况下"才适用。欧洲法院认为，考虑到那些使其认为第5条1款适用的因素，第5条5款也必须视为已经满足。本法官将在讨论 *Infopaq II* 案时对这一点重新展开讨论。

Infopaq II 案

20. 与 *Infopaq I* 案一样，*Infopaq II* 案是同一个案件中的第二个先决裁判请示。它涉及第三、第四和第五个条件，这些条件在前一个先决裁判请示中没有直接涉及。欧洲法院基本上重复了其在 *Premier League* 案中就第5条1款（b）项下的"合法性"测试所给的陈述，并借此裁定认为第四个条件得到了满足。这里无需再对这一点进行进一步讨论。其他问题涉及第三个条件（技术过程内在且必要的组成部分）、第五个条件（没有独立的经济意义）和第5条5款的效力。

21. 丹麦法院对第三个条件提出的问题是，欧洲法院以前强调不得有人为干预，这似乎排除了第 5 条 1 款适用于启动这一过程的扫描件，因为原件必须由人工放入扫描仪。在处理这一问题时，欧洲法院指出，其在 *Infopaq I* 案中所强调的是删除临时复制件不得依赖人为干预，但并未规定任何阶段都不能有人为干预（见第 32 段）。由此可知，法院无需考虑用户启动该过程（如通过启动计算机或访问特定网页）这一个人决定。

22. 在处理完这一问题后，欧洲法院借此机会，更为全面地探究了复制应当是"技术过程内在且必要的组成部分"这一要求：

"第 30 段 '技术过程内在且必要的组成部分'这一条件要求临时复制行为必须全部在实施技术过程中进行，也就意味着，无论是全部还是部分的临时复制行为，都不能在这一技术过程之外进行。这一条件还假定临时复制行为必然是一个闭环过程，没有这一闭环过程，有关技术过程就不能正常和高效地运作（类似表述见 *Infopaq International*❶ 案判决书第 61 段）。

第 37 段 最后还需注意，如果没有相关的临时复制行为，技术过程就无法正常和高效运作。该技术过程旨在识别报纸文章中预先设定的关键词，并将它们提取存储在数字媒介上。因此，此类电子检索需要将这些文章从纸质媒介转换成数字数据，这种转换是识别数据、发掘和提取关键词所必需的。"

23. 欧洲法院在处理第五个条件关于缺乏"独立经济意义"时，又回到了这个主题：

"第 48 段 在这方面，应当回顾，第 5 条 1 款意义上的临时复制行为旨在使人们能够获取并利用受保护作品。由于这些作品具有特定的经济价值，因此对它们的获取和利用必然也具有经济意义（类似表述见 *Football Association Premier League* 案，《欧洲共同市场判例汇编》2012 年第 1 卷，起始页 769，第 174 段）。

第 49 段 此外，从第 2001/29/EC 号指令序文第 33 段中可以明显看出，临时复制行为——如实现'浏览'和'缓存'的行为——旨在促进作品的利用，或提高其利用效率。因此，这些行为的一个固有特征是实施这些行为能够实现效率增益，进而增加收益或降低生产成本。

---

❶ 此处应指的是 *Infopaq I*。——译者注

第50段 但是，这些行为不得具有独立的经济意义，也即实施这些行为所产生的经济利益不得与合法使用有关作品所产生的经济利益不同或相分离，也不得产生超出利用受保护作品本身的额外经济利益（类似表述见 Football Association Premier League and Others 案，第175段）。

第51段 实施临时复制行为所产生的效率增益，如主要诉讼程序中争议的效率增益，并没有这种独立的经济意义，因为实施临时复制行为所产生的经济利益只有在利用被复制的标的物时才能体现出来，因此这些效率增益既未区别于利用被复制标的物所产生的利益，也做不到与之分离。

第52段 另一方面，只有作者本人实施了特定临时复制行为并从中获取了经济利益，才能称得上不同或相分离的经济利益。"

24. 最后，欧洲法院在 Infopaq II 案中进一步拓展了其在 Premier League 案中对第5条5款的认识：

"第56段 在这方面，只要这些复制行为符合欧洲法院判例所阐释的第2001/29/EC号指令第5条1款的所有条件，就足以认定这些复制行为不会与作品的正常使用相冲突，且未不合理地侵害权利人的合法利益（见 Football Association Premier League and Others 案，第181段）。

第57段 因此，第七个问题的答案是，第2001/29/EC号指令第5条5款必须解释为，在'数据抓取'过程中实施的临时复制行为，如那些在主要诉讼程序中争议的行为，只要它们满足指令第5条1款中规定的所有条件，就必须视为未干扰作品的正常利用，也未不合理地侵害权利人的合法利益。"

25. 最后这一结论乍看起来很奇怪，因为它意味着第5条5款相较于第5条1款没有任何新加内容。但是，当人们意识到第5条5款再现的是欧盟及其成员国所必须遵守的《伯尔尼公约》之第9条2款时，便释然了。根据该条，公约签署国有权立法明确某些不被视为侵权的复制行为，但这些例外不得与作品的"正常"利用相冲突，且不会"不合理地"侵害作者的"合法"利益。第5条1款就属于此等立法。欧洲法院指出，起草该条的目的是在立法上确定哪些利用行为应视为对作品的正常利用，以及哪些影响作者垄断性权利的行为应视为合理合法。这并不意味着第5条5款是冗余的，其作用是对第5条1款进行严格解释以符合其立法目的（见 Infopaq I 案判决书第 58 段）。但无论如何，在试图对其进行解释前，必须首先考虑其立法目的。

欧洲法院裁决的效果

26. 欧洲法院这一权威机构，就此问题的裁决结果总结如下：

（1）遵从本法官将在后文总结的限制，第 5 条 1 款中的例外情形适用于作为"技术过程"（特别是数据的数字处理）中一个内在且必要的组成部分而存在的复制件。在这里，如果制作复制件的行为能够使这一技术过程"正常和高效"工作，则它就是这一过程的"必要"组成部分（见 *Infopaq II* 案判决书，第 30 段和第 37 段）。

（2）这些复制件必须是临时的。第 5 条 1 款紧接着用以下文字解释并界定何谓"临时"：复制件的制作必须是"短暂或附随的，并且是技术过程中内在且必要的组成部分"。这意味着：①存储和删除版权资料须是用户决定启停相关技术过程的自动结果，而不是依赖于人的择机干预；②复制件的存续期间应限于完成相关技术过程所必需的时间（见 *Infopaq I* 案判决书第 62 段和第 64 段）。

（3）这一例外不限于为使能够在网络上通过中间媒介传播资料而进行的复制行为，也适用于目的仅在于实现其他用途而实施的复制行为，前提是这些其他用途是合法的。此处的"其他用途"包括网页浏览（见 *Infopaq I* 案判决书第 63 段和 *Infopaq II* 案判决书第 49 段）。

（4）就第 5 条 1 款而言，无论是否经过版权人授权，只要利用版权资料的行为符合欧盟关于复制权的立法（包括第 5 条 1 款本身，见 *Premier League* 案判决书第 168 段至第 173 段，以及 *Infopaq II* 案判决书第 42 段），则这一利用行为就是合法的。不能仅因为未经版权人的授权使用该版权资料就简单地认定为非法。

（5）制作临时复制行为不得具有"独立的经济意义"。这并不意味着其一定没有商业价值——它可以有商业价值，只是不得具有"独立"的商业价值，也就是说，不得有除通过数字传输或查阅资料所获得价值之外的价值（见 *Premier League* 案判决书第 175 段，以及 *Infopaq II* 案判决书第 50 段）。

（6）满足所有这些条件，则自动满足第 5 条 5 款。

对本案的适用

27. 首要的基本问题是，第2001/29/EC号指令第5条1款是否完全适用于终端用户使用互联网生成的临时复制件。代表"报纸许可协会"出庭的皇家大律师豪依先生认为并不适用。他辩称，指令第5条1款仅适用于在网络上传输资料过程中生成的复制件，如在路由器和代理服务器缓存中生成的复制件。在本法官看来，这一论点站不住脚。首先，从指令的序文，特别是序文第33段可以清楚地看出，指令所指的例外应"包括确保浏览以及缓存实现的行为"。浏览不是传输过程的一部分，浏览是终端用户使用网络浏览器查看网页，从本质上讲，这属于面向终端用户的功能。所谓"行为"，是指在指令序文开头所指的"临时复制行为"，这一所指贯穿整个序文。促成用户浏览网页的临时复制行为因而是指在终端用户硬盘驱动器的网络缓存中和屏幕上制作临时复制件的行为。因此，序文明确表明，例外将适用于终端用户浏览网页情形。其次，如果豪依先生的主张是正确的，那么例外的范围将仅相当于第5条1款（a）项所涵盖的那一部分过程（在互联网上通过中间媒介在第三方之间传输）。而实际上，缓存涉及的是在互联网中传输资料，因为缓存的目的在于通过缓解容量限制来提高互联网运行效率（见上第2段）。但无论如何，例外的范围要广于此，因为它也适用于第5条1款（b）项所涵盖的操作（合法使用）。"合法使用"是指对受版权法保护作品的使用。正如欧洲法院在 *Premier League* 案和 *Infopaq II* 案中所明确的那样，"合法使用"也包括"不受相关法律禁止的使用"，无论是否获得版权人的授权。这必然包含终端用户浏览互联网时对作品的使用。最后，豪依先生的主张与 *Premier League* 案的判决直接冲突，在该案中，法官将指令第5条适用于墨菲女士在电视上播放版权资料的行为。她是终端用户，她和她的顾客正在消费产品。第五个条件要求复制件不应具有独立的经济意义，欧洲法院在判决书第176段中讨论了在电视屏幕上展示复制件的状况，因为欧洲法院总法律顾问曾提出，屏幕上展示的复制件可能具有缓存中复制件所不具有的独立经济意义（见总法律顾问意见第95段）。在第179段，欧洲法院指出，如果第5条1款不能适用于电视终端用户观看版权资料，这就意味着"在未获得版权人授权的情况下，此类观众将被阻止接收广播"，这将"阻碍新技术的实际传播和贡献，甚至致其瘫痪，这有悖于欧盟立法机构在序文第 31 段中所表达的愿景"。为此，无需区分对待在电视屏幕上观看版权资料和在计算机上观看相同资料。

28. 一旦人们能接受第 5 条 1 款的部分目的是为使终端用户能在互联网上查看版权资料而实施的复制行为授权，则该条所规定的各种条件就必须尽可能以与该目的一致的方式来解读。如果例外情况之间是一致的，那么第 5 条第 1 款也必须适用于与互联网浏览相关的一般技术过程。

29. 在本法官看来，就本案而言，满足第 5 条 1 款中的第三、第四和第五个条件并不存在争议。第三个条件是，在网络缓存和屏幕上制作复制件应当是技术过程"内在且必要的组成部分"。很显然是的。在指令发布之时并且时至今日，这些仍然是现代计算机设计的基本特征。毫无疑问，有可能设计出不在互联网浏览过程中缓存资料的计算机，但用 *Infopaq II* 案判决的话来说，如果没有相关复制行为，浏览互联网所需的技术过程就无法"正常并高效"地运作（见判决书第 30 段和第 37 段）。适用于像融文集团客户那样的终端用户，第四个条件要求其使用是合法的。根据 *Premier League* 案和 *Infopaq II* 案中的裁决，一旦确立未经版权人授权的对作品的利用属于合法利用，也就等于是明确满足了第四个条件。满足第五个条件（即复制行为不得具有独立的经济意义）的原因与 *Premier League* 案相同，即复制行为对融文集团的客户来说没有独立的经济价值。这是因为，除非他们下载或打印出资料（毫无疑问，在这些情况下他们需要授权），否则他们通过融文集团网站上获取信息所产生的唯一经济价值是通过在屏幕上阅读信息获得的。

30. 这些讨论无疑解释了为什么豪依先生的陈词主要针对前两个条件，即浏览网站所涉及的技术过程中产生的复制件是否为"临时"且具有"短暂或附随"性。并不是说"短暂"和"临时"有什么不同，在本法官看来它们是一样的。"短暂"只是"临时"后面被修饰词语的部分意义。

31. 正如欧洲法院已认定的那样，如果在互联网上浏览版权资料是符合第 5 条 1 款规定的利用方法，并且在网络缓存中或在屏幕上进行临时复制对于正常高效地操作浏览所涉及的技术过程是不可或缺的，那么法律再认为这些复制件在正常运作过程中算不上"短暂的"或"附随的"进而不符合条件就很奇怪了。正如本法官上文中援引 *Infopaq I* 案判决给出的分析那样，

相关要求是：①版权资料的存储和删除须是自动发生的结果，而非依赖于人的择机干预，以及②复制行为的持续时间应限于"完成相关技术过程所必需的时间"（见第62段和第64段）。"存储"资料，即在缓存中或屏幕上创建复制件，是浏览互联网的自动结果。除了要人为决定访问相关网页外，它不需要其他人为干预；同样，删除资料是随着时间推移和继续使用浏览器而自动发生的结果。"相关技术过程"是指伴随网页浏览必然发生的过程，包括在缓存中留存资料。它所留存的时间不会超过互联网正常使用的持续时间。现在将对欧洲法院所用语言的细致分析暂放一下，就不难发现这些语言的目的非常简单，那就是要将使用计算机或其他设备来查看相关资料与使用计算机或其他设备来记录资料区分开来。将复制件限于"短暂的"或"附随的"特征，是不希望版权保护的这一例外被用于保护下载或其他形式的数字或物理复制。对于后者，在用户选择删除或销毁复制件之前，复制件一直存在，因此可以根据用户意愿永久存在。

32. 豪依先生的观点是，缓存资料并不是"短暂的"或"附随的"，因为用户可以自行决定关闭计算机，从而将资料无限期地保留在缓存中，直至再次启动浏览器；或者，用户可以调整设置，扩大缓存容量，这样即使用户还在使用浏览器，也可延长资料留存在缓存中的时间；用户还可以访问一个网页，保持计算机在开启状态，在屏幕上无限期显示该网页。豪依先生所列举的确实都是人为择机干预的例子，但与本案无关，因为这些操作只是人为地延长了相关"技术过程"的持续时间，并不涉及用户是否自行决定将资料保留在缓存中。目前需要从三个方面回应。首先，在浏览过程中必须根据计算机或浏览器的正常操作情况来判断在网络缓存中或屏幕上创建复制件的效果。仅凭在法庭上通过精巧设计展示，以在某种程度上延长原本具有临时性的复制件的留存时间是不够的。其次，是否需要人为干预删除资料是个问题（见 *Infopaq I* 案判决书第66段）。就第5条1款所确立的目标而言，至关重要的一点是，人为决定延长自动过程中资料的留存时间，与在浏览过程中存储资料复制件以确保其永久存在（除非并且直至用户自行决定将其删除或销毁），这两者之间是有区别的。欧洲法院的多个裁决表明，前者一般满足第5条1款中的前两个条件，而后者则不满足。最后，被上诉人所举的这些例子本身就已经说明很多问题。如果仅仅因为一般而言可以通过关闭计算机、更改浏览器设置以扩大网络缓存容量或无限期地将图像留存在屏幕上，就可以阻止适用第5条1款，那么，第5条1款将永远不可能适用于互联网浏览。这将违背立法的初衷。

33. 在本法官看来，如果在网络缓存中或屏幕上的复制件是"短暂的"，严格来说，就没有必要再考虑这些复制件是否也是"附随的"。但本法官认为它们很明显是附随的。计算机软件将网页展示在屏幕上及放入缓存中，以实现合法利用版权资料（即查看版权资料）的目的。复制件的创建完全附随于所涉技术过程。

34. 一旦确定了这些事项，就可以同时满足第5条5款的要求。

后果

35. 欧盟的政策是维持"高水平的知识产权保护"。这一政策在指令本身（见序文第4段和第9段）和判例（如 *Premier League* 案判决书第186段）中均得以体现。本法院面对的争论意见是，如果在网页上观看版权资料无需版权人的许可，那么，版权人将面临大规模且难以发现或阻止的盗版行为。

36. 本法官不认可这一争论意见，而且显然欧洲法院在连续几个相关案例中的裁决对此也不予认可。诚然，对版权人权利的任何削弱，都必然缩小其就作品所享有的保护范围。但我们却有必要在一定程度上限制版权人的权利。一是，第5条1款是版权人控制作品复制权的例外，它准许某些未经版权人授权的复制行为，这些复制行为原本会侵犯版权人的权利。二是，无论是在英国法还是在欧盟法中，仅是查看或阅读以实体形式存在的侵权文章，从不会构成侵权。这种情况在第2001/29/EC号指令第2条、第3条和第4条中对版权人权利的列举中得到了确认，但从未有人认为这种情况与对知识产权的高水平保护相矛盾。第5条1款所主张的，只是将在互联网上查阅版权资料的方式与查阅实体形式资料的方式等同对待，尽管所涉及的技术过程附随包括在所用电子设备中进行临时复制的行为。三是，如果仅浏览版权资料而不去下载或打印就属于侵权，那么，原则上浏览互联网时很可能只要查看了载有版权资料的网页，就无意中违反了民事法律。这种结果似乎令人无法接受，它将使欧盟无数个出于个人或商业目的使用浏览

器和搜索引擎的普通互联网用户变成侵权人。四是，第5条1款中的任何内容都不影响融文集团事先征得许可，方得以将版权资料上传到其网站上或以其他方式制作非临时复制件。目前，融文集团支付的许可费是基于其客户从报纸发行商处获得个人许可，并且该服务仅提供给获得报纸发行商许可的终端用户。如果终端用户不用获得报纸发行商的许可，则融文集团应付给报纸发行商的许可费很可能会大幅提高（本法官对此不作决定），因为在此情形下融文集团被许可的价值将显著提高。被上诉人已经据此另行向版权裁判所提出了索赔。在本法官看来，根据版权价值大小向将版权资料置于网络平台者支付一笔大额许可费，要比从成百上千个零散的互联网浏览者（在有些情况下可能是数百万）那里单独收取小额费用更方便。五是，不将仅仅是浏览网页的行为视为侵权，并不意味着版权人没有针对盗版行为的有效救济措施，这只是意味着救济措施必须是针对那些看起来更有明显过错的人。第5条1款中的任何内容均不影响版权人对那些非法将版权资料上传到互联网的人提起诉讼的权利，正如版权人始终有权起诉那些制作或分发书籍、电影、音乐或其他受保护作品的盗版件者。第2001/29/EC号指令本身在第三章和第四章就包含重要条款，详述了打击盗版行为的程序和处罚。

下级诸法院的决定

37. 普劳德曼法官判决认定，融文集团的客户无论是通过电子邮件接收监测报告，还是浏览网站以获取报告，都需要征得版权人的许可。她的理由是：①在浏览过程中，终端用户在其计算机上的复制行为无论持续时间有多短暂，都不是技术过程的一部分，因为复制行为是"因他自己的意愿发生的"，即是他自愿决定访问网页；②之所以不是技术过程的一部分，还有一个原因是，复制行为事实上只是这一技术过程的末端结果，毕竟它是"终端用户"看到的；以及③查阅这些复制件并不构成"合法使用"，因为它们未经版权人授权（见第109段）。这些原因当然是相关的，并且用普劳德曼法官自己的话说，这三个原因加起来得出的结论为"在此情况下，被告可援引的抗辩理由是复制的目的，即在互联网上通过中间媒介（通常是互联网服务提供商）实现第三方之间的高效传输"（见第110段）。上诉法院同意她的观点,尤其是她论述的理由①。上诉法院认为,"复制行为是因人们主动访问网页所引起的行为"(见第 35 段)。在效果上,这等于是支持了普劳德曼法官的观点,即未经许可,浏览互联网永远不能满足第 5 条 1 款的条件。很明显,如果普劳德曼法官和上诉法院能从欧盟法院 *Premier League* 案和 *Infopaq II* 案的判决中获得启发,他们就不会得出这些结论。特别是欧洲法院在这些案件中赋予了"合法使用"这一概念更广阔的含义,使得不可能将例外的范围局限于互联网的内部系统中。一旦接受了将第 2001/29/EC 号指令第 5 条 1 款扩展适用于未经许可的终端用户为浏览目的而进行的临时复制行为,各下级法院就会摒弃他们所接受的很多争论意见。

向欧洲法院请示先决裁判意见

38. 欧洲法院在其就先决裁判意见所作出的最新建议(2012 年 11 月 6 日欧盟官方公报 C338)中注意到,尽管欧盟成员国国内法院可能认为现有欧洲法院判例已经集聚足够的规则来指导裁决案件,但新问题的出现使得对欧盟法律的解释对在欧盟范围内统一适用法律具有普遍利益时,或者如果现有判例法不能适用于新情况时,成员国国内法院可以请示欧洲法院出具先决裁判意见。根据欧洲法院迄今对第 2001/29/EC 号指令所作的解释和适用,本法官已在本判决书中作出判决。然而,本法官认识到,这一问题具有跨国性,并且将版权法应用到互联网环境中对欧盟数百万使用这一基础技术设施的人有着重要影响。考虑到这些因素,任何有关于此类问题的决定,都应提请欧洲法院出具先决裁判意见,以便在整个欧盟范围内统一解决这一关键问题。本法官认为,在就本上诉作出任何裁决之前,本法院应向欧盟法院请求指示第 2001/29/EC 号指令第 5 条 1 款的条件,即复制行为应是①临时的,②短暂的或附随的,以及③技术过程内在且必要的组成部分;是否在本判决第 2 段和第 31 段、第 32 段所述的技术特征中得到满足,尤其是这样一个事实:在互联网的一般应用过程中,在浏览行为完成后,版权资料的复制件将在缓存中留存一段时间,直至被其他资料所覆盖,并且屏幕复制件将保留在屏幕上,直到用户终止浏览行为。

39. 本法官将邀请律师就拟提请指示的问题发表意见,并且起草或(有可能的话)商定一份先决裁判意见草案,以供本法院参考。

[2013] UKSC 18
On appeal from: [2011] EWCA Civ 890

Public Relations Consultants Association Limited (Appellant) v. The Newspaper Licensing Agency Limited and others (Respondents)

before

Lord Neuberger, President
Lord Kerr
Lord Clarke
Lord Sumption
Lord Carnwath

JUDGMENT GIVEN ON

April 2013

Heard on 11 and 12 February 2013

https://www.supremecourt.uk/cases/docs/uksc-2011-0202-judgment.pdf

Public Relations Consultants Association Limited (Appellant)v.
The Newspaper Licensing Agency Limited and others (Respondents)

LORD SUMPTION (with whom Lord Neuberger, Lord Kerr, Lord Clarke and Lord Carnwath agree)

The issue

1. This appeal raises an important question about the application of copyright law to the technical processes involved in viewing copyright material on the internet. The owner of a copyright has the exclusive right to do or to authorise a number of acts defined in sections 16 to 26 of the Copyright, Designs and Patents Act 1988. Broadly speaking, it is an infringement to make or distribute copies or adaptations of a protected work. Merely viewing or reading it is not an infringement. A person who reads a pirated copy of a protected book or views a forgery of a protected painting commits no infringement although the person who sold him the book or forged the painting may do.

2. The ordinary use of the internet will involve the creation of temporary copies at several stages. Copies will be created in the course of transmission in internet routers and proxy servers. Where a web-page is viewed by an end-user on his computer, without being downloaded, the technical processes involved will require temporary copies to be made on screen and also in the internet "cache" on the hard disk. The screen copy is self-evidently an essential part of the technology involved, without which the web-page cannot be viewed by the user. It will remain on screen until the user moves away from the relevant web-page. The function of the internet cache is somewhat more complex. It is a universal feature of current internet browsing technology. It would be possible to design browsing software without an internet cache, but in the present state of technology the result would be that the internet would be unable to cope with current volumes of traffic and would not function properly. The cache may be deliberately cleared by the end-user, but otherwise it will in the ordinary course be overwritten by other material after an interval which will depend on its capacity and on the volume and timing of the end-user's internet usage. The above is a crude, but for present purposes sufficient, description of the technical processes. Like most things in the digital world, their operation is capable of being modified. The capacity of the internet cache may within limits be modifiedby altering the browser settings on the user's computer. Deleted material can sometimes be retrieved by special software or highly proficient techni-

cians. But this refinement is not characteristic of the ordinary use of the internet and can for present purposes be ignored. The important point is that in none of these cases does the end-user set out to make a copy of the web-page unless he chooses to download it or print it out. His object is to view the material. The copies temporarily retained on the screen or the internet cache are merely the incidental consequence of his use of a computer to do that. The question which arises on this appeal is whether they are nonetheless infringing copies unless licensed by the rights owner.

3. The appellant is a professional association of public relations professionals who, among other things, monitor news coverage on behalf of clients. One way of doing this is to use on-line monitoring or search services. This appeal is about the services provided to members of the association by the Meltwater group of companies. The Meltwater companies use automated software programmes to create an index of words appearing on newspaper websites. Meltwater's customers provide them with search terms of interest to them, and Meltwater produces a monitoring report listing the results of a search of the index for those keywords. For each search hit, the monitoring report will present the opening words of the article, the keyword together with several words on either side of it, and a hyperlink (in the form of a reproduction of the headline) which enables the user to access the article on the relevant source website. It should, however, be noted that if that website has a paywall, the link will not enable the user to avoid it. He will have to pay for access to the material behind the paywall on the same terms as anyone else. Meltwater sends the monitoring report to the customer by email or the customer accesses it on the Meltwater website.

4. A number of points are common ground. It is common ground that Meltwater agreed to take a licence from the publishers of the newspapers to provide their service on terms which have been settled by the Copyright Tribunal. It is also common ground, and has been from an early stage of these proceedings, that Meltwater's customers require a licence to receive the service in its present form. This is because in its present form the service automatically involves the transmission of the monitoring report by e-mail. The email copy is not temporary. It is stored on the recipient's hard drive until the end-user chooses to delete it. The real question on this appeal is whether Meltwater's customers would need a licence to receive its service if the

monitoring report were made available only on Meltwater's website. Obviously, to the extent that the customer downloads the report from the website he is making a copy that will infringe the newspaper's copyright unless he is licensed. But what if he merely views the material on the website? Proudman J held that he also needed a licence for that, and the Court of Appeal agreed with her. The issue has reached this court because it affects the operation of a service which is being made available on a commercial basis. But the same question potentially affects millions of non-commercial users of the internet who may, no doubt unwittingly, be incurring civil liability by viewing copyright material on the internet without the authority of the rights owner, for example because it has been unlawfully uploaded by a third party. Similar issues arise when viewers watch a broadcast on a digital television or a subscription television programme via a set-top box.

Directive 2001/29/EC

5. Temporary copies created as part of the technical processes involved in viewing copyright material on a computer are dealt with by section 28A of the Copyright, Designs and Patents Act 1988. Section 28A was added to the Act by regulation in 2003 to give effect to Directive 2001/29/EC of 22 May 2001 on "the harmonisation of certain aspects of copyright and related rights in the information society." It is not disputed that the effect of the Directive and the English statutory provision is the same, and it is convenient to refer to the terms of the Directive.

6. Directive 2001/29/EC originated in Commission Green Paper on Copyright and Related Rights in the Information Society, published in July 1995, which identified as an issue the use of data processing systems to reproduce copyright material "in a form which cannot be apprehended directly by the human senses", i.e. as digital code. This would make it necessary to decide, among other things, whether the right of a copyright owner tocontrol the reproduction of his work "should come into play in the ordinary use (digitization, intermediate copies, downloading into main memory) of the computers and other equipment which characterize the information society. " This was followed, after a period for consultation, by a proposal of the EC Commission issued in its final form in December 1997, which identified very clearly

the problem which has arisen on this appeal. It addressed the prospect of the commercial transmission from digital databases of music, films or other copyright material as digital signals over the internet or other high-speed networks for display or downloading, which would dispense with the need for physical media of transmission and storage such as books, disks, tapes, and the like. On the one hand the EU has traditionally afforded, as a matter of policy, a high level of protection for intellectual property rights, and the widespread use of these technologies was likely to facilitate piracy. On the other, it is clear that there was concern that the over-rigid application of copyright law devised for physical media of transmission or storage would retard the commercial development of the internet and other form of electronic media technology. In particular, there was uncertainty about the status of "temporary or incidental reproductions in the electronic environment."

7. Article 9(2) of the Berne Convention for the Protection of Literary and Artistic Works authorised signatory states to legislate for limited exceptions to the author's exclusive right to authorise the reproduction of his work:

"It shall be a matter for legislation in the countries of the Union to permit the reproduction of such works in certain special cases, provided that such reproduction does not conflict with a normal exploitation of the work and does not unreasonably prejudice the legitimate interests of the author."

The problem, as the Commission saw it in 1997, was that different member states had made use of the liberty conferred by article 9(2) to legislate in different ways for the treatment of copyright works made available in digital form and these differences were liable to impede the development of the internal market. The purpose of the Directive, a draft of which was annexed to the proposal, was to harmonise the rules across the EU.

8. Directive 2001/29/EC was an internal market measure designed to "adapt and supplement" existing copyright law to "respond adequately to economic realities such as new forms of exploitation" (Recital 5). Its object was to ensure a "high level of protection for copyrights", while modifying those rights to allow the ordinary use of the internet. Recital 31 declared:

"A fair balance of rights and interests between the different categories of rightholders, as well as between the different categories of rightholders and users of protected subject-matter must be safeguarded. The existing exceptions and limitations to the rights as set out by the Member States have to be reassessed in the light of the new electronic environment."

Recital 33 referred directly to the problem of temporary copies in the following terms:

"The exclusive right of reproduction should be subject to an exception to allow certain acts of temporary reproduction, which are transient or incidental reproductions, forming an integral and essential part of a technological process and carried out for the sole purpose of enabling either efficient transmission in a network between third parties by an intermediary, or a lawful use of a work or other subject-matter to be made. The acts of reproduction concerned should have no separate economic value on their own. To the extent that they meet these conditions, this exception should include acts which enable browsing as well as acts of caching to take place, including those which enable transmission systems to function efficiently, provided that the intermediary does not modify the information and does not interfere with the lawful use of technology, widely recognised and used by industry, to obtain data on the use of the information. A use should be considered lawful where it is authorised by the rightholder or not restricted by law."

9. Chapter II of the Directive deals with "Rights and Exceptions". The rights of the copyright owner are dealt with separately in articles 2, 3 and 4 under three heads: reproduction rights, communication rights and distribution rights respectively. Article 5 then qualifies these rights. Article 5.1 creates an exception for temporary copies which applies only to the reproduction right defined by article 2. It provides:

"1. Temporary acts of reproduction referred to in Article 2, which are transient or incidental [and] an integral and essential part of a technological process and whose sole purpose is to enable:

'(a) a transmission in a network between third parties by an intermediary, or

(b) a lawful use of a work or other subject-matter to be made, and which have no independent economic significance, shall be exempted from the reproduction right provided for in Article 2.'

...

5. The exceptions and limitations provided for in paragraphs 1,2,3 and 4 shall only be applied in certain special cases which do not conflict with a normal exploitation of the work or other subjectmatter and do not unreasonably prejudice the legitimate interests of the rightholder."

Chapters III and IV then make extensive provision for the enforcement of copyright owners' rights in the digital world.

The case law of the Court of Justice

10. The Court of Justice of the European Union has considered article 5.1 in three recent cases which have laid down broad principles for application by national courts. They are, in the order in which they were decided, (Case C-5/08) *Infopaq International A/S v. Danske Dagblades Forening* ("*Infopaq I*") [2010] F. S. R. 495; (Case C-403/08) *Football Association Premier League Ltd v. QC Leisure and Others and* (Case C-429/08) *Karen Murphy v. Media Protection Services Ltd* ("*Premier League*") [2012] 1 CMLR 769; and (Case C-302/10) *Infopaq International A/S v. Danske Dagblades Forening* ("*Infopaq II*"), 17 January 2012. It should be noted that only the first of these cases was cited to Proudman J or the Court of Appeal. Neither the *Premier League* case or *Infopaq II* had been decided at the time when they gave judgment.

Infopaq I

11. In *Infopaq I* [2010] F. S. R. 495, at [54], the Court of Justice paraphrased article 5.1 as making the exemption for an "act of reproduction" dependent on five conditions being fulfilled:

"— the act is temporary;

— it is transient or incidental;

— it is an integral and essential part of a technological process;

— the sole purpose of that process is to enable a transmission in a network between third parties by an intermediary of a lawful use of a work or protected subject-matter; and

— the act has no independent economic significance."

This formulation has been repeated in this form in the subsequent case-law, and it is undoubtedly convenient. It is, however, important to remember that it is a paraphrase. Notwithstanding that the five conditions are laid out in five separate sub-paragraphs, they are not free-standing requirements. They are overlapping and repetitive, and each of them colours the meaning of the others. They have to be read together so as to achieve the combined purpose of all of them. This is, as the case-law demonstrates, what the Court of Justice has always done.

12. In particular, it was the approach of the Court of Justice in *Infopaq I* itself, which was a reference from Denmark concerning commercial media monitoring service, Infopaq, which was not unlike Meltwater's. The issue was about Infopaq's "data capture process", i. e. the electronic search process by which it identified relevant newspaper extracts. It was not, as the present case is, about the method by which the result of the search was communicated to Infopaq's clients. However, Infopaq's methods did make it necessary to consider generally how article 5. 1 applied to the storage and viewing of digital data. They involved the creation of copies at four successive stages: (i) the creation of a scanned image of the original article, (ii) the conversion of that image into a searchable text file, (iii) the extraction of the keywords from that text file together with the five words on either side, and their storage as a text file, and (iv) the printing out and retention of copy (iii). The issue turned on the temporary or transient character of copies made in the course of this procedure. It was held that article 5. 1 might apply to (i), (ii) and (iii), if the national court was satisfied that these copies were deleted automatically, i. e. without any discretionary human intervention, when the technical need for them had passed. On the other hand, (iv) was not "transient" because the print-outs were destroyed only when a human agent decided to destroy them.

13. Although the Court of Justice was directly concerned only with the first two conditions, it construed them in the light of the third. In substance what the court

held was that the requirement of the third condition that the copying should be an "integral and essential part of a technological process" meant that it could only be regarded as "temporary" or "transient" if it was inherent in the technological process that the copy would be deleted when that process was complete. The court's analysis began by drawing attention to the fact that the exception in article 5.1 was a derogation from the rights conferred on copyright owners:

"56 For the interpretation of each of those conditions in turn, it should be borne in mind that, according to settled case-law, the provisions of a Directive which derogate from a general principle established by that Directive must be interpreted strictly (*Criminal Proceedings against Kapper* (C-476/01) [2004] E. C. R. 1-5205, ECJ at [72], and *Commission of the European Communities v. Spain* (C36/05) [2006] E. C. R. 1-10313 ECJ at [31]).

57 This holds true for the exemption provided for in art. 5(1) of Directive 2001/29, which is a derogation from the general principle established by that Directive, namely the requirement of authorisation from the rightholder for any reproduction of a protected work.

58 This is all the more so given that the exemption must be interpreted in the light of art. 5(5) of Directive 2001/29, under which that exemption is to be applied only in certain special cases which do not conflict with a normal exploitation of the work or other subject matter and do not unreasonably prejudice the legitimate interests of the rightholder."

At paras 61-64 the court summarised the position in this way:

"61 The court finds, in the light of the third condition referred to in [54] of this judgment, that a temporary and transient act of reproduction is intended to enable the completion of a technological process of which it forms an integral and essential part. In those circumstances, given the principles set out in [57] and [58] of this judgment, those acts of reproduction must not exceed what is necessary for the proper completion of that technological process.

62 Legal certainty for rightholders further requires that the storage and deletion of the reproduction not be dependent on discretionary human intervention, particular-

ly by the user of protected works. There is no guarantee that in such cases the person concerned will actually delete the reproduction created or, in any event, that he will delete it once its existence is no longer justified by its function of enabling the completion of a technological process.

63 This finding is supported by recital 33 in the preamble to Directive 2001/29 which lists, as examples of the characteristics of the acts referred to in art. 5(1) thereof, acts which enable browsing as well as acts of caching to take place, including those which enable transmission systems to function efficiently. Such acts are, by definition, created and deleted automatically and without human intervention.

64 In the light of the foregoing, the court finds that an act can be held to be 'transient' within the meaning of the second condition laid down in art. 5(1) of Directive 2001/29 only if its duration is limited to what is necessary for the proper completion of the technological process in question, it being understood that that process must be automated so that it deletes that act automatically, without human intervention, once its function of enabling the completion of such a process has come to an end."

Addressing the question of copy(iii) (the text file containing the keyword extracts), the court added,

"66 ...It is for the national court to ascertain whether the deletion of that file is dependent on the will of the user of the reproduction and whether there is a risk that the file might remain stored once the function of enabling completion of the technologicalprocess has come to an end."

The Premier League case

14. In the important case of *Football Association Premier League Ltd v. QC Leisure and Karen Murphy v. Media Protection Services Ltd*[2012]1 CMLR 769, the ambit of article 5.1 arose in the context of a dispute about the fourth and fifth conditions, which had not been considered in *Infopaq I*. It was, however, impossible to form a view about the effect of those conditions without construing article 5.1 as a whole, and examining the function of each of the five conditions. This is what the Court of

Justice did.

15. The facts were that Mrs. Murphy had subscribed to a pay TV service in Greece and acquired a Greek satellite decoder, but used it without the authority of the rights owner to receive broadcasts of football matches in her pub in the United Kingdom, where they were viewed by her customers. The copies said to infringe were the temporary copies made in the memory of the decoder and on the television screen in the course of the streaming of the material. Functionally, these were similar to the copies made in the internet cache and on the screen of a personal computer. On any view, the infringement alleged was against the "consumption" of the copyright material by Mrs Murphy and the customers in her pub as end-users. At paras 162-164, the court reminded itself that while any exception from the prima facie right of the copyright owner to control reproduction must be strictly construed, that right had to be balanced against the purpose of the exception, which was to encourage the development and operation of new technologies and the rights of users who wished to use those technologies. It was held that Mrs. Murphy was protected by article 5(1).

16. The first question was whether the allegedly infringing copies made in the cache of Mrs Murphy's decoder were made for one of the two purposes specified in sub-paragraphs(a) and (b) of article 5.1. Since they were not made for the purpose of the transmission of the material through a network, it was necessary for Mrs Murphy to rely on sub-paragraph(b). This required her to establish that the copies were made to enable some other use which was lawful. The court held that they were. It put the matter in this way:

"168 As is apparent from recital 33 in the preamble to the Copyright Directive, a use should be considered lawful where it is authorised by the right holder or where it is not restricted by the applicable legislation.

169 Since in the main proceedings the use of the works at issue is not authorised by the copyright holders, it must be determined whether the acts in question are intended to enable a use of works which is not restricted by the applicable legislation.

170 In this regard, it is undisputed that those ephemeral acts of reproduction

enable the satellite decoder and the television screen to function correctly. From the television viewers' standpoint, they enable the broadcasts containing protected works to be received.

171 Mere reception as such of those broadcasts—that is to say, the picking up of the broadcasts and their visual display—in private circles does not reveal an act restricted by EU legislation or by that of the United Kingdom, as indeed follows from the wording of Question 5 in Case C−403/08, and that act is therefore lawful. Furthermore, it follows from [77]−[132] of the present judgment that such reception of the broadcasts must be considered lawful in the case of broadcasts from a Member State other than the United Kingdom when it is brought about by means of a foreign decoding device.

172 Accordingly, the acts of reproduction have the sole purpose of enabling a 'lawful use' of the works within the meaning of art. 5(1)(b) of the Copyright Directive.

173 Acts of reproduction such as those at issue in the main proceedings thus satisfy the fourth condition laid down by that provision. "

17. This section of the judgment is critical to an understanding of the current issue and to the whole of the jurisprudence of the court upon it. EU law might have treated any use of copyright material apart from its transmission through a network as unlawful, if it lacked the authority of the copyright owner. A suggestion was in fact made by the Economic and Social Committee that the Commission's original proposal should be amended ("expanded and clarified") so that "[a]ny reproduction that in effect is consumption of the work" should be unlawful if it occurred without the copyright owner's authority: see OJ C 407/32, 28. 12. 98, at paragraph 3.7.1.2. The suggestion was not, however, adopted, and in the *Premier League* case the Court of Justice decisively rejected an attempt to arrive at the same result on the construction of article 5.1 as issued. Because Mrs. Murphy's use of the material was not contrary to the "applicable legislation", it was held to be lawful for the purpose of article 5.1 (b) even though it was not authorised by the rights owner. In a later section of its judgment, the court went on to hold that Mrs Murphy's use of the material infringed

the separate communication right defined by article 3 of the Directive, and was to that extent unlawful. That did not, however, affect its conclusion that her use of the material was lawful for the purpose of article 5.1(b). This was because article 5.1 was concerned only with the ambit of the reproduction right defined in article 2. The only requirement was therefore that the relevant use should be consistent with EU legislation governing the reproduction right, including article 5.1 itself.

18. The court then turned to the fifth condition, which is concerned with the "economic significance" of the use made of the material. The Court interpreted this condition as meaning that the use made of the material by the alleged infringer must not have any economic value other than that which was inherent in its mere reception and viewing:

"174 So far as concerns, finally, the fifth condition laid down by that provision, these acts of reproduction carried out in the course of a technological process make access to the protected works possible. Since the latter have an economic value, access to them necessarily has economic significance.

175 However, if the exception laid down in art. 5(1) of the Copyright Directive is not to be rendered redundant, that significance must also be independent in the sense that it goes beyond the economic advantage derived from mere reception of a broadcast containing protected works, that is to say, beyond the advantage derived from the mere picking up of the broadcast and its visual display.

176 In the main proceedings, the temporary acts of reproduction, carried out within the memory of the satellite decoder and on the television screen, form an inseparable and non-autonomous part of the process of reception of the broadcasts transmitted containing the works in question. Furthermore, they are performed without influence, or even awareness, on the part of the persons thereby having access to the protected works.

177 Consequently, those temporary acts of reproduction are not capable of generating an additional economic advantage going beyond the advantage derived from mere reception of the broadcasts at issue.

178 It follows that the acts of reproduction at issue in the main proceedings

cannot be regarded as having independent economic significance. Consequently, they fulfil the fifth condition laid down in art. 5(1) of the Copyright Directive.

179 This finding, and the finding set out in [172] of the present judgment [that the copying had the purpose of enabling a lawful use], are moreover borne out by the objective of that provision, which is intended to ensure the development and operation of new technologies. If the acts at issue were not considered to comply with the conditions set by art. 5(1) of the Copyright Directive, all television viewers using modern sets which, in order to work, need those acts of reproduction to be carried out would be prevented from receiving broadcasts containing broadcast works, in the absence of an authorisation from copyright holders. That would impede, and even paralyse, the actual spread and contribution of new technologies, in disregard of the will of the EU legislature as expressed in recital 31 in the preamble to the Copyright Directive. "

19. Finally, the court dealt briefly with the requirement of article 5.5 that the exception should be applied only in "special cases which do not conflict with a normal exploitation of the work or other subject-matter and do not unreasonably prejudice the legitimate interests of the rightholder." It held that in view of the considerations which had led it to hold that article 5.1 applied, article 5.5 must be regarded as satisfied also. I shall return to this point in the context of *Infopaq II*, where the reasoning is repeated in expanded form.

Infopaq II

20. *Infopaq II* was a second reference in the same case as *Infopaq I*. It concerned the third, fourth and fifth conditions, which had not been directly in issue on the previous reference. The court substantially repeated what it had said in the *Premier League* case about the test of "lawfulness" under article 5.1(b) and it decided on that basis that the fourth condition was satisfied. No further discussion of that point is called for here. The other issues related to the third condition ("integral and essential part of a technological process"), the fifth condition (no "independent economic significance"), and the effect of article 5.5.

21. The Danish court's problem with the third condition was that the court's previous emphasis on the absence of human intervention appeared to rule out the application of article 5. 1 to the scanned copy which initiated the process, since the original article had to be manually inserted into the scanner. In dealing with this question, the court pointed out that in *Infopaq* 1 it had been concerned to emphasise that it was the *deletion* of a temporary copy which must not depend on human intervention. It had not said that there must be no human intervention at any stage: see para 32. It followed from this that the discretionary nature of the user's decision to initiate the process(for example by switching on his computer or accessing a particular web-page) was irrelevant.

22. Having dealt with this point, the court took the opportunity to deal more generally with the requirement that the copying should be an "integral and essential part of a technological process":

"30 The concept of the 'integral and essential part of a technological process' requires the temporary acts of reproduction to be carried out entirely in the context of the implementation of the technological process and, therefore, not to be carried out, fully or partially, outside of such a process. This concept also assumes that the completion of the temporary act of reproduction is necessary, in that the technological process concerned could not function correctly and efficiently without that act(see, to that effect, *Infopaq International*, paragraph 61).

37 Finally, it should be noted that the technological process in question could not function correctly and efficiently without the acts of reproduction concerned. That technological process aims at identifying predefined key words in newspaper articles and extracting them on a digital medium. Such electronic research thus requires a transformation of those articles, from a paper-based medium, into digital data, since that transformation is necessary in order to recognise that data, to identify the key words and to extract those key words."

23. The court returned to this theme in dealing with the fifth condition about the absence of "independent economic significance":

"48. In that regard, it should be recalled that the acts of temporary reproduction, within the meaning of Article 5(1), aim to make access to the protected works and their use possible. Since those works have a specific economic value, access to them and their use necessarily has economic significance (see, to that effect, Football Association Premier League [2012] 1 CMLR 769, paragraph 174).

49. Furthermore, as is apparent from Recital 33 in the preamble to Directive 2001/29, the acts of temporary reproduction—like the acts enabling 'browsing' and 'caching'—have the purpose of facilitating the use of a work or making that use more efficient. Thus, an inherent feature of those acts is to enable the achievement of efficiency gains in the context of such use and, consequently, to lead to increased profits or a reduction in production costs.

50. However, those acts must not have independent economic significance, in that the economic advantage derived from their implementation must not be either distinct or separable from the economic advantage derived from the lawful use of the work concerned and it must not generate an additional economic advantage going beyond that derived from that use of the protected work (see, to that effect, Football Association Premier League and Others, paragraph 175).

51. The efficiency gains resulting from the implementation of the acts of temporary reproduction, such as those in issue in the main proceedings, have no such independent economic significance, inasmuch as the economic advantages derived from their application only materialise during the use of the reproduced subject matter, so that they are neither distinct nor separable from the advantages derived from its use.

52. On the other hand, an advantage derived from an act of temporary reproduction is distinct and separable if the author of that act is likely to make a profit due to the economic exploitation of the temporary reproductions themselves."

24. Finally, the court in *Infopaq II* expanded on what it had said in the *Premier League* case about article 5.5:

"56. In that regard, suffice it to note that if those acts of reproduction fulfil all the conditions of Article 5(1) of Directive 2001/29, as interpreted by the case-law of the Court, it must be held that they do not conflict with the normal exploitation of the work or unreasonably prejudice the legitimate interests of the rightholder (Football Association Premier League and Others, paragraph 181).

57. Consequently, the answer to the seventh question is that Article 5(5) of Directive 2001/29 must be interpreted as meaning that, if they fulfil all the conditions laid down in Article 5(1) of that directive, the acts of temporary reproduction carried out during a "data capture' process, such as those in issue in the main proceedings, must be regarded as fulfilling the condition that the acts of reproduction may not conflict with a normal exploitation of the work or unreasonably prejudice the legitimate interests of the rightholder."

25. This last conclusion may at first sight seem odd, since it means that article 5.5 adds nothing to article 5.1. But the apparent oddity disappears when one appreciates that article 5.5 reflects the terms of article 9(2) of the Berne Convention by which both the EU and its member states are bound. Under that article, signatories have a right to authorise by legislation copying which would otherwise be an infringement, in "special cases" provided that this does not conflict with the "normal" exploitation of the work and does not "unreasonably" prejudice the "legitimate" interests of the author. Article 5.1 is the legislation in question. The Court of Justice is pointing out that it has been drafted so as to determine legislatively what exploitation is to be regarded as normal, and what derogations from the author's exclusive rights are to be regarded as reasonable and legitimate. This does not make article 5.5 redundant. Its effect is to require article 5.1 to be as narrowly construed as is consistent with its purpose: see *Infopaq I* at para 58. But its purpose must nevertheless be at the forefront of any attempt to construe it.

The effect of the CJEU decisions

26. The effect of this body of authority can be summarised as follows:

(1) Subject to the limitations which I shall summarise in the following sub-paragraphs, the exception in article 5.1 applies to copies made as an integral and necessary part of a "technological process", in particular the digital processing of data. For this purpose, the making of copies is a "necessary" part of the process if it enables it to function "correctly and efficiently": *Infopaq II*, at paras 30, 37.

(2) These copies must be temporary. This requirement is explained and defined by the words which follow, namely that the making of the copies must be "transient or incidental and an integral and essential part of a technological process". It means (i) that the storage and deletion of the copyright material must be the automatic consequence of the user's decision to initiate or terminate the relevant technological process, as opposed to being dependent on some further discretionary human intervention, and (ii) that the duration of the copy should be limited to what is necessary for the completion of the relevant technological process: see *Infopaq I*, at paras 62 and 64.

(3) The exception is not limited to copies made in order to enable the transmission of material through intermediaries in a network. It also applies to copies made for the sole purpose of enabling other uses, provided that these uses are lawful. These other uses include internet browsing: *Infopaq I*, at para 63 and *Infopaq II*, at para 49.

(4) For the purpose of article 5.1, a use of the material is lawful, whether or not the copyright owner has authorised it, if it is consistent with EU legislation governing the reproduction right, including article 5.1 itself: *Premier League*, at paras 168–173, *Infopaq II*, at para 42. The use of the material is not unlawful by reason only of the fact that it lacks the authorisation of the copyright owner.

(5) The making of the temporary copy must have no "independent economic significance". This does not mean that it must have no commercial value. It may well have. What it means is that it must have no *independent* commercial value, i. e. no value additional to that which is derived from the mere act of digitally transmitting or viewing the material: *Premier League*, at para 175, *Infopaq II*, at para 50.

(6) If these conditions are satisfied no additional restrictions can be derived from article 5.5.

Application to the present case

27. The first and fundamental question is whether article 5.1 applies at all to temporary copies generated by an end-user's use of the internet. Mr. Howe QC,

who appeared for the Newspaper Licensing Agency, submitted that it did not. He argued that it applied only to copies made in the course of the transmission of the material within a network, for example in the caches of intermediate routers and proxy servers. In my opinion, this is an impossible contention. In the first place, it is clear from the Directive's recitals, and in particular from recital 33, that it was intended that the exception should "include acts which enable browsing as well as acts of caching to take place." Browsing is not part of the process of transmission. It is the use of an internet browser by an end-user to view web pages. It is by its very nature an end-user function. The "acts" referred to are the "acts of temporary reproduction" referred to at the outset of the recital, with which the whole recital is concerned. The acts of temporary reproduction which "enable" browsing to occur are accordingly the making of temporary copies in the internet cache of the enduser's hard drive and on his screen. It follows that the recital expressly envisages that the exception will apply to end-user viewing of web-pages. Secondly, if Mr Howe is right the scope of the exception corresponds only to that part of the process which is covered by article 5.1(a) ("transmission in a network between third parties by an intermediary"). In fact, caching is concerned with the transmission of material in a network, because its purpose is to make the operation of the internet more efficient by easing constraints on its capacity: see paragraph 2 above. But the exception in any event is wider than that, for it also extends to operations covered by article 5.1(b) ("lawful use"). Lawful "use" refers to the use of the work which is the subject of the copyright. It extends to use, as the Court of Justice made clear in the *Premier League* case and *Infopaq II*, whether or not authorised by the copyright owner, which is "not restricted by the applicable legislation". This necessarily includes the use of the work by an end-user browsing the internet. Third, Mr. Howe's submission is directly contradicted by the judgment in the *Premier League* case, where article 5 was applied to Mrs Murphy's use of the copyright material by displaying it on her television. She was the end-user. She and her customers were consuming the product. In the context of the fifth condition, that the copy should have no independent economic significance, the court considered at para

176 the status of the copy made on the television screen, because it had been suggested by the Advocate-General (at AG95) that the screen copy might have an independent economic significance that the cached copy lacked. At para 179, the court pointed out that if article 5.1 did not apply to the viewing of copyright material by a television end-user, such viewers "would be prevented from receiving broadcasts... in the absence of an authorisation from copyright holders", which would "impede and even paralyse the actual spread and contribution of new technologies in disregard of the will of the EU legislature as expressed in recital 31." For this purpose, there is no rational distinction to be made between viewing copyright material on a television screen and viewing the same material on a computer.

28. Once it is accepted that part of the purpose of article 5.1 is to authorise the making of copies to enable the end-user to view copyright material on the internet, the various conditions laid down by that article must be construed so far as possible in a manner consistent with that purpose. It must, if the exception is to be coherent, apply to the ordinary technical processes associated with internet browsing.

29. There is, to my mind, no room for argument on the facts of this case about the third, fourth and fifth conditions in article 5.1. The third condition is that the making of copies in the internet cache and on screen should be an integral and essential part of a technological process. Manifestly it is. These were at the time of the Directive and remain today basic features of the design of modern computers. It would no doubt be possible to design computers that did not cache material in the course of internet browsing, but in the words of the judgment in *Infopaq II*, the technological processes required to browse the internet could not function "correctly and efficiently" without the acts of reproduction concerned: see paras 30 and 37. The fourth condition, as applied to end-users like Meltwater's customers, is that its use should be lawful. Once it is established, as it is by the decisions in the *Premier League* case and *Infopaq II*, that this means lawful apart from any lack of authorisation by the copyright owner, it is equally clear that this condition is satisfied. The fifth condition, that the copying should have no independent economic significance, is satisfied for the same reason as it was satisfied in the *Premier League*

case, namely that it has no *independent* economic value to Meltwater's customers. This is because unless they download or print out the material (in which case it is not disputed that they require a licence), the sole economic value which they derive from accessing information on Meltwater's website is derived from the mere fact of reading it on screen.

30. These considerations no doubt explain why Mr. Howe's submissions were addressed mainly to the first two conditions, that the copies generated by the technical processes involved in browsing should be "temporary" and "transient or incidental". It is not suggested that "transient" means anything different from "temporary", and in my view they are the same. "Transience" is simply part of the elaborate explanation of "temporary" which follows that word.

31. If, as the Court of Justice has accepted, browsing copyright material on the internet is a method of using it which is within the scope of article 5. 1, and if the making of copies in the internet cache or on screen is indispensable to the correct and efficient operation of the technical processes involved in browsing, it would be strange if the law said that the period of time for which these copies will exist in the ordinary course of that operation was insufficiently "temporary" or "transient" to qualify. As I have explained above by reference to the judgment in *Infopaq I*, the relevant requirements are (i) that the storage and deletion of the copyright material should be automatic, as opposed to being dependent on "discretionary human intervention", and (ii) that the duration of the copy should be limited to what is "necessary for the completion of the technological processes in question": see paras 62 and 64. The "storage" of the material, i. e. the creation of copies in the cache or on screen, is the automatic result of browsing the internet. It requires no other human intervention than the decision to access the relevant web-page. Its deletion is the equally automatic result of the lapse of time coupled with the continuing use of the browser. The "technological processes in question" are those necessarily associated with web browsing, including the retention of material in the cache. It is retained there for no longer than the ordinary processes associated with internet use continue. Standing back for a moment from this fine verbal analysis of the language

of the court, the purpose of these formulations is plain. It is to distinguish between the use of a computer or other equipment simply to view the relevant material, and its use to record it. The object of the restriction to "temporary" or "transient" copies is to ensure that the exception does not apply to protect downloading or other forms of digital or physical copying which will remain in existence until the user chooses to delete or destroy them and are therefore as permanent as he chooses to make them.

32. Mr Howe's argument was that cached material was not "temporary" or "transient" because the user could make a discretionary decision to close down the computer, thereby leaving the material in the cache indefinitely until the browser was used again. Or he could adjust the settings so as to enlarge the cache, thereby extending the period for which material might remain in it even while the browser was in use. He could also access a web page and leave his computer on with the web page on screen indefinitely. These are certainly examples of discretionary human intervention, but they are irrelevant because they do not involve a discretionary decision whether to retain the material in memory or not. They are merely rather artificial ways of extending the duration of the relevant "technological processes". They call for three comments in the present context. The first is that the effect of creating copies in the internet cache or on screen in the course of browsing, must be judged in the light of the normal operation of a computer or its browser. It is not enough that forensic ingenuity can devise a method of extending to some extent the life of copies which are by their nature temporary. Secondly, the question is whether human intervention is required to delete the material: see *Infopaq I* at para 66. There is a difference, which is fundamental to the object of article 5. 1, between a discretionary decision to extend the duration of what remains an automatic process, and the storage of a copy of material in the course of the browsing in a manner which will ensure that it is permanent unless and until a discretionary decision is made to delete or destroy it. The decisions of the Court of Justice show that in principle the former satisfies the first two conditions in article 5. 1 whereas the latter does not. Third, the Respondents' examples, as examples go, prove too much. If the mere

fact that it is in principle possible to close down a computer, alter the browser settings to enlarge the internet cache or leave an image on screen indefinitely were enough to prevent article 5.1 from applying, then it would never apply to internet browsing. This would frustrate the purpose of the legislation.

33. If, as I consider, the copies made in the internet cache or on screen are "transient", it is strictly speaking unnecessary to consider whether they are also "incidental". But I think it clear that they are. The software puts a web-page on screen and into the cache for the purpose of enabling a lawful use of the copyright material, i.e. viewing it. The creation of the copies is wholly incidental to the technological process involved.

34. Once these matters are established, it follows that article 5.5 is also satisfied.

Consequences

35. It is the policy of the EU to maintain a "high level of protection of intellectual property". That policy is acknowledged both in the Directive itself (see recitals 4 and 9), and in the case law (for example, *Premier League* at para 186). We were pressed with the argument that if the viewing of copyright material on a web-page did not require a licence from the copyright owner, he would be exposed to large-scale piracy of a kind which would be difficult to detect or prevent.

36. I am not persuaded by this argument and nor, it is clear, was the Court of Justice on the successive occasions when it has dealt with this issue. Of course, any diminution in the rights of copyright owners necessarily narrows the scope of the protection which they enjoy for their works. But we need to keep this point in proportion. In the first place, article 5.1 is an exception to the copyright owner's right to control the reproduction of his work. It necessarily operates to authorise certain copying which would otherwise be an infringement of the copyright owner's rights. Secondly, it has never been an infringement, in either English or EU law, for a person merely to view or read an infringing article in physical form. This state of affairs, which is recognised in the enumeration of the copyright owner's rights in arti-

cles 2, 3 and 4 of the Directive, has never been thought inconsistent with a high level of protection for intellectual property. All that article 5.1 of the Directive achieves is to treat the viewing of copyright material on the internet in the same way as its viewing in physical form, notwithstanding that the technical processes involved incidentally include the making of temporary copies within the electronic equipment employed. Third, if it is an infringement merely to view copyright material, without downloading or printing out, then those who browse the internet are likely unintentionally to incur civil liability, at least in principle, by merely coming upon a web-page containing copyright material in the course of browsing. This seems an unacceptable result, which would make infringers of many millions of ordinary users of the internet across the EU who use browsers and search engines for private as well as commercial purposes. Fourth, nothing in article 5.1 affects the obligation of Meltwater to be licensed in order to upload copyright material onto their website or make non-temporary copies of it in some other way. At the moment, the licence fee payable by Meltwater is fixed on the basis that its customers need a licence of their own from the publishers and that the service will be supplied only to end-users who have one. It seems very likely (although I am not deciding the point) that the licence fee chargeable to Meltwater will be substantially higher if end-users do not need a licence because on that footing the value of the rights for which Meltwater is licensed will be significantly higher. The respondents have lodged an alternative claim with the Copyright Tribunal on that basis. In my view it is altogether more satisfactory that a single large licence fee should be payable representing the value to the person who puts the material onto the internet, than that tiny sums should be separately collectable from hundreds (in other cases it may be millions) of internet viewers. Fifth, if merely viewing a web-page is not an infringement, that does not leave the copyright owner without effective remedies against pirates. It simply means that his remedy must be found against others who on the face of it are more obviously at fault. Nothing in article 5.1 impairs the copyright owner's right to proceed against those who unlawfully upload copyright material onto the internet, just as the copyright owner has always been entitled to proceed against those who make or distribute pirated copies of books, films, music or other protected works. The Directive itself contains in Chapters III and IV important provisions enlarging the range of procedures and sanctions available against piracy.

The decisions below

37. Proudman J decided that Meltwater's customers needed a licence both to receive the monitoring reports by email and to access them on Meltwater's website. Her reasons were (i) that the making of copies, however temporary, in the end-user's computer in the course of browsing was not part of the technological process because it was "generated by his own volition", i. e. by his voluntary decision to access the web-page; (ii) that it was outside the scope of the technological process for the additional reason that it was in reality the end result of that process since it was what the end-user viewed; and (iii) that the viewing of these copies did not constitute "lawful use" because they were not authorised by the copyright owner: see para 109. These reasons are of course related, and all three of them lead to the conclusion that, in the judge's words, the "kind of circumstance where the defence may be available is where the purpose of the copying is to enable efficient transmission in a network between third parties by an intermediary, typically an internet service provider" para 110. The Court of Appeal agreed with her, essentially on her ground (i). In their view the "acts of reproduction are those occasioned by the voluntary human process of accessing that web-page" para 35. For practical purposes, this amounted to an endorsement of Proudman J's view that unlicensed internet browsing could never satisfy the conditions in article 5. 1. It will be apparent that Proudman J and the Court of Appeal could not have arrived at these conclusions if they had had the benefit of the judgments in *Premier League* and *Infopaq II*. In particular, the far broader meaning given by the Court of Justice in these cases to the concept of "lawful use" makes it impossible to confine the scope of the exception to the internal plumbing of the internet. Once it is accepted that article 5. 1 extends in principle to temporary copies made for the purpose of browsing by an unlicensed end-user, much of the argument which the courts below accepted unravels.

Public Relations Consultants Association Limited (Appellant)v. The Newspaper Licensing Agency Limited and others (Respondents)

Reference

38. In its recent recommendations in relation to references, OJ C338, 6. 11. 2012, the Court of Justice of the European Union has observed that while a national court may consider that sufficient guidance is available in the existing case-law of the Court of Justice to enable a case to be decided, a reference may be useful where there is a new question of interpretation of general interest for the uniform application of European Union law or where the existing case-law does not appear to be applicable to a new set of facts. I have set out in this judgment the conclusions that I have reached on the effect of the Directive, as the Court of Justice has interpreted and applied it to date. However, I recognise the issue has a transnational dimension and that the application of copyright law to internet use has important implications for many millions of people across the EU making use of what has become a basic technical facility. These considerations make it desirable that any decision on the point should be referred to the Court of Justice for a preliminary ruling, so that the critical point may be resolved in a manner which will apply uniformly across the European Union. In my view, before making any order on this appeal, this court should refer to the Court of Justice the question whether the requirements of article 5. 1 of the Directive that acts of reproduction should be(i) temporary, (ii) transient or incidental and(iii) an integral and essential part of the technological process, are satisfied by the technical features described at paragraphs 2 and 31-32 of this judgment, having regard in particular to the fact that a copy of protected material may in the ordinary course of internet usage remain in the cache for a period of time after the browsing session which has generated that copy is completed until it is overlaid by other material, and a screen copy will remain on screen until the browsing session is terminated by the user.

39. I would invite Counsel to comment on the proposed issue to be referred and to prepare and if possible agree a draft reference for consideration by this court.